THE PRISON POEMS OF
NIKOLAI BUKHARIN

T0345230

Преображение
Мира.
(Стихи о веках и людях)

Bukharin's 'cover design'—birds on a roof-like structure, perhaps as seen from his prison window.

THE PRISON POEMS OF NIKOLAI BUKHARIN

TRANSFORMATION OF THE WORLD
(VERSE ABOUT THE AGES, AND ABOUT PEOPLE)

Translated by George Shriver

LONDON NEW YORK CALCUTTA

Seagull Books, 2018

Translations © George Shriver, 2008

ISBN 978 0 8574 2 581 2

British Library Cataloguing-in-Publication Data
A catalogue record for this book is available
from the British Library

Typeset by Seagull Books, Calcutta, India

Printed and bound by Leelabati Printers, Calcutta, India

Contents

CONTENTS

Translator's Introduction

In these translations I have, for the most part, not attempted to reproduce the rhyme schemes of the original poems. Occasionally I have rhymed some lines, but almost all of the translations are in free verse. Among the exceptions to my choice of non-rhyming translation are the poems 'Sirin and Alkonost' and 'Night'. But even in those cases I use only occasional rhymes, whereas Bukharin almost always used a standard rhyme scheme, usually *abab*, but sometimes *abba* or *aabb*, or more complex rhyming patterns.

In a few cases, Bukharin did *not* use rhyme in his Russian text—for example, in 'Life and Death', 'Ancient Landscape' and 'Rádunitsa'. (In the case of 'Rádunitsa' I have given the transliterated Russian wording, interspersed line by line with my English rendering, to give the reader a rough idea of the sound of the original, in which Bukharin echoes Russian folk poetry.)

As in his use of rhyme, Bukharin's use of certain types of vocabulary and imagery was fairly conventional, not particularly innovative. The same can probably be said of his use of meter and length of line. In each poem I have tried to employ meter and length of line in a manner corresponding to the original, though not always exactly. Sometimes the demands of meaning or a complicated image or thought required lines to be lengthened or shortened and meter to be shifted.

My primary aim has been to render clearly the author's ideas and imagery, while attempting to convey something of the rhythm and tone of the Russian original. Here and there I felt it necessary to add or omit a small detail, so that the poem, as I saw it, would 'work' better in English, but I tried to keep such modifications to the minimum. Perhaps being too faithful to the Russian text results in a poem 'less beautiful' in English, however . . .

CHIEF VALUE OF THE POETRY MANUSCRIPT: ENLARGING OUR KNOWLEDGE OF AN IMPORTANT HISTORICAL FIGURE

The chief value of the poetry manuscript, in my opinion, is that it enlarges our understanding of Nikolai Bukharin, who with all his strengths and weaknesses was a major historical figure, one of the leaders of the Russian revolution, which will always occupy a large place in human history as the first attempt to reconstruct society on a socialist basis.

The main interest of this manuscript, then, is not the high or low quality of the verse, but what it shows about Bukharin as an individual, what it reveals about his intellectual and emotional condition and concerns during the last year of his life, the thoughts and feelings that were most vital and urgent for him in prison in the year 1937.

THE THEMATIC 'CYCLES', OR 'SERIES', OF BUKHARIN'S VERSE

In the Russian typescript Bukharin himself specifies a number of different 'cycles', or 'series' (using the terms more or less interchangeably). The headings for these groups of poems delineated the themes or motifs that were most important for him at the time. Many of those same themes were taken up in his other three prison manuscripts, as well as in his earlier writings.

For example, Bukharin gave to a cluster of 32 poems the title 'Nature—Mother of All' (*Prámater— Priróda*; alternative translation, 'Nature—The Primal Mother'). As his autobiographical novel also shows, Bukharin loved the natural world and knew it quite well. Philosophical themes akin to 'the philosophy of nature' form a subset of the Nature poems. These echo topics that he discussed in the book *Philosophical Arabesques*, which he was writing during the same months when he wrote these poems.

The poems that we have are dated from late June to early October 1937—with one poem, the very last, very short one, dated in November 1937. He began work on his autobiographical novel in November, having finished his philosophical work by then. His book-length manuscript entitled *Socialism and Its Culture* was the first work he wrote in prison, probably from mid-March to mid-May 1937 (see the preface to that work by the daughter who survived him, Svetlana Gurvich-Bukharina). In other words, he produced these poems *while* he was writing *Philosophical Arabesques* and *after* he had completed *Socialism and Its Culture*. I would argue that the more personal focus of the poems foreshadowed his turn towards the final work, the autobiographical novel.

One of the major themes of Bukharin's verse is 'Heritage' (in Russian, *Nasledstvo*), the achievements and advances of human culture. He pays tribute to the cultures of China, India and the indigenous civilizations of the Americas, among others, not limiting the sources of the human 'Heritage' to the Near East, the Mediterranean and Europe. (That is, he was not consciously and deliberately 'Eurocentric'.)

Related to the theme of 'Heritage' is the theme 'Emancipation of Labour', which could be used as a title for Bukharin's many poems about socialist aims and achievements in the USSR. These achievements include, as he saw it, the emancipation of women and of oppressed nationalities, in addition to progress in industry and agriculture. Verse on these themes is grouped mostly under the heading 'Epoch of Great Works'.

Also related to the theme of 'Heritage' are two sets of poems addressed to particular historical figures, trends or schools of thought (the Greek materialist thinkers Democritus, Heraclitus, Archimedes; the Renaissance, Leonardo da Vinci, Shakespeare, Bacon, Newton; the Encyclopedists, Darwin, Hegel, Beethoven, Pushkin, Tolstoy, et al.). Perhaps his poems 'in imitation of' Horace, Ovid and Ausonius belong here too, although their content and tone more properly place them with the personal poems about love and loss, the series he entitled 'Lyrical Intermezzo' (more about which below).

Another cycle related to 'Heritage' is what Bukharin called 'Precursors', human events or social movements of past centuries prefiguring the world's first socialist revolution, the Bolshevik revolution of 1917. Included among 'Precursors' is his retelling of an Iranian tale, 'The Blacksmith's Apron', and an ancient Egyptian priest's lament about a slave revolt. All but two of the poems in the 'Precursors' cycle appear together, as a solid block in the Russian typescript, pages 209–242, and were written from 12 to 15 September 1937.

Another cycle follows in the typescript right after the 'Precursors' series. It consists of 16 poems dealing with the 1917 Revolution and the Russian Civil War of 1918–21. (A poem about the kulaks, who were 'eliminated as a class' in the period roughly from 1929 to 1933, is attached as a kind of final note after the group of poems he entitled 'Civil War'.) These poems also were written as a solid block, right after the 'Precursors' group, from 15 to 22 September 1937.

Although the 'Precursors' and 'Civil War' series were written later, Bukharin decided to put them first in the book as he conceived it. This is made clear by his handwritten 'Systematic Listing' of the poems, which we reproduce at the end of this book.

ANTI-NAZI AND ANTI-CAPITALIST POEMS

Another cycle—in this case the poems belonging to it were scattered chronologically throughout the manuscript—consists of *anti-Nazi poems*. Closely related to these are poems foreseeing a Nazi-Soviet war, which Bukharin overoptimistically saw as 'the final conflict', ending in the near-complete liberation of humanity. His prose 'Preface' to the book of poetry particularly emphasizes this theme of final conflict.

Related to the anti-Nazi poems are a large number describing the evils of the capitalist world. A subset of the poems about capitalism are four poems about capital cities that Bukharin was familiar with: London, Paris, New York and Berlin. In contrast to those are his poems on the two Soviet capitals, Leningrad and Moscow ('Capital of the World'). This brings us to another series of poems, which might be called 'Military-Patriotic Verse', portraying proud, bold, unpretentious young workers and peasants of the Red Army, Air Force and Navy who Bukharin felt sure would crush the Nazi menace under their boot heels. This series includes several poems about young Soviet women paratroops, who especially captured his imagination.

A recurrent theme throughout the book is the suppression or execution of those who questioned prevailing dogmas or rose in rebellion against the existing social order. Obviously this theme is suggestive of his own situation, and he is drawn repeatedly to images and descriptive accounts of such events.

His poetry about the Soviet Union of the 1930s emphasizes the theme of progress and prosperity after years of difficult and desperate struggle. He accentuates the positive and dares not directly violate the taboo on mentioning anything negative about the rule of the Soviet bureaucracy under Stalin. Of course, he knew all too well about this negative side of existing conditions in the USSR. In his 'Letter to a Future Generation of Party Leaders' (which was kept secret until the 1960s), he vividly describes the 'infernal machine that seems to use mediaeval methods, yet possesses gigantic power [and] fabricates organized slander', etc.

THE OBLIGATORY LAUDING OF STALIN

The least attractive motif, which appears in a few of the poems, or passages in poems, has to do with the praising of Stalin, in fact a cruel dictator who was about to be Bukharin's executioner.

It must be explained in regard to obeisance paid to Stalin—passages praising him or attributing great things to him (which were usually not true)—the inclusion of such material was obligatory for anyone who wished to be published under Stalin's increasingly totalitarian rule in the 1930s. And it seems that Bukharin did have the vain hope that his prison works might be published, and even that his life might be spared. Above all, the praise of Stalin was intended as insurance to protect the lives of family members.

It seems that Bukharin made a deliberate decision to try and flatter 'Koba'. (That was Stalin's old revolutionary party name, and the one by which Bukharin and others had often addressed him when they were secondary party leaders before and after the revolution. Later, Bukharin and Stalin were allies in the top party leadership, roughly 1925–28.) In prison Bukharin actually wrote a long narrative poem glorifying Stalin. It is referred to in the 'Chronological Listing' as *Poema o St.* ('Poem about Stalin'). He was going to make it the first poem in the book, coming immediately after the 'Author's Preface'. (At the end of this book, we have reproduced Bukharin's 'Chronological Listing', indicating the order in which he wrote the poems, as well as his 'Systematic Listing', which groups the poems thematically and indicates the order in which he wanted them to appear in the book.)

Such prominent figures in Soviet life under Stalin as Boris Pasternak and Osip Mandelstam also wrote fawning verses in honour of the 'Great Leader'—in an effort to save their own lives and the lives of others. Mandelstam's life was not spared, but Pasternak's was (though no one knows exactly why). At any rate, no doubt gritting his teeth and swallowing his pride, Bukharin wrote his *'Poema o Staline'*—probably well after completing the other poems. When photocopies of the poetry manuscript were delivered to Anna Larina in 1992—primarily as the result of Stephen F.

Cohen's lobbying efforts with a high-level official of the Yeltsin regime, as Cohen reports in his 'Introduction' to the 2008 Russian edition of the prison manuscripts—Larina decided, and I think quite rightly, that this fulsome '*Poema o Staline*', the result really of pressure, extortion and abasement of the individual, should not be included in published versions of Bukharin's poetry.

THE 'LYRICAL INTERMEZZO'

An important theme touched on in poems that appear chronologically towards the end of the book (poems written mostly in August and September) is that of love and loss, a motif expressed especially in his poems for or about his beautiful young wife, Anna Larina. For this group of poems Bukharin chose the title 'Lyrical Intermezzo'.

The son of Larina and Bukharin, Yuri Nikolaevich Larin, was born, incidentally, less than a year before the Soviet leader's arrest at the end of February 1937. That fateful arrest was followed by a year of imprisonment (the time when he wrote his last four book-length manuscripts) and then a show trial and execution in March 1938. (For more on 'The Bukharin–Larina Relationship', see below, the separate section with that heading.)

BUKHARIN'S TITLES FOR HIS GROUPS OF POEMS

In the end Bukharin decided to arrange his poems into nine groups, although the first group, with 14 poems, is missing. (We know of that first group because he included the titles of those poems as the first 14 in his 'Chronological Listing', which the reader may consult at the end of the present edition.)

We have used Bukharin's titles for the eight remaining groups of poems that appear in this book. All together, the typescript we worked from has a total of 173 individual poems, some quite short, some fairly long. At the end of each poem, the author carefully inserted the date, and sometimes an indication of the time of day ('morning', 'night, early hours of such-and-such day', etc.)

For more on how the poems are arranged in this edition, see our note to Bukharin's 'Systematic Listing' at the end of this book.

In his 15 January 1938 letter to his wife, Anna Larina, Bukharin wrote: 'A *plan* is attached to the poems. On the surface, they seem to be chaotic, but they can be understood.' His 'Systematic Listing' groups the poems, precisely in a way that 'can be understood'.

Of course many of the concerns and aspirations expressed in Bukharin's other three prison manuscripts appear in the poems as well, in altered form. (See below for a listing of the other three prison manuscripts, with information on when and where they have been published in English.)

However, some of the topics Bukharin takes up in his poetry were *not* discussed in the other prison manuscripts, at least not in any detail. This observation applies to his poems about the Russian Revolution of 1917 and the Civil War of 1918–20 (the 'cycle' that begins with the poem 'Smolny' and ends with 'Perekop'). It applies as well to his poem about the 1905 revolution in Russia and some of the other poems about revolutionary events that he viewed as 'Precursors' to the Russian Revolution.

His poems for and about Anna Larina are also unique to this manuscript, dealing with an intimate part of his life not discussed in other works for publication. As he says in the letter to Anna Larina cited above, '. . . many of the poems are related to you, and you will feel through them how [closely bound to you I am] (*kak ya tebe privyazan*).'

Bukharin apparently hoped that Anna Larina and his father would be allowed to edit and publish this and the other three book-length manuscripts that he wrote in prison during his final year.

As things turned out, of course, the four prison manuscripts remained hidden in Stalin's personal archive, then in the secret archives of Stalin's heirs, the leaders of the Communist Party of the Soviet

Union, and then, under 'post-Soviet' President Boris Yeltsin, in the Presidential Archive, under the watchful eye and continuing presence of the Russian state security services. Only as a result of a campaign by the Bukharin family together with Bukharin's American biographer, Stephen F. Cohen, were copies of these manuscripts finally obtained from the secret archives in 1992. (See below for Cohen's detailed account of this victory.)

This book of poetry is the last of Bukharin's four prison manuscripts to be published. The other three manuscripts were first printed in book form in Russia in the 1990s, and with the appearance of the present work, English translations of all four prison manuscripts will be available. Editions in English of Bukharin's other prison manuscripts are as follows:

Socialism and Its Culture (London, New York, Calcutta: Seagull Books, 2006).

Philosophical Arabesques (New York: Monthly Review Press, 2005).

How It All Began (New York: Columbia University Press, 1998; also distributed in South Asia in a separate edition by Seagull Books).

HOW THE PRISON MANUSCRIPTS WERE UNEARTHED
After being buried in secret government archives for decades, Bukharin's prison manuscripts were, as we have said, finally brought to light in 1992. It is worth-

while to reproduce here the relevant passages about this remarkable victory for freedom of information from Cohen's essay 'Bukharin's Fate', first written as an Introduction to the English edition of Bukharin's autobiographical novel, *How It All Began*. That account, published in 1998, has now been updated. We now reproduce the relevant excerpt from that updated version, which appears in a new collection of Cohen's essays, *Soviet Fates and Lost Alternatives: From Stalinism to the New Cold War* (New York: Columbia University Press, 2009).

Cohen explains that after Bukharin's execution Stalin buried the four book-length prison manuscripts 'deep in his personal archives'. He adds: 'They were excavated, at my initiative, 54 years later, in 1992.' His account continues as follows:

> The role I unexpectedly played in this saga was an outgrowth of my biography of Bukharin, first published in the United States in 1973 and eventually in the Soviet Union in 1989, and my close personal relationship with his widow and son from the time we first met surreptitiously in 1975 in pre-glasnost Moscow. While researching that book from afar, I came across reports that Bukharin had written some kind of manuscript in prison, as indeed he hinted at the trial, but neither I nor his family, who were still living with an official stigma, could learn anything more for many years. Only in 1988 did an aide to Gor-

bachev, who had read and publicly remarked on my book, tell me privately that not one but four such manuscripts existed in closed archives.

On behalf of Anna Larina, her artist son Yuri Larin, and myself, I began asking for the manuscripts. Gorbachev, although sympathetic to the request, was already locked in a bitter political struggle with Communist Party opponents who resented his revelations about Soviet history and particularly about these kinds of 'Party documents'. Nonetheless, I still was optimistic in 1991 that he would soon authorize release of the manuscripts. Suddenly, however, with the end of the Soviet Union and his own office, Gorbachev no longer controlled any of the archives.

In 1992 Anna Larina, now almost eighty and ill with cancer, and I took a different approach. Believing that the Bukharin family was the legal and moral heir to his works, and had a juridical right in the 'new, democratic Russia' to examine all files related to his case, she formally named me her proxy and requested that relevant archives give me full access to the materials. To our surprise, the former NKVD/KGB archive, under the Ministry of Security, responded promptly and more or less positively. My work in that storehouse of historical horrors soon began.

I quickly learned, however, that not even the top archive officials of the new Russian state could authorize access to the Presidential Archive, where the manuscripts and other essential mate-

rials were held. It could be done only by some-
one at the highest levels of the Yeltsin govern-
ment. Nor was it a good political moment. The
end of Communist rule had diminished public in-
terest in all the Soviet founding fathers, and the
new government seemed interested only in
archival documents that would discredit Gor-
bachev and enhance its upcoming trial of the
Communist Party. The prison writings of a mar-
tyred founding father embraced by the last Soviet
leader served neither purpose.

Through a mutual Russian friend, I had earlier
met a person who now had the power and per-
haps the inclination to help, Gennady Burbulis.
One of Yeltsin's closest and most influential
aides, he had become a high-ranking official in
the first post-Soviet government. In July 1992,
ironically during the opening session of the Com-
munist Party trial, I approached him in a corridor
and asked for his help. Though not a politician
with any sympathy for the Soviet founding fa-
thers, Burbulis knew Anna Larina's saga through
her best-selling 1988 memoirs [entitled *Nezabyvae-
moe* (literally, 'The Unforgettable'), serialized in a
popular magazine in late 1988, and published as
a book in 1989] and was moved by her desire to
learn everything about her husband's fate. Only
very recently have I felt free, with his permission,
to name and publicly thank Gennady Burbulis.

Within minutes I was in his office while he spoke
on the phone to archive administrators, and

within a few weeks photocopies of the four man-
uscripts were in our hands. Another large batch of
materials from the Kremlin Archive soon fol-
lowed, just before its doors again slammed shut.

[In the 2008 Russian edition of the prison man-
uscripts Cohen has the following footnote: 'The top
archive administrators with whom I met, R. G.
Pikhoya and A. V. Korotkova, welcomed the decision
to release the manuscripts and gave me their support.
I wish to express special thanks to Yu. G. Murin, who
at that time was senior archivist of the Presidential
Archive. His expert evaluations, knowledge of the
documents and their history, and his human compas-
sion were a great help to us.' (See *Uznik Lubyanki:
Tiuremnye rukopisi Nikolaia Bukharina* [Inmate of
Lubyanka: The Prison Manuscripts of Nikolai
Bukharin], Moscow: AIRO-XX; RGTEU, 2008, 1,011
pages. This contains the complete Russian texts of *So-
cialism and Its Culture*, *Philosophical Arabesques* and the
autobiographical novel, but only 13 of the 187 poems,
the book-length verse manuscript that Bukharin enti-
tled 'Transformation of the World—Verse About the
Ages, and About People'.)]

Thus were Bukharin's widow, son, and daughter,
the historian Svetlana Gurvich, able to encounter
him anew across an enormous chasm of time and
suffering. For Anna Larina, who died in 1996,
there was just enough time left, with the help of
family and friends, to help prepare her husband's

last writings for publication in his homeland.

That is the end of the excerpt from Stephen Cohen's account of how the prison manuscripts were unearthed.

THE BUKHARIN–LARINA RELATIONSHIP

Anna Larina was born on 27 January 1914, 10 years to the day before Lenin's death; she died in 1996, only a few years after receiving copies of the prison manuscripts, including the verse her murdered husband had written for and about her.

The relationship between Nikolai Bukharin and Anna Larina has rightly been called one of history's remarkable love stories. It was movingly portrayed for English-speaking audiences in the television documentary *Widow of the Revolution*, which was shown nationally on the PBS network in the United States in August 2000, with Vanessa Redgrave as the voice of Anna Larina, reading excerpts from Larina's memoirs. This documentary, made by Rosemary Reed, was reported and narrated by Stephen Cohen.

Anna and Nikolai became lovers in 1930, then after a falling-out and some rough spots in their relationship, became a couple for good in 1934 and had a son, Yuri, in 1936. But at the end of February 1937 they were parted forever when Bukharin was arrested and, after a year in prison, was tried and executed (March 1938). Before Bukharin's arrest Anna memorized his 'testament', a letter entitled 'To a Future Generation of Party Leaders'. (See the English translation of her memoirs, *This I Cannot Forget*, New York: Norton, 1993.)

She kept this text alive in her memory through 20 years of prison, Gulag and exile. When she was allowed to return to Moscow, under Khrushchev, after his 1956 'secret speech' denouncing many of the crimes of Stalin, she finally dared to write down the text of Bukharin's letter, rather than holding it in memory alone.

In 1961, she delivered the text of Bukharin's testament to the Central Committee of the Soviet Communist Party, but the top party authorities still declined to clear Bukharin of the fabricated charges made against him in the Moscow trial of March 1938.

Throughout the 1960s and 1970s and into the 1980s, Anna Larina repeatedly 'sought his rehabilitation from senior Party leaders and in the highest Party echelons, the presidiums of Party Congresses, but without result' (*This I Cannot Forget*, p. 345). Not until 1988, under Gorbachev, was her long-dead husband, to whose memory she remained ever faithful, finally exonerated.

Her unswerving commitment to the man she had loved and married half a century earlier is expressed in her memoirs: 'I am glad I lived to see this day. Justice has triumphed. But nothing has dimmed my memory. And [to this day] the words Bukharin addressed to the future live in my soul: "Know, comrades, that the banner you bear in a triumphant march toward communism contains [also] a drop of my blood . . ."' (ibid., p. 346).

In her memoirs Anna Larina describes, among other things, two high points of their relationship that are also described in some of Bukharin's poems.

In the Crimea in 1930, at the age of 16, she went to visit him at his vacation home in Gurzuf a few hours' drive from Mukhalatka, where she and her father were on vacation. That was where and when their adult love relationship began. As a family friend, Bukharin had been a frequent visitor to the home of Yuri Larin, Anna's father, and a warm friendship had long existed between the child Anna and the older, but childlike Nikolai.

The Sixteenth Congress of the Soviet Communist Party was under way in summer 1930, but Bukharin did not attend, having borne the brunt of a campaign by Stalin and his faction accusing him, along with Rykov, Tomsky and others, of heading a 'Right Opposition'. He stayed away from the party congress also on account of illness, and went to the Crimea to recover. A photo in the English edition of Larina's memoirs captioned 'Bukharin during his illness in the Crimea, 1930' shows him stretched out on a bed, looking feverish.

Yet the romance between the 16-year-old Anna and the 42-year-old Nikolai began then. It is interesting to read his description of this in his poem 'Beginnings' and to compare that with her much more detailed account in *This I Cannot Forget* (pp. 107–112 and 128–9).

Another high point in their life together, after their decision to stay together as a couple, was their trip to Siberia in the late summer of 1935, described by Larina in her memoirs (pp. 79–85) and referred to by Bukharin in at least three poems: 'Together', 'Altai Rapids' and 'Conception'.

> Nikolai Ivanovich spent his vacation, as usual, immersed in nature, asserting his love of life to the full. He swam in cold mountain streams with floating chunks of ice and hunted for wild ducks from rafts bobbing down the Katun [River], which was certainly not without risk . . .

Bukharin's poem 'Altai Rapids' clearly derives from the same summer 1935 vacation. It describes the risky riding of a raft down the Biya River. (The Biya and Katun are neighbouring rivers. Both flow from the Altai mountain ranges and converge to form the Ob, which runs north through all of Siberia to the Arctic.)

In telling of their 1935 Siberian vacation Larina also recalls:

When we took a car up the Chuisky road [or Chuya highway, in the Chuya mountain range] to the Mongolian border, he hunted roe deer.

This may be the hunting trip Bukharin describes in the poem 'Car Chase'.

It was during that Siberian vacation that she became pregnant with their son, born nine months later, in April 1936, and named Yuri after her father, Yuri Larin. Anna omits any mention of this intimate aspect of their Siberian vacation, but Bukharin proudly titles his poem about it 'Conception'.

BUKHARIN AS POET

A friend to whom I showed some draft translations of *The Prison Poems* commented: 'Bukharin was not by nature a poet.'

I disagree. There is a bit of the poet in most all of us. There seems to be an innate human appreciation of rhythmical, musical language combined with vivid imagery and expressing or eliciting strong feelings. Also, there seems to be an innate urge to produce this kind of language, found in most human cultures in the world. What else is the source of folk songs and oral epics, not to mention 'the blues' that originated among African Americans? Why else are popular songs, with their lyrics and melodies, so popular? With or without music, they are poetry.

The *quality* of the poetry is another question. Often in deciding whether or not a poem is of high quality, the subjective tastes and preferences of the reader enter in.

Thus, in Julia Ward Howe's *Battle Hymn of the Republic* some of the lines strike me as poetry of high quality:

> *He is trampling out the vintage where the grapes of wrath are stored.*
> *He has loosed the fateful lightning of his terrible swift sword.*

It is rhythmical and musical, it can be sung, and its imagery seems to me quite successful. The quality of the phrase 'grapes of wrath' in fact is almost universally acknowledged. It has become virtually a standard phrase in American English.

Supporters of the Confederacy probably looked with jaundiced eye on those lines and denied any poetic value to them.

Yet I think some of the lines Bukharin wrote in Russian, though they may be regarded as politically tendentious, are of as high quality as Ms Howe's. (Whether I have been able to render them into English well enough for their quality to be appreciated is a separate question.)

Recently I chanced across a poem by the abolitionist William Lloyd Garrison, probably of 1850s' vintage, quoted by Frederick Douglass in his famous oration, 'What to the Slave is Your Fourth of July?' In its spirit, tone and style it reminded me of some of

Bukharin's verse.

Here is a sample stanza:

God speed the hour, the glorious hour,
When none on earth
Shall exercise a lordly power,
Nor in a tyrant's presence cower,
But all to manhood's stature tower,
By equal birth!
That hour will come, to each, to all,
And from his Prison-house, from thrall,
Go forth.

Much of Bukharin's poetry—with the exception, of course, of appeals to the deity—is in the same spirit and style. Though many might dismiss such verse as 'doggerel', it does nevertheless seek to express with rhythmic and rhymed language, vivid imagery, and emotion-inducing phrases, a higher aspiration, a vision and commitment to human solidarity, liberty and equality.

(It is, of course, ironic—and perhaps subversive of the quality of Bukharin's poetry—that he frequently refers to the Soviet Union as a 'land of freedom', even as he himself was languishing in prison on false charges concocted by the tyrannical ruler of the Soviet Union at that time, Joseph Stalin, chief bureaucrat in a system by then dominated by a privileged party/state bureaucracy. And Bukharin would soon face a frame-up trial and totally unjustified execution

in that 'land of freedom' of which he sang so elo-
quently, as if his wish could make it so.)

It should also be noted that Bukharin was an
artist, quite a skilled and talented painter, and the
painter's eye can often be detected in the poet's im-
agery. For example, his image of Mount Elbrus, re-
peated at the beginning and end of his poem on
Kabardá ('Pearl Necklace') seems consistent with a
painting he did of Elbrus, which Anna Larina de-
scribes as follows:

> We were sitting on the couch. Above it my fa-
> vorite watercolor [by Bukharin] still hung: *The El-
> brus at Sunset.* I . . . wiped the dust from the glass
> with a rag. At once the two-headed icy blue peak
> of the Elbrus was revealed, radiating in the rosy
> glow of sunset.

Similarly, a Bukharin painting of the Crimea, with
its mountainous rock cliffs plunging into becalmed
waters of the Black Sea, is reproduced in the Russian
edition of Larina's memoirs. That painting's visual im-
agery is echoed in several of *The Prison Poems*, in par-
ticular, 'Crab', 'Beginnings' and 'Black Sea'.

Much in Bukharin's past made him intimately fa-
miliar with the great works of literature in the cultural
heritage of humanity, and that includes poetry of
course. He placed the highest value on that cultural
heritage, as these poems show. He had a good feel for
and appreciation of poetry and quality literature from

many different lands and traditions. This truth is illustrated by the epigraphs, not only in Russian but also in Latin, Greek, German, French, Italian, and even in English (from Shakespeare), which he used to introduce many of his poems. (He did not always specify the source of an epigraph, and in some cases we have not been able to locate the original in German, French, etc. In such cases we have simply made back-translations from Bukharin's Russian version.)

In an autobiographical sketch that he wrote in the late 1920s he states that as a schoolchild (quite an exceptional one, we must say) he devoured all the plays of Molière.

Some of Bukharin's poems in this book have epigraphs related to that great French humorist.

Bukharin's autobiographical novel, written in prison *after* he wrote these poems, confirms the strong influence on the young Bukharin of the great German poets Goethe and, especially, Heine. That influence is expressed in many of *The Prison Poems*, including 'Eyes of Zeus' about Goethe and 'Lyre of Irony' about Heine.

Like many members of the Russian intelligentsia, Bukharin was surrounded by poetry from his earliest days. The family Bukharin grew up in treasured poetry, and literature in general. They were schoolteachers from whom he surely inherited his own appreciation of the human cultural heritage.

This was reinforced by the classical education he received in the Russian secondary school he attended in Moscow. The Russian *gimnaziya* was of course named after the *gymnasion* of ancient Athens, and like similarly named schools in Germany and other European countries it prepared students for university education, providing them with a wide cultural background. The *gimnaziya* introduced him to ancient Greek, and to Latin, including, in all likelihood, such Latin poets as Ovid, Horace, Virgil and Ausonius, whom he cites in *The Prison Poems*. But he also pursued this interest on his own. Throughout his life, he seems to have been a person full of curiosity and an independent thirst for knowledge.

Many other leaders of the Russian revolution, Lenin and Trotsky in particular, were well versed in literature and the human cultural heritage generally. In 1925, after Lenin's death, when the ruling Communist Party decided to adopt an official policy on the contending schools of literature that had emerged in Soviet life, it was none other than Bukharin, along with Trotsky, who was assigned to draft the official Party resolution. That is, among Party leaders Bukharin and Trotsky were seen to be the most substantial authorities on literary matters.

Later, after Trotsky had been expelled from the party (1927) and then deported from the Soviet Union (1929), Bukharin remained as perhaps the best qualified party leader on the subject of literature. Even though in 1929–30 Bukharin was ousted from top leadership posts and reviled as head of a supposed 'Right Opposition', mainly because of his (sensible and correct) opposition to forced collectivization of peasant agriculture, his expertise in the field of literature was so widely acknowledged that he was authorized to give a major speech at the founding congress of the Union of Soviet Writers in August 1934. The opening section of his speech was on 'Poetry, Poetics and Problems of Poetry in the USSR'. An English translation of this extensive discussion of poetry by Bukharin may be found in Maynard Solomon (ed.), *Marxism and Art* (New York: Vintage, 1974), pp. 205–14.

Bukharin's 1934 speech at the Soviet Writers' Congress demonstrates once again his vast and intimate acquaintance with poetry, ranging from a discussion of 'the mystical interpretation of poetry and poetic experience', as expressed in treatises on poetry from ancient India and ancient China, to a Marxist, sociological analysis of poetic creation.

One may argue, of course, that even if a person has a solid grounding in the many varieties of poetry worldwide and an ability to present a well-informed discussion of poetry and poetics, that does not mean that such a person will be a good poet.

A good drama critic is not necessarily a good playwright.

But in Bukharin's case, I think he had absorbed from his wide reading and close familiarity with poetry a sense of the elements that go into versification, developing poetic skills of his own. The elements of poetry that he had dealt with so much in his life became a part of him. He was driven by the emotions and contradictions of his own personal situation, in prison, to seek solace in the writing of poetry, perhaps also seeking to impose order and perspective on this experience. The result was often of high quality, in my opinion, just as his prose work, *How It All Began* (the autobiographical novel), is of high quality.

A further comment should be made on his relation to folk poetry. Anna Larina relates that at one point during the terrible emotional strain of their last days together, just before his arrest, which they knew was coming, she broke down sobbing.

In an effort to console her Bukharin began singing a folk song, a favourite of theirs, which they had often sung together with their chauffeur, Klykov. (Earlier she had quoted parts of many other folk songs they and Klykov had sung together.)

The Russian text of the song Bukharin sang to her, in transliteration, goes like this (with accent marks over the stressed syllables):

Chudny mésyats plyvyót nad rekóyu,
Vsyo obyáto nochnói tishinói.
Nichevó mne na svéte ne nádo,
Tolko vídet tebyá, mily mói!
A wondrous moon's afloat above the river,
The still of night holds all in its embrace.
There's nothing in this world that I have need of,
Nothing but to see you, oh my love!

Many of the lines of Bukharin's verse are written in this spirit, even with a similar vocabulary, especially in the 'Lyrical Intermezzo' part of the book. (His poem 'The Road', is an example.)

In his autobiographical novel he has the following passage about this form of folk poetry: 'Full of melancholy were these Russian folk songs. They sang of "evil fate", oppression, parting, sorrow, orphanhood, unlucky love, and poverty, as the autumn winds sing sadly in the trees. Nowhere are the typical features of our life registered so expressively as in our folk songs . . .'

(See Bukharin's discussion of Russian folk songs in *How It All Began*, pp. 122–4. In those pages he quotes half a dozen or more such songs, including the one he sang to Anna Larina when she broke down crying during their last days together—although he does not allude to that occasion.)

In the torment and horror of the time of Stalin's Great Terror, often unbearable emotions found vent in poetry.

Larina describes how Bukharin reacted to the news of Sergo Ordzhonikidze's suicide, not long before Bukharin's own arrest: 'He was composing a poem dedicated to Sergo's memory, an expression of shock and grief at this heavy loss.'

Bukharin's poem to Ordzhonikidze was confiscated by Stalin's secret police when they searched the Bukharins' apartment shortly after his arrest. Larina, who had typed the handwritten poem, could remember, decades later, only the last two lines:

Solid as granite in the flaming sea,
He cracked like lighting in the foaming waves.

The imagery and rhythms are similar to many lines in *The Prison Poems*.

This source of Bukharin's poetic expression might be seen as a variation on Wordsworth's comment that poetry 'takes its origin from emotion recollected in tranquility'. Unfortunately, in Stalin's Russia there was little tranquility for such recollecting. Bukharin, in prison, apparently did have moments, snatches of time, for recollection, often at night. The dating of many of his poems is phrased this way: 'night, early hours of . . . [such-and-such a day]'.

Against this background, Bukharin's poetry may be more highly appreciated.

In conclusion, I wish to acknowledge and express my gratitude to Stephen F. Cohen and Katrina van den Heuvel, to Naveen Kishore and Sunandini

Banerjee of Seagull Books, and to the Chekhov Foun-
dation, whose assistance helped make possible this
work of translation. I also thank the many friends—
David Ray, Alicja Mann, Paul Le Blanc, Dara Noyes,
Joseph Auciello, and others too numerous to men-
tion—for reading or listening to draft translations of
the poems and providing helpful feedback.

* * *

AVAILABILITY OF THE RUSSIAN TEXT OF THE POEMS

The Russian originals of these poems have not been
published—except for the 13 poems included in the
2008 Russian edition of the prison manuscripts.
(Somehow the title of one of those 13 became gar-
bled in the process of publication. It appears in the
2008 Russian edition, incorrectly, as *Gnilye vorota*
['Gates of Decay'] when in fact Bukharin's title was
Gnilye bolota ['Swamps of Decay'].)

Readers wishing to consult the Russian originals
can turn to the typescript of 173 poems (typed by
Anna Larina's daughter-in-law Tonya from photo-
copies of Bukharin's handwritten manuscript deliv-
ered to the Bukharin family from the official archives
of the Russian government in 1992).

One copy of the typescript is on deposit at Co-
lumbia University Library in New York, in the
Bakhmeteff Archive of Russian and East European

History and Culture, in the Rare Book and Manuscript Library.

Another copy is on deposit in Moscow at the Moscow city archives—that is, Tsentralyi Moskovskii Arkhiv-Muzei Lichnykh Sobranii [Central Moscow Archive-Museum of Private Collections] (www.Mosarch.mos.ru), which is part of the Glavnoe Arkhivnoe Upravlenie Goroda Moskvy [Main Archival Administration of the City of Moscow].

Author's Preface*

Yes, these surviving remnants or descendants of the Teutomanes of 1815, the super-German blockheads who have merely rearranged their old costumes and trimmed their long ears a bit—all my life I've hated these types and fought against them, and now as the sword is slipping from the dying man's grasp, I am consoled by the sure conviction that Communism, across whose path they will be encountered first, will deal them the final blow. And that young giant will not just knock them flat with a cudgel, but will crush them underfoot the way you crush a repulsive reptile.

—Heinrich Heine

We live in an iron age. Behind us are dreadful but victorious struggles and colossal victories. The world is an enormous holding tank of fermentation, and

Communism is the life-giving leaven in that tank, the great fermenting force that produces new life.

After all, it is precisely for life, for ardent, passionate, joyful life that a worldwide struggle is now going on. Its enemies have called up from the darkness all the vampires of the past that have greedily sucked the blood and drained the hearts of humankind. Look, my friends, how many flocks of gloomy spirits, malicious gnomes and goblins, are swarming in the foul and stinking pit of fascism? What poisonous potions they are brewing to conjure up their death-dealing fogs, with which they wish to extinguish our rising radiant sun!

They no longer even need Christ, however well varnished, plastered over, and touched up with rouge his figure may be; Christ wearing a crown of worthless bank notes painted gold in service of Mammon.

They have called for assistance from the god of the hangman's noose, the bloodthirsty old god Wotan, and this drunken god is brandishing his sword, shouting hoarsely and berserkly, and mouthing filthy curses. He has let loose from the gates of Valhalla his savage, vengeful Valkyries. They have resurrected the blonde beast imagined by Nietzsche, that mad prophet of hatred, and with it the cruel lustfulness of aristocratic robbers, the gentlemen for whom the blood of slaves is a life-sustaining fluid.

Wherever they wander, the smoke of giant bon-
fires marks their path. With iron sword these murder-
ers of the soul wish to pierce the heart of our new
world, our country, which has raised itself up like a
young giant from the very depths of poverty, oppres-
sion, barbarism and grief, carrying the lofty banner of
the most noble ideals and unparalleled accomplish-
ments. They want to drown our luxurious meadows in
a sea of scarlet blood and tears of salt, our meadows
with their wondrous flowers of joy and creativity,
beautiful flowers that have opened wide their magical
eyes and are gazing at the limitless blue sky. Flowers
that are living and breathing and glorifying life.

Along the highway of robbery and plunder these
so-called Aryans, these killers, have linked up with the
evil dragon of Oriental mediaevalism, to whom God
himself points out with his wrinkled, long-nailed fin-
ger how to dig their way into someone else's pocket.
And oh, yes, there's another person who can't be left
out of this equation, the Pope, the most Holy Father,
who in the shape of a crumbling mummy with the
trembling hands of an old man blesses the Nordic-
Japanese-Roman crusade of Christ and Wotan against
the light-bearing rays of the sun!

Then there are the worshipers and admirers of
the ancient she-wolf who with her milk of iron suck-
led the babes Romulus and Remus, the ancestors of
those who today are suppressing ancient Ethiopia.

They have forgotten about the time when their country and the *urbs*, the great city of Rome, lay in ruins at the feet of harsh Teutonic hordes. All of them are united by a fierce hatred of the bright new life whose silver wings gleam so miraculously in the brilliance of the dawn of humankind.

* * *

Yes, we are living in an age of iron. Two worlds stand face to face, two great armies, and a battle is in the making on whose outcome depends the entire future life of people on this earth, a billion and a half working people scattered across the planet.

'The pyramids are looking at you, soldiers,' said Napoleon addressing his troops at the time of his Egyptian expedition. The entire past-present-and-future is looking at us. And our fighters know this, our men of steel, our falcons and eagles, and our whole country knows it—a remarkable country at whose head stand iron people with minds that see across centuries, with hearts aflame like fire and with wills of granite.

Ah no, you spirits of gloom! You are going to break your teeth, and your own people are going to lift you up on the points of their lances, and you will end your lives in shame, and no one will sing dirges for you, and your accursed graves will be grown over by the weeds of oblivion while the collective heart of a united human race goes on happily beating.

Yes, friends, we live in an iron age. And our cause is one of iron, and our swords should be strong and sharp: we should forge them from the very best steel, so as to sever the heads of the enemy in the raging thunderstorm of battle.

But does that mean we should feed ourselves on filings of iron instead of bread and meat? Drink machine oil instead of wine? Deprive ourselves of the joys of life? Put on the sad faces of the Lenten fast? Place our hopes in the scant forces of heaven? But science has long since cleared those imaginary forces from the skies, having proven that what exists there is nothing but a terrible coldness. And even if a stern God the Father *was* located there, he would long since have turned into a clinking doll of ice, so that he could neither help nor curse human beings (and he did the latter, according to Holy Writ, much more often than the former).

Are those the things we should do? No! It is with joy and under the banners of the bright blood-red of life itself that our country prepares for battle. The blood pulses ardently through our country's veins, and the pounding of its great heart can be heard around the world. Across its vast spaces songs can be heard, and ever new varieties of flowers are blooming on its fields and meadows. More and more new forms of beauty reveal themselves for the millions of our people.

Let there be more happiness, joy and creativity! There is power in this; it builds our might, our self-confidence, daring and loyalty. A joyful song is also an inspiration to bravery. Love and friendship mean reliability and faithfulness in battle. There is happiness in fighting for a life of creativity, life consecrated to beauty.

The poets of the world that is dying, the frail, slender singers of the aromas of death, who reek of the past's festering lily, have called for a retreat into an ivory tower and for locking oneself away in that tower so that the noises of the street will not interfere with one's total devotion to the sweet passion of decay, the corpse-like voluptuousness of doomed and dying parasites.

Our poets too sometimes go off into a tower. But that tower is a very high watch tower, a proud Mt Everest of the world, from which all past centuries are visible, and also visible is the disposition of the armies on the field of battle today, with their banners and their troops, and from that tower it is even possible to see into a future that is illumined by golden rays.

The new master of the world has arrived, its collective owner, the proletariat, which is growing into and becoming the people as a whole, is being transformed into the human race itself. It is the owner and master of everything. From billions and billions of bricks it is building temples of life and temples of glory. It gathers construction materials from everywhere, but only if they are solid and firm, and have withstood testing.

The proletariat searches everywhere, in the West and in the East, in the North and in the South— searches for flowers, herbs and grasses, and trees, which it can plant in its own great Garden of Life, where golden apples are already beginning to store up their juices and where a new earthly paradise will flourish. But there will be no serpent in this Garden of Eden. On the other hand there will be attractive clothing of good quality and many other truly superlative things that were never suspected or imagined in the old holy book of the Hebrews, bound in pigskin. That book's savage and vengeful God, that foul-tempered oldster, having created man so that he could punish him, and having created man's lovely companion so as to beat her with whips, that obnoxious old man in the sky turns out to be totally beside the point. No one any longer will call him by name, either by his last name or his first.

So then, Comrades! I had the chance to hike among the mighty mountain peaks where the sun was shining, and down below me on the Alpine meadows I saw various flowers growing. I gathered them in a basket and wove a wreath of them, which I propose to lay on the communal grave of those who have given their lives in the affirmation of Life Itself, for the cause of our country, for the happiness and earthly joys of the peoples of the world.

Perhaps I did not succeed in weaving this wreath as it should have been woven. Perhaps some of the flowers have withered along the way, their little crowns drooped, and their sweet smell vanished in the air. But you know, I tried so hard to gather them and bring them to you! And besides, I have brought roots and seeds. Others too may plant them, so that they can grow.

Feci quod potui. Faciant meliora potentes!

(I have done what I could. May others who can, do better!)

[*NOTE: The 'Author's Preface' appears in the typescript after 'Berlin Zoo', dated 3 October 1937, and before 'Ancient Landscape', dated 4 October 1937. Thus the preface was apparently written 3–4 October 1937—G. S.]

PRECURSORS

[Bukharin gave the above title to the 13 poems that he designated as 'series II', but since 'series I', with its 14 poems is missing, this is the first group of poems in the present edition.—G. S.]

An Egyptian Priest's Lament
(From an Ancient Papyrus)

The Plaint of Ipuwer:
O great gods, divinities majestic! O Osiris!
O Isis, our great mother,
Have mercy on us! Save us!
Crush the rebellious foul corruption!

Our last days, the final times, have come,
With sacred temples lying in the dirt
The names of all the pharaohs are defiled.
Accursed boorish louts are everywhere.

Slaves are covering their bodies
With rich cloth of priceless value
While princes of the blood wear stinking rags.
One closes one's eyelids in fear.
The corpses of nobles are flung about in corners

And hungry dogs lick at them.
Slaves in the palaces are burning the incense of
others
To win credit from the gods for themselves.

The grain has been robbed from the emperor's
granaries.
The slave women stole it away.
O divine luminaries! Wine and perfume
From the priests and the princes were taken!

Among us the louts have grown insolent. They live
With the noblest wives of the highborn,
And they rub their rough hides with the finest
perfumes,
And they dress in the clothing of others.

And children with well-born family names
Are serving as couriers to former slaves.
O gods! Send down to us shackles and manacles
Instead of fair lotuses and tender lilies!

Thus lamented the Egyptian priest Ipuwer
After the slaves had won power.
The hieroglyphics reveal to us
This exemplary ancient historic event.

No one knows what happened next.
That's been hidden away forever,
But the ancient papyrus shows us clearly
The priest with his frantic yammering.

In the land of the pyramids, dreadful battles
happened,
Clashes with the rabid owners of slaves.
That's what this papyrus is relating.
It tells us of our nameless precursors,

Of slaves, madly daring, courageous fighters,
And the rich people's furious hatred,
The impotent priests, long since turned to dust,
Their bellies still bursting with malice.

(night, early hours of 12 September 1937)

The Blacksmith's Apron
(A Legend from Ancient Iran)

In the sources of antiquity, in great Iran,
There lived a cruel king, Zohak by name,
Eating away at the country like liver cancer,
Like a bloody, suppurating wound.
Of all the kings, perfidious and cruel,
Who trampled common people into dust
No more evil monster could be found
Than the terrible monster named Zohak.
In his luxurious palace, at temple or bazaar,
On the balance beam of his shoulders he carried
Two repulsive burdens, always with him,
Two giant snakes with scaly patterned skins.
These were by no means ordinary serpents,
But loyal servants of tormentor-kings.
They ate but one thing—they ate the thick,

Fresh brains of any person they had crushed.
Throughout the land mad terror held its sway,
But in night's silence, there built up resistance.
With painful, slow effort of thought, the people
Began to sharpen their axes against the king.
Among others in those days lived Kaweh,
A huge man and a blacksmith of great skill,
A mighty warrior. From him the snakes had stolen
Seventeen sons the way that wolves steal sheep.
Only one son remained, only one son,
For that one too the ruler was licking his lips.
The blacksmith brought all working folk together
With their hammers and chisels and saws.
His leather apron, forged from animal skins,
With powerful mitts, he nailed to a sturdy tree,
Made it the banner of the workers' cause,
The greatest cause of all, the fight for freedom.
And valiantly he led a rebel march
With his folk, workers of the crafts and trades.
The people of labour defeated the king,
Who by some miracle escaped with his life
And fled in fright to the mountain Demavend,
But there the god Feridun fastened him
To a volcano by a set of chains.
And when they saw the end of evil times
The people celebrated just like children.

* * *

For centuries the simple leather apron
Was honoured as the people's victory banner.
But then the rich purloined the leather flag
And ushered in a time of new misfortune.

They covered the apron with a fancy shawl
Of diamonds and sapphires shining like stars,
Of rubies and turquoise and Tyrian purple
And gifts set in weighty cases.
Such a heavy burden. No one could lift it.
No one could see the paths that formerly
Led to the simple apron of the blacksmith,
The man who fought for the good of the people.

* * *

The evil years—they've set in once again.
Over the land reign poverty and need,
But the time will come—and somewhere someday
The people of Iran will find their banner!

(morning, 20 July 1937)

Spartacus

'Your favorite hero?'
'Spartacus.'
—Karl Marx [in reply to a questionnaire
compiled by his daughters]

In giant Rome great tumult reigns. Swollen and
voracious,
Its belly roars its victories.
The idle crowd's dense mass has given rise
To black fruit hanging from war's bloody tree.

With heavy tread, to all ends of the earth
Rome's legionnaires have marched, victorious,
Dragging behind triumphal chariots
In dirt and dust full many a conquered throne.

The Roman land is jammed with captive slaves.
With piles of tribute sent from everywhere,

The price of slaves has fallen to mere pence,
Crowds of them herded, lassos round their necks.

The people fill the sumptuous circuses,
A living mass that stirs in happy waves.
Bloodthirsty beasts from distant Africa
Are brought out here to tear the flesh of slaves.

To please the idle crowd the gladiator
With iron sword cuts down his very brother.
The emperor, depraved, from his plush cushion
Cries hoarse-voiced, *Vae victis*!—shrugging his
shoulder.

But Spartacus rebelled and raised the banner:
Freedom for slaves from torment and abuse.
The clans and tribes of nations with different
tongues
Gathered like brothers in rebel regiments.

A great and sacred battle then began
Against Rome's host of stern centurions.
In the unequal fight, though Spartacus fell,
His name lives on through all the centuries.

(12 September 1937)

Peasant War

When Adam delved
And Eve span
Who was then
The gentleman?

—English folk song

'Our forefather Adam, the son of the Lord,
He did the plowing, and Eve did the spinning.
Where were you in those days, noble landlord,
What work were you doing?'

Thus sang the peasants, children of want,
Bitterly cursing their fate,
They peacefully sat in their huts, and were deaf
To appeals for battle, to take up the axe.

The princes, the barons, the full-bellied priests
Swarmed over them, greedy as horseflies,

Stuffed their craws to the full with their blood and
their sweat
Tore the skin off their backs without mercy.

Round the clock knights in armour on highways
robbed them,
And the greedy priest gathered his tithe.
The baron, while taking away their cattle,
Said, 'Don't set your foot on my land.'

Never unsoiled were their calloused hands
As they worked off the burden, corvée.
On the baron's rich fields for the baron's whole tribe
The peasant would labour away.

On the cliffs overhead stood the fearsome castle,
Overlooking the downtrodden village.
Like a bird of prey, the landlord swooped down,
His angry bass voice full of curses.

From Holy Scripture the learned priest read,
Instructing the peasants like children,
Spelling out by letter and syllable
What was sacred in God's strict commandments.

At last in the villages peasants had reached
The bloody-lined limits of patience,
Angrily clenching their fists they vowed
To put an end to their sufferings.

They sharpened their axes both day and night,
Their pitchforks and knives, scythes and lances.
The leaders had lived to see the dread day.
Bloody dewdrops shone red in the morning.

The rebel flag was a peasant's shoe,
Worn down and crude and coarse.
Poorboy Conrad—he marched on those dogs of barons
To knock out their sharp canine fangs.

Baronial castles then burst into flame.
The estates of the princes were burning.
The ring of fire and blood closed around them.
Crimson wedding dances were playing.

In bloody waves the battles were waged.
The peasants fought stubbornly onward.
Against them the barons' formations were rallied
In armour of steel, on spirited steeds.

The peasants were crushed by these princely formations,
Superior weapons, and crafty deception.
All the rebels were killed, put to death savagely
And a bloody fog covered the land.

The towns of the rebels were taken by storm
Where journeymen formed their communes.
In the village smoke rose over garden and home
The priests' false beliefs were victorious.

An endless row of black gallows arose,
And loud was the cawing of carrion crows.
For the orphan children, the peasants' kids,
Life's harness traces were broken . . .

Dark people of labour remember well
The savage and vicious reprisals.
They say to the powers: 'We will not forget.
For this you will pay in full!'

(12 September 1937)

Pugachóv Encaged

Bright falcon fated never more to fly,
Grey eagle never more to take his prey,
His fate, enclosed in iron cage to sit,
The pain of death upon the block to bear.

'The brigand has been trapped! We've caught you,
villain!'
'A long career of thieving you've had, Cain!'
'The honest folk are gonna let you have it.'
'We hope you're firmly fastened by that chain.'

Around the cage the mob crowds close,
Feet stamping. Stares of curiosity.
A mash of bodies. Fox fur. Ladies' bare skin.
Bared sabres. Shouts and cries. Reproaches.
The entire Bolotnaya Plaza's astir,
Filled to its limits with people.

The plaza hums like an angry hive
With irrepressible buzzing and chatter.

Pugachóv sadly looks for a friendly face
Among the many-eyed crowd.
Metallic clang of shackles and chains,
An ill-met reward for his battles and pains.

Ah, but those were great days,
Those were the years!
All the flowers were blooming,
Cares and worries fled!
Like schools of fish in the sea
The poor peasants flocked together
In the fight for land and freedom.
How brightly our battle flared!
What dashing young fellows
Were then at my side!
Where are you now, bronze cannon?
Fighters for freedom, where are you?
The Bashkirs and the Cossacks
And lads from the factories,
Who forged sturdy pole-axes
Against the satanic foe.
Ah, how we took the towns at one swoop
And took captives with us—disrobed boyars.
Freedom clung to our chests like our shirts.
Red was the glare of fires burning.

Ah, how we drove the gentry from their nests,
Smoking them out with flame and sword.

A lucky star stood over us then,
Liberty-loving, free peasant people.
On their trellised porches of fine design
The generals trembled to face our courts.
And ours, fully ours, was the noble's rich home,
Songs of praise were sung to our fine, daring fellows!

Rage and black torment
Burned in his eyes.

On the chopping block adroitly
The headsman sharpened the axe.

(night, early hours of 13 September 1937)

Precursors

Since long ago great minds have dreamed
About a bright and better future,
Looked far ahead and sometimes grumbled
At a common sight, the beggar's pouch.

And from the depths of the 'lower orders'
Where passion turbulently bubbled,
From the dark and bloody abyss of woe
Where poverty's maw gaped wide,
A flame sprang up—and sprang up more than once—
The flame of new doctrines and principles,
And a banner was lifted to the skies
And a mighty lion's wrath roared out.

In peasant revolts of the Middle Ages,
Among journeymen in the towns,

In times of harsh and bitter battle
A bright sun was shining in their minds.

Not only the Taborite pioneers,
But Thomas Müntzer and John of Leiden—
They were leading a caravan
Of brave and audacious dreams.

And the fighting Levellers of England
Added their voice to the chorus.

The enemy viciously settled the score.
The headsman's axe fell on all their necks . . .

And Campanella with sad gaze
Dreamed of the City of the Sun
While in a dungeon underground
The hapless captive's light burned low.

Sir Thomas More's sharp thought produced
A brilliant work, Utopia,
Showing how life would look—some day—
In a cheerful future paradise.

Babeuf's Conspiracy of Equals
Rang out, both menacing and strong,
Against the foul, unequal foundations
That Capital was laying down.
And like the breath of a new-forming mass,
Like tender fruit, as yet unripe,
The stubborn bent of Fourier's mind

Was present in the new line of thought.
Sardonic, brilliant, bold, to the point,
His sharp-tongued critical commentary
And his unlimited flights of fancy
Rose from the depths of an unhappy world.

The well-phrased passion of Saint Simon,
Prophet of the new in darkest times,
Like a crown in full resplendence,
Shone forth for all, a vision bright.

The sober, simple considerations
That Robert Owen presented us—
They reinforced golden dreams of old
With plain and sturdy, well-forged iron.

Yes, those were only golden dreams
And they had many holes in them,
But already outlines could be seen,
Landmarks presaging a brighter future.

The unripe kernel, with time's passing,
Has changed into the richest fruit.
In clashes with inveterate enemies
The workers have matured, grown firm and strong.

(early hours of 13 September 1937)

Thunderstorm
(The French Revolution)

LOUIS XVI: *Une rivolte?*
COUNT LIANCOURT: *Non, Sire . . . une révolution.*
HEGEL: It was a splendid rising of the sun.

All courtiers were overcome with fright, with
deathly terror,
With trembling at the knees.
The people summoned willpower on an awesome
scale and, roaring,
Rose up with sword in hand.

Shaking behind their modish masks, the palace fops
fell silent.
Wigs toppled,
Powder spilled on the floor, and cold ice froze their
brains
As stiff as armour.

Battalions of the people stormed the Bastille.
Plebeian bayonets
Gleamed in the sunshine like gold crowns,
And fists waved.

A raging fury echoed in the flood of noisy streets
In boisterous city squares,
In the shouts of *enragés*, in madly fierce
And fiery speeches.
All the rotted-out laws went flying off to hell,
Along with monarchs' thrones,
With coats of arms of marquis, count and lowly squire,
And glittering princes' crowns.

And proudly from below an awesome power arose
At a moment of crisis
To crush the foes' attacks, the hordes from hostile
countries,
The National Convention.

Combating the Gironde, the knife's sharp blade was
set to work
By the Mountain, by Robespierre.
The Marseillaise rang out and cannon smoke curled up
From desperate battles.
Plebeian fighters struggled, passionate, brave and firm,
On every border battlefield.

In the insurgent country famine reigned—dark,
terrible.
Not enough force was being used.

Vile thieves of bread, of money and markets, met
with threats,
The people's hammer of reprisal.

Marat quite rightly sounded the alarm, unceasingly,
In his *Ami du people*,
But the people's tribune fell, slain in a wicked plot.
A dagger killed the fighter.

Alarming times crept up, the enemy tightened ranks.
They guillotined Robespierre.
An aristocracy of wealth began its greedy reign
With measures against the poor.

* * *

Against the gloomy background of a red sky, dark
and stormy,
Upon a heap of crowns,
A spectre loomed, distant, then close, on horseback,
then enthroned,
The former corporal, Napoleon.

(13 or 14 September 1937)

The Dreamer
(Charles Fourier)

> Nothing great in this world is achieved without passion.
>
> —Hegel

A humble, lowly dreamer, somewhat eccentric,
With wild imagination's giant power,
Not at all timid, not simple-minded,
Brilliantly sharp and cuttingly smart,
He knew the world of commerce's living secrets,
The swindling on the bourse and in the shop,
In offices and banks, where coins ring out,
And in the general toils of capitalism.
He tore the cover off of all deceit,
All base and foul and hypocritic lying,
Luxurious depravity, the chains of want,
His skilful pen lashed out against them all.

Cold-bloodedly he laid bare with his knife
The vices of the civilized but blind
And saw the thresholds of new times to come
After these blighted shores are left behind.

Morality, family life, bowing and scraping,
Fawning and feigning, fake servility,
The rottenness of laws, shot through with lies,
Enslavement of women, the damaging of children,
Sternly he thundered against them with burning
words,
With beautifully vivid, fire-breathing phrases,
For all who would listen or had eyes to see.

His prose was ardent and his style direct.
He dreamed of new life, fired by passion,
Of fragrant seas and perfumed oceans,
Of anti-lions and anti-tigers,
And souls of stars, pure, crystalline.

He listed the passions of every kind, and urged
Each one be given its work to do,
So that the lice eggs of vice would disappear,
The satisfaction of needs would destroy care.

He longed for a full new life for people,
Using the model of a whole new system,
A new home for all, a 'phalanstery'
Among the trees and flowers like a garden.

Stubbornly he sought the aid of the wealthy,
The aid of men of influence and power,
A means to reach this new millennium
Where folks could freely live in love and friendship.

He didn't see the mighty force (the working class)
That could in fact transform the world,
And in the end his ventures came to naught.
In poverty he died, still longing. . . .

(night, early hours of 14 September 1937)

1848

A majestic year. Despite Saturnalias of blood
In battles for power
In capitals of the world the working class first
stepped forward
To win or die!
Paris, Vienna, Berlin—all of them rose up in fury.

Upon the paving stones
Arose barricades of lumber. Bullets whistled
And ominous fights impended.

Pale with fear in the face of universal indignation,
Ministers and princes
Lost the feathers from their tails and in swift retreat
Saw the shreds of their powers burn.

The lawyers, doctors, writers, blabbermouths for the
bourgeois,

Calmed down right away.
And the workshops' sons marched forward, a
proletarian assault
On the lords and gentlemen.

The liberals then began to howl, like dogs gone mad,
And made a change of front.
Bloodthirsty Cavaignacs appeared on the scene,
Horizons darkened.

Grapeshot and cannon went wild, and without let-up
They blasted the barricades' bodies.
Mountainous rows of corpses built up
In piles on the pavement.

Vilely vengeful, the shopkeepers howled with
malicious glee.
It was their victory!
For capital, for money, for landed property,
The bastards shed the workers' blood!

The heroes who fell and fought in that glorious year
We crown with laurel wreaths.
For now we've lived to see the great dawn—our
victories
Over all the frenzied foe!

(night, early hours of 14 September 1937)

John Brown (A Ballad)

The land was conquered by the sword
And everything around destroyed.
From Europe, Capital had arrived,
With cross in hand, and crucifixion.

To the New World it brought from Africa
Black slaves in the bottoms of ships,
With iron chains for bracelets,
Letting them rot by the thousands.

In the new land it kept them like cattle
Beat them with bludgeons, batons.
Foreheads were seared with iron brands,
And men crushed down beneath the iron heel.

The spirit of savage Christians,
The ones whose skin was white,

Was scornful towards all black-skinned folk,
Holding the nose, saying, 'Oh my god!'

Among those dogs of Puritans
There lived a farming man, John Brown,
And he had offspring, two strong sons,
And both of them he dearly loved.*

He also loved all who were poor,
And it made his good blood boil
When he saw slaves being brought
Out onto the auction block.

Alone he rose against it all.
Fiery he was and bold.
He called on blacks to follow him
To heroic feats and glorious deeds.

And long did this proud lion fight,
Kept up an unexampled battle,
But his inspired rage was crushed
In that barbaric land.

Into the enemy's hands he fell,
And torture him they did.
They fell upon him, hacked his flesh
As though to make ragout.

But he kept standing straight and proud,
And his great forehead shone
With sacred strength of true ideas
His eyes still held their gleam.

And when they led him out to die,
He noticed in the crowd
A black child sitting in the dust
Beside a farmer's house.

He gave the little child a kiss.
A tear gleamed in his eye.
The hangman placed a noose around
His neck and drew it tight.

(30 August 1937)

[*NOTE: John Brown in fact had 20 children. Two of his
sons took part in the raid on Harper's Ferry in 1859 and
were killed in the fighting.—G. S.]

Chernyshevsky on the Scaffold*

Russia's great scholar and critic . . .
—Karl Marx (in reference to Chernyshevsky)

Alas, Nikolai Gavrilovich!
Who can bear to see you like this?
Your misfortune is no small thing.
It makes tears start from every eye.
They've stood you up next to the block.
Imagine! You, the pride of Russia,
Like a thief, a killer, an evildoer,
In the thrall of the tsar's savage power.

Your learned and enlightened mind,
So penetrating and clear-sighted,
Your stubborn will, and deeds that add up
To a daring exploit of lasting value,
Bringing light to a dark, enormous land,

Whispering, 'Moujiks, take up arms,
Wage a merciless peasant war
Against landlord and priest and tsar.'

Beloved idol of all the youth,
Master of science, thought and word,
They sent him in chains to be buried alive
In the realm of hard labour—dark grave.

The drum rolls,
A paper is read,
And an officer numskull
Breaks a sword over his head.
The crowd trembles and freezes in place
In an agony of fear and awe,
As though courage and conscience had died in
them all
At the sight of the martyr's fall.

From the depths of the motley crowd,
Like a bird, flowers fly to the scaffold,
And tender red roses touch the shirt
That bears the emblem of disgrace.
A smile bloomed on his face of pain
And his lips were seen to move.
The gendarmes with their sabres bared
Rushed forward, rudely shoving.

The carriage bearing him starts to rumble,
The escort troops swing round,

And the crowd runs after.
Dear friend, farewell!

(14 September 1937)

[*NOTE: In this poem Bukharin describes the 'civil execution' to which the writer, critic and revolutionary democrat Nikolai Gavrilovich Chernyshevsky (1828–89) was subjected on 19 May 1864, at Mytnaya Square in St Petersburg. Under tsarist rule, 'civil execution' (*grazhdanskaya kazn'*) was an official ceremony in which the condemned person was led onto a scaffold before a large crowd, as though to be executed. But the 'execution' was only symbolic, a public humiliation in which the condemned was officially stripped of all civil rights and any rank or title previously held. He was forced to kneel down, a sword was broken over his head, and then he was chained to a pillar with a sign saying 'State Criminal' hung around his neck. After such a ceremony, Chernyshevsky was sent off to 20 years of hard labour and exile in Siberia. An eyewitness account describing the 'civil execution' of Chernyshevsky may be found in Franco Venturi, *Roots of Revolution* (New York: Grosset & Dunlap, 1966), pp. 180–1 and 749 (NOTE 136).—G. S.]

The Paris Commune

History has never known such an example of
heroism.

—Karl Marx

Wherever you cast a glance
A shameful sight you see!
The generals all turned tail,
Those dashing, bold *canaille*,
Leaving Frenchmen to their fate
To be beaten, beaten, beaten.
The news carries like thunder
Of one rout after another.

Napoleon III was surrounded,
Defeated and disarmed.
Marshall MacMahon surrendered
In time for supper with Bismarck!

The swindler army-suppliers
Feed the soldiers what trash they can grab.
They're stealing everywhere
And feasting everywhere.

* * *

The Prussians have laid siege to Paris.
They're going to starve out the city.
What will come next?
Who here can guess?

* * *

Paris, the giant, is full of alarm.
The winged rumours fly and swarm.

Thiers & Co. want to surrender,
Deaf to the people's grumbling.
They want to harness Parisians
Like slaves to the German chariot.

But no, that will never happen!
Such trickery and treachery!
We say 'No' to a shameful captivity!
Thiers issues a fateful order:
'Turn over the National Guard cannon
Immediately to the Germans!'

'What's this? What game are you playing?
The hell! We won't give up our cannon.

We'll cope with these bastards ourselves!'
'Lousy dwarf! What did you want to do?
A demon of wheeling and dealing, that's what you
are!'

* * *

Many-headed Paris is boiling and bubbling,
The steam of anger rising from the cauldron.
Choose a centre for the Commune!
Let the Commune be proclaimed!
The journeymen, master craftsmen,
And the poor of all the dark quarters,
The soldiers, the dashing guardsmen,
Poor students from their garrets,
And dwellers in gloomy, dank cellars
And writers, intellectual fellows—

The entire plebeian host stands up
As one under Communard banners.

* * *

Thiers' government fled to Versailles.
Dammit, why didn't they catch 'em?
Take the *canaille* alive,
Tickle 'em with a gun barrel.

* * *

The work is humming everywhere.
Paris is concerned about the poor
And about its sacred defenses,
Must get ready for victory's battle.
Decree on decree is issued
On wages, on labour,
On education and aid to the needy,
Whatever help can be given in time of disaster.

* * *

At Versailles the wild howling of wolves:
'The Communards are robbers; they're scum.
Bismarck, come help us. Come!'

* * *

The city's completely transformed.
A new order has arisen.
The thieves' den atmosphere,
So foul and deadening, is gone.
The coquettes, priests and courtesans,
And aristocratic dandies,
Hyenas of the banks and bourses,
And the baldness of heads with tonsures—
A great wave has swept them away.
They've slunk off to Versailles
Without taking their soap.

* * *

And now the great city is serious, stern
It's got something to teach and something to learn.
From the forts echo sharp shouts of guards.

* * *

Thiers and Bismarck have formed a bloc.
The march from Versailles has begun.
They'll shed a sea of the workers' blood.
The powers that be want to keep what they've got.

* * *

Over paving stones cannon are rumbling.
The bayonet's gleam speaks of savage revenge.

* * *

Everyone to arms!
Make every house a fortress!
Don't let the ravens
Peck out the heart of Paris!

* * *

And a cruel struggle begins,
A bloody and fateful battle.
Grenades and shells explode.
The walls of the houses are spattered
With patches of blood.

Torn-off heads and limbs
Lie in pieces beside
Blasted barricades.

The people keep fighting like lions.
After each barricade there's an ambush.
From the windows of attics and garrets
Fire pours on the pigs from Versailles.
Amidst the whistling of grapeshot
In hellish clouds of smoke
A boy lifts onto his shoulder
A sackful of cartridges,
Lugs it over to his father,
Old fighter in a workman's blouse.

In a leaden downpour of bullets,
For the men's mouths, grown hot and dry,
The stern-faced women bring water,
Relief for the lips of the men.

* * *

But Paris the warrior—his strength is worn down.
The homes are destroyed with no let-up
By artillery shells
And the cannons belch death from their bellies.

Old man Delescluze now has fallen,
His cap spilling from his head.

And Varlin—they took him captive,
Then up against a wall they killed him.

* * *

Reprisal of the beasts has begun.
One firing squad after another.
The corpses form vast hecatombs,
Expressions on faces frozen forever.

And nowhere to put all this human flesh.
The *grandes dames* and elegant dandies
Come to poke at the dead with umbrellas.
They laugh and chortle and yammer
At this world-historic drama.

* * *

Go on, laugh, you elegant vermin.
Today is your day. Celebrate!
Your nerves are calm, composure regained,
And your saucy lover awaits you.

But the dead ones' pale faces are speaking:
'You should wait before laughing so quickly.
The one who laughs last will laugh best.
Comes the day when you'll see this yourselves.'

(14 September 1937)

1905

I

Grey, gloomy fields are stretched out far and wide,
With ruined oats or rye clumps jutting up,
A land of loamy soils, cheerless, depressing,
And by the ditches, in the thorny bushes
The only sound's the chattering of magpies.
Dilapidated huts huddle together
Like aged birds of tattered feather.
The sweep at the well makes a tiresome creak
As women pour water from a rusty bucket.

'Today's our last day at home!' The full-lunged
bawling
Of new recruits is carried through the village.
Yevseyevna, procuress, the soldier's chum,
Is at the lads' disposal all day long.
They have caroused and drunk up their last penny.

Ekkh, what an evil, troubled life we have!
The last cow has been driven from the yard
And now it's time to drink, or lay down to die!

II
In gold-embroidered uniforms
With stars and satin ribbons
A pack of the tsar's most dangerous wolves
Is at the cabinet minister's plush apartment.
Grey-headed generals sport aiguillettes
Alongside financiers with beefy brows
And speculators from the Far East borders.
Heroes of a bloody springtime sowing,
They look at the map and calculate.
They're trading in cannon fodder,
Figuring gains from concessions in China, Korea,
Each aiming to outsmart the other,
And in cold blood deciding: 'It will be war!'

'We'll drown those Japs
In a sea of our caps.'
'They're stifling our growth.
We'll teach them for that.
Victory's already in the bag.'

III
A sea of grey, a million strong,
Shaved heads and soldiers' greatcoats.
The age-old misery of the peasant

Solidly overlays their minds.
'What the hell'd they send us out here for?
Just think! To the ends of the earth!
No good's gonna come of this, for sure.
Good thing we have our icon with us.'

Meanwhile officers, eating and drinking
Flirting and playing their hands at cards,
Sing their drunken songs in the garden
While the quartermaster crowd is busy stealing.

At headquarters among the grey-haired
Father-commanders no one is worried,
And the priests with their chubby fingers
Are carrying icons larger than life.

IV
Defeats arrive, one after the other,
And always the news reports say:
'Strategic considerations today required
Withdrawal from the present engagement.'
The same lie, a hundred times over.
No one believes it.
It's enough to look at the liars' faces.

Remember the terrible blow at Tsushima.
The scandal involving Stessel.*
The battle of Mukden. Blood-drenched are the fields
Where kaoliang sorghum grows.

The army is one vast bleeding wound.
'The tsarist scum, they'll pay for this.
It's not the same as when the gendarmes
Lashed people with Cossack whips back home.
Not something to drink away with a bottle of rum.
Wait and see, something big's gonna happen.
The only reasoning between them and us is the axe!'

V

Crowds of workers march to the Winter Palace
Watched by ever-vigilant eyes.
To appeal to the tsar, eyes shining with hope.
It's just that life's grown so dark and hard.
Good Gapon wrote up a paper for us,
A request for the tsar to intercede.
He'll give us help. Now's a good time to ask.

What the heck is this, bayonets all around us?
They won't let us through, whether walking or riding.
Brothers, let us through. We've come to see the tsar.
We're bringing our humble appeal to him!

Volley after volley, once and again.
A man falls to the ground, head covered with blood.
From a tree a boy plunges, shot dead.
A burial mound of blood-soaked bodies.
There's shouting and weeping. And also cursing.
The soldiers have shot down their faith in the tsar.

VI

Throughout the country, indignation
Crying out, yelling for revenge.
It flows like turbulent spring waters,
It surges like a roaring river,
No barrier dams will stop this flood.
The universities' doors have been
Thrown open wide for the masses.
The old authorities' obscurantism
Has suddenly disappeared.
The working class is everywhere,
And everywhere are stormy meetings.
They openly call for insurrection,
While through the hamlets and villages
The red cock flies with redoubled force.

VII

A general strike. Everything grinds to a halt.
The shop hands withhold their labour.
The sound of revolutionary arias
Has started to rumble and roar.
Tumultuous Russia's worker now is singing
In full voice for the first time.
Trains and wagons on rail and road
Have all stopped.
At night the cities are dark,
Not even a dog on the loose.
On strike to the very last man,

They're voting against the tsar.
Workers, teachers, engineers, fashion models,
Opera singers, high-school students,
The whole country has reared up,
Bearing the banner of sacred struggle

VIII

'Arise ye prisoners of starvation
Arise ye wretched of the earth . . .'
Our despot, turned coward, broke into a sweat,
A real cold sweat, with fever and chills.

He issued the October manifesto,
Granting free vote for a Duma.
The good-for-nothing liberals
Grabbed onto it at once,
Took the bait without hesitation.
The workers glumly held their tongues.
That little piece of paper was a big trick.
It wasn't worth a tinker's damn.

The Black Hundreds began their pogroms
With the tsar as their recognized leader.
The corn-chandler thugs took the offensive,
Called on the troops to back them up.

Strikes break out again, and demonstrations
Moscow and St Petersburg are seething.

IX

With every day the fight grows fiercer.
A new strike. The roar of demonstrations.
Here and there shots ring out. Pogroms are all
around.
A flood of delegations takes up arms.
Soviets arise in both capitals,
Enormous 'Unions of Unions'.

But the Constitutional Democrats draw back.
They call for a peaceful outcome.
They've come to terms with the authorities.
They've had a whiff of sharing power
And their mouths are watering for more.
The maw of the autocracy is not averse
To devouring the people, head and all.

Moscow ominously hunkered down,
As nature does before a storm,
And in Moscow the storm burst out
In the people's December insurrection.

X

White snow. Freezing cold.
The crackle of revolvers.
The whole city seems overgrown
With rows of barricades. On city squares
They've dug out iron gratings.
Mauzers with stubby handles

Stick out from under their clothing—
That's what the workers' guard relies on.

An exchange of fire is under way.
The minute hand on the tower clock
Is bent by a ricochet bullet.
Troops of the Rostov regiment
Maintain an angry silence.
They haven't come out of their barracks.
A brouhaha's going on inside.
On street corners here and there
Lie those who have been killed,
Their arms flung out
In the last torment of death.

XI

Admiral Dubasov dashes off a message
To St Petersburg:
'Situation extremely serious.
My forces are insufficient.
Threatening, suspicious silence
Is encountered all around.
The Rostov regiment can't be counted on.
It's not at all reliable for us.
Only one solution exists.
Otherwise I feel I'm in trouble.
Send me two other regiments,
Semyonovsky and Preobrazhensky.

Otherwise I'll be caught short, and may
Have to dress like a woman to escape.'

As bad luck would have it,
The two elite regiments,
Masters of bayonet and gun,
Are sent immediately from Petersburg.

XII

The crash of cannon, the rattle of machine guns.
Bullets and shells fly down the street.
The insurgents are smashed in the centre of town,
The barricades taken by bayonets.
The fighting units of workers
Withdraw from all sides to Krasnaya Presnya,
Their home neighbourhood.
They flood into houses and gateways of courtyards.
Loud singing of workers' songs has subsided.
The enemy surrounds the workers' quarter
With the thunder of his many guns.
Arms, heads, chests
Are swimming in scarlet bloody pools.
Black smoke curls upward.
The whole sky has turned copper
As houses go up in flames.
Presnya is ablaze with blood.

The frenzied tsarist Cain has turned
The homes and hearths of people

Into a black mound of ruins,
A dismal pile of ashes.

XIII

Death's punitive detachment,
The phalanx of butchers has passed by.
Tormenters of varied rank
Have fed the people a hail of lead.
Rows of gallows form a line
Along the railroad tracks.
Foul predatory birds
Peck at the corpses of the hanged.

The two-headed tsarist eagle now
Has both heads sitting on straight.
But only a few years later, a stake
Will be driven through its heart for good.

(night, early hours of 15 September 1937)

[*NOTE: For a useful account of tsarist Russia's expansionist policies, speculation and concession-seeking in Korea and Manchuria, northeastern China, with direct participation by the imperial family and backing by French capital, see Michael T. Florinsky, *Russia: A History and an Interpretation*, VOL. 2 (New York: Macmillan, 1958), pp. 1262–70. Also see pp. 1270–9, on the events of the Russo-Japanese War of 1904–05 and its outcome. In particular, Florinsky describes the Russian setbacks in the battles of Liaoyang (August 1904) and Mukden (February–March 1905), as well as the crushing defeat of the Russian fleet in the Straits of Tsushima on 27 May 1905. His summation of the Stessel scandal is worth quoting in full:

> On December 19, 1904, after a siege lasting 148 days, the [Russian] commander of Port Arthur, General A. M. Stessel, surrendered the fortress to the enemy. The besieged troops had fought gallantly and had inflicted heavy losses on the Japanese . . . [The] capitulation does not seem to have been justified because the garrison still had some 25,000 able-bodied men and adequate supplies of food and munitions. According to some authorities, the prolongation of the resistance until the arrival of the Baltic fleet then on its way from Europe might have altered the outcome of the war. Stessel acted on his own responsibility, in disregard of the views of other senior officers of the Port Arthur command.

[A trial in 1908 found Stessel guilty of wrongfully surrendering Port Arthur and sentenced him to death. The sentence was commuted to 10 years imprisonment, and in 1909 he was pardoned by Tsar Nicholas II.—G. S.]

CIVIL WAR [1917–1920]

[Bukharin gave the title 'Civil War' to the 15 poems that he designated as 'series III' of his book of poetry. (The subject matter is actually the 1917 Russian Revolutions, of February and October, as well as the civil war and foreign intervention consequent to the Bolshevik revolution.)
—G. S.]

Smolny*

Languid affectations of minuet couples,
The lace and bouquets and throwaways,
Young girls' secrets in sheltered dorm rooms,
Stylish maids of honour with haughty gait.

All that has been swept off and sent to hell
By the uprising wave of the masses.
Proletarian cohorts with iron tread
Stepped up and took the dance classes.

This workers' anthill is swarming with people,
Regiments being dispatched to the front.
Smolny is humming—unquenchable buzz.
Rifles, bayonets, hang from the shoulder.

Under the corridors' vaulted ceilings
Black leather jackets flow in streams.

They spring from a source with many brave hearts,
With audacious vision, rebel energies.

The spirit of rebel factories reigns here.
Here life is boiling, life's fermenting.
Immense, tempestuous, new freedom's thought,
Like the reddest of suns—here it's shining.

Revolution's stubborn, persistent will
Subdues all things with its stern stride.
Let olden times sigh for the past that's been lost.
No matter. The insolent foe will be smashed!

Insurgent, the people will not be mowed down
Or picked off like game birds by hunters.
Up top is Ilyich, who knows how to listen,
And he's leading the troops into battle.

At an entrance to the large old building
The guards oversee admission.
Black and stern, like vigilance personified,
A machine gun's barrel stands ready.

(15 September 1937)

[*NOTE: In Petrograd (St Petersburg) in 1917 the Smolny
Institute for the Daughters of the Nobility was taken over
by the revolution and became the seat of the Councils of
Workers', Soldiers', and Peasants' Deputies, the Soviets.
—G. S.]

Sabotage

Quos ego!
　　—From Virgil, unfinished threat uttered by
　　　　　　　Jupiter: 'Them, I will . . .'

The factories are ours. Everything in them is part of
the uprising.
The workers stand together like a solid wall,
But in the old offices—Lord a mercy!—what
pernicious chaos there is!
Old, fire-eating warriors of the tsar, the gentry, the
people of rank,
And entire hordes of intellectuals
Are holding malicious council,
Gossiping, frittering away the time,
Sighing over the lost world of interest rates,
And pulling dirty tricks wherever they can,
Some of them cautiously, others foaming at the
mouth.

It's the underground work of blind old moles,
With slowdown strikes against the workers
Or outright sabotage
To set things rocking dangerously
So the workers won't be able to shoulder the load,
The difficult new tasks of governing.

They know no limit in the stupid arrogance
Of their meagre minds.
When all the towns and villages
Are voting in action for Soviet power,
This mouth keeps repeating that is has to eat.
'Just try getting by without us!'

And the workers reply with a threat,
'We'll deal with them!' (*Quos ego . . .*)
And seriously, audaciously
The workers appoint their own people
And send these old fleas and lice
Off to the devil's grandmother.

(early hours of 16 September 1937)

Lenin at a Factory

The workshops of a giant factory.
There isn't room to breathe,
Such a crush of people.
It's downright awful.
Nobody stayed home,
Even outsiders came.
They all want to hear Ilyich,
The Sovnarkom's chairman,
Their leader and native son.

Black, sweaty faces.
The smile of shining eyes.
'If only we had some water to drink.'
'It's so damn hot in here.'
Suddenly the crowd makes way
As the word spreads like lightning
'His car has arrived . . . Here he comes.'

* * *

The people start swaying back and forth
Then with a sharp splash a storm
Of hand-clapping breaks out,
A declaration of ardent love.
Like a fuse to powder
It sets things off; it ignites
The entire mass all around.
The cheering grows and grows
Till it's a hurricane's crashing thunder.

* * *

In a hurry Ilyich runs up
Onto a wooden platform.
The stormy sea of love caresses him.
He stands there simply, no affectation,
Reliable and dearly loved,
Straight and true, from top to toe,
Spirit of a troubled epoch,
A leader superb for all these fighters
'With this man you can't go wrong.'
'With him you can go to your death!'
So much love they won't let him speak.
Lenin stands there,
Wiping the brow of his mighty cupola,
Tentatively touching the microphone,
'Comrades . . .' His speech has begun.

Thought now begins to take wings.
With simple words, like nails,
Ilyich hammers his message home.
One's whole head grows clear
As though everything was wiped clean,
A brick scraping mould from copper plating.

* * *

From behind his whiskers
Someone whispers
'The way he talks—it seems so simple.'
'Who would have thought it?'
'Stuff we didn't know before,
And he just lays it out.'

* * *

Thousands of eyes, like augers,
Drill into Ilyich,
This genius of the labouring masses,
A mind unbounded, and hot-blooded.

* * *

He's finished. And quickly slips down,
Wild ovations exploding around him.
The workers surround him, dogging his steps
As delegates from other plants

Cry: 'Comrade Lenin! Vladimir Ilyich!
'Come to our plant! All our guys are asking!'

An older worker, a wise grey owl,
Takes charge, getting Lenin back in his car.
Everyone's smiling. And through the glass
Lenin raises his hand in farewell.
A sea of ardent love has flowed,
Selfless and wholehearted love.

(night, early hours of 16 September 1937)

The Tauride Palace

The Tauride Palace, fine creation
Of Empress Catherine. 'Twill stand for ages . . .
The groaning of serfs, the torments of servants,
But also the feasts,
The arrogant shouts of the Empress' favourite,
The fawning speeches by all the spongers,
And half-mad prattle by 'Fools of God',
The patterned ceiling and golden cornice,
The staff in constant fear and trembling,
The clowns, the Negroes, the dwarfs in dunce caps,
The bay of borzoi hounds, the pet bear's growl,
The host of precious stones on bony wrists,
The gleam of countless candles in the mirrors,
Amorous whisper of mattresses carefully picked,
Ballrooms and dances and masquerades,
The drunken cheer of saint's day festivals

Insanely expensive promenades,
The kissing of the pretty servant girls,
And lovely music from fair Italy,
The crafty favourite, 'Holy Prince of Tauria',
Voluptuary of the pompous Catherine,
The boundless servility of courtiers,
Along with haughtiness and arrogance—
All of this past has long since flown away
Into the limitless span of the ages.

* * *

The Tauride Palace . . . The Duma held its sessions
here.
Here the last-born tsar held forth in speech,
When the Petersburg worker was grimly preparing
New battles, and in fury holding his tongue.

Here the insolent fop Purishkevich
Carried on in his affected ways.
From here Stolypin the Hangman uttered his lies,
Here Petrunkevich was wont to burst into warbling,
And the bison Markov belched out his black fumes.

Here Pavlov the prosecutor uttered
His winged phrase: 'So has it been, so will it be.'
While the Left shouted 'Shame! Get out of here!'
Their fists were clenched, chests all a-tremble.
The peaceful Trudoviks were here in session,

Here the Kadets set their traps for the people,
From here the Bolsheviks put into circulation
Their daring speeches, wall-bursting battering rams.
The tsarist dogs seized them,
          sent them off to forced labour.
Their voices, bright and bold, fell silent then.

* * *

But long-awaited dawn at last arose
And revolution's storm began to roar.
Now reigning in the Tauride was sly Milyukov
And that unbearable blabbermouth, Kerensky.
The stern time of the Bolsheviks arrived
All dregs were swept away, a pile of trash.

* * *

The Petersburg potholes are filled with snow,
An icy wind is blowing,
The struggle has gone beyond all limits,
But the Proletariat-Messiah
Keeps up its noble spirit.
Like granite is the stubborn will
Of all impoverished Russia,
Though burdened down by foulest fate

* * *

Now in the Tauride Palace
The Constituent Assembly congregates.
The SRs and Kadets intend to try
Repairing the broken wine-press of Capital,
Imposing limits on the Revolution.

* * *

There's flame and fire in the meeting.
The passions are white-hot. Don't touch.
In the Bolshevik speeches, a conflagration.
Their opponents' equipment's a little rusty.

The atmosphere is simply steaming.
Will shooting break out at any moment?
A battle of fists and bullets is near.
There's gunpowder, sulfur in the air.
The Palace is kept under guard by sailors
With rifles and bayonets at the ready.
They narrow their eyes as they watch the charade,
Clicking and cocking their triggers.

Ilyich sits, leaning back, relaxed,
On the long steps of a stairway
As though he isn't bothered by
The buzzing of the wasp's nests.

* * *

In a small, glass-enclosed room
Of the Palace, the CC huddled,
Deciding what measures to take
To strike the enemy down.
They listened and they decreed:
'Sailors, shut down the Assembly!'
All were sick to the stomach from
The endless flux of Contra speeches.
The people were tired of it all.
Ilyich laughed till tears came to his eyes.
'Summon the sailors at once,' he said.
'Send out the call to arms.'
Long had the Kronstadters waited
Just to be given this signal.
Zheleznyák, with his sailor's firm hand,
Turned out the lights in the hall.
The wolves started howling, full voice,
Made a huge fuss . . . and then dispersed.
The sailors laughed: 'Encore!'
'We'd like to do that again.'
'That's what we call real work!!'

* * *

Our Russia is a land immense.
She has need of Soviet power.
She's willingly bucking fate
On her way to Paradise gates.

The enemy wants civil war.
The worker does not fear it.
With his blood he'll water the earth.
Berserkly he'll fight the foe
Till victory's golden day,
Defeat of the repulsive Whites.
They're a dark disaster. They must be crushed
Beneath the Sovnarkom banner!

(night, early hours of 17 September 1937)

Predators

From all our borders, near and distant,
From the lands of White bourgeoisie,
Packs of hellhounds came rushing against us
And countless hawks of steel flew down.
The wild dogs bayed with throats of iron
And flooded all our roads with blood.
The hawks belched forth their fire and lead
All over our Red virgin ground.
They tore at our body day and night,
Those fiendish, hellish beasts of prey.
On our fields, in our towns, heaps of bones
gleamed white,
The bones of our dear, dead kin, both women and
men.
With our last bit of strength we drove off the
plagues,

While shedding our last drop of blood,
But we pulled out the teeth of those predator
hounds,
With our sabres cut hawk meat to bits.
Those were sacred days, heroic, grand,
Never can or will they be forgotten.
Firm imprints stamped our memories well
In those years of glory triumphant.

(night, early hours of 17 September 1937)

In the Coils of the Constrictor

In the coils of a huge and fierce constrictor,
The cruel embrace of fire and iron,
Bloody vengeance against the revolution,
In spasms of pain our country is writhing.

On the White Sea, Brits have landed. In the East,
There's Kolchak with the crafty Japanese,
Plus generals of the Entente, and near them,
The United States' star-spangled banner.

In the South, the French and Englishmen
Brought battleships with regiments,
Forging chains to make of Russia a slave,
And hired Whiteguard bayonets to serve them.

In the West, Yudenich's degenerates
Suck up goodies supplied by 'civilized' Powers,

Taking into their drunken bandit ranks
Adventurers and titled riff-raff.

White hordes of the Czechoslovak Legion,
Lackeys in service to plunder—they fight us.
And far away from any front-line danger
Old generals' decrepit mugs jut up.

Krasnov, Kaledin, German troops and Poles,
Denikin, Wrangel (a baron with a 'von'),
These are imperialism's haughty swordsmen
All aiming for the ancient tsarist throne,
For oil, for grain, for coal, for leather
For land to be snatched back from peasant owner,
For factories and plants, so that the peace
Of capitalists and counts won't be disturbed.

Behind them a worthy gypsy camp comes dragging,
A motley crew, ex-owners of the land.
Here we find counts and princes, gentry with
pedigrees,
Families with coats of arms and genealogies,
Factory owners and landlords, and also cocottes
And dubious wheeler-dealers, as well as bishops,
Kadet professors, and all kinds of speculators,
Priests and puffed-up merchants, the Russia of old,
People who love to sleep, have a bite to eat,
To ride someone else's back, and suck their blood,
Listen to gossip while resting on puffy pillows,
And even while resting, always filling their pockets.

They bring death with them, high mountains of
corpses,
Their path's adorned with rows and rows of gallows,
Their unrestrained and drunken packs of hounds
Sow bloody terror everywhere they go.

* * *

Miner's bodies hang in blackened rows,
Every tenth one, shot against a wall.
They've fertilized the soil here with 'Jewboys',
Mowing them down by the hundreds, Israel's sons.
These beasts have a taste for blood, inflicting torture,
And in the case of captured Communists
Often they tore the skin right off their hands,
Making gloves of flesh, and then put out their eyes.
Thus people died in dreadful agonies,
The last groan wrenched from the expiring chest.

They cut the Revolution from its source of life,
The regions giving meat and grain and warmth.
The poor folk in rebellion, the poor of Russia,
Suffered without end for their Motherland.
From lack of fuel their houses had turned cold.
No bread, no flour. From skinny shoulders there hung
The old, familiar beggar's canvas pouch.
The worker sits to eat; there's only thin gruel.
An eighth of a pound of bread is his whole ration,
But his gleaming eye reveals a will of steel.

He keeps his rifle cocked and at the ready.
Hungry and cold, the proletariat is seething,
A mighty volcano, against the enemy.

The workers send new units to the Red Army.
Stubborn as granite, they reinforce front lines.
In factories, there's the hum of workers' meetings.
All forces mobilize against the foe.
No whining here, no groaning or complaints.
From here they see the shores of victory.
Invincible exertions of firm will,
Invincible the fighters' fervent faith.
Hateful to them the generals' well-groomed mugs,
Along with the hefty bellies of the merchants.
'Give back all land to landlords once again?'
'Give back the factories? Never, no! No, never!'
'Traitors! We will punish them, but good!'
'The White disaster with its chains won't beat us!'

And they keep sending out their brave battalions.
Of all our armies they're the solid backbone.
Carefully testing cannon, rifle, cartridge.
Denikin and Kolchak won't soon forget them!

With worn-out shoes, no boots, and sometimes
shoeless,
The peasant poor keep fighting for the land,
For they remember well the chains and muzzles
The landlords used to wrap around their mouths.

'Fearless we go to battle for Soviet power!'
The song is heard on front lines and at home.
On ramparts, generals and professors hear it,
And sour grimaces twist across their faces.
'We're not afraid of any Whiteguard threats,
We're not afraid of hunger, cold, or typhus,
Not even tears of widows and of orphans.'

The creative masses' outburst is grand and sacred.
This mighty hurricane sweeps all before it.
It can't be stopped by anyone, anything.
The worker in his greatcoat old and torn
Is making a new world for everyone.

(17 September 1937)

White Church Bells

Ding ding ding Bong
Ding ding ding Bong
Bong
Bong

The heavy, rich peal of the church bells
Proclaims victory coming soon
And chiming in are the ringing spurs
Of grey-haired generals.

The priests are strutting about
With churchly banners and crosses.
They stick their bellies out,
Make holy signs with fingers.

Ding ding ding Bong
Ding ding ding Bong

'Within a week we'll be drinking tea
In hundred-steepled Moscow

With God's help we'll come marching in
Greeted with praise and glory
And we'll hear the pealing of bells
From the holy Kremlin churches.
We'll scourge the land of Bolsheviks,
Those vile and unclean creatures.
We'll find our friends of old again
And shoot down all our enemies.
The peace of ancient times we'll win,
Restoring Holy Russia.'

Ding ding ding Bong
Ding ding ding Bong

Denikin stood outside Oryol
Celebrating his success
When suddenly all hell broke loose
And all his comforts fled.
The Red ranks struck, and struck again,
Determined, stern and deadly.

Better to flee and head for home
Take off, before it's too late.
The wolfpack hosts went rolling back,
Not looking round, just ran for it!

Yessir, our guys have learned to fight,
Our well-trained factory hands!

(night, early hours of 18 September 1937)

Raven

Why do you croak, ill-omened one,
Black-coated raven, evil thing?
That is a human eye you're pecking.
You're tearing at a golden mind.

I peck a sternly gazing eye
And tear at thicknesses of brain
But 'twas not I with bloodied hand
Who has this living person slain.

It was not I who tortured him
Out on the vast and open plain.
About that you'd do best to ask
Among those cruel Whiteguard men.

Yes, I am Raven, thing of black,
And I peck at those who've died

But Whiteguards are the ones who torture
The peasant poor without restraint.

And croak I do as I go flying
Through the sky, dark blue and light,
But I know nobody so cruel
As those behind the Whiteguard lines.

(morning of 18 September 1937)

*Osmushka** (Eighth of a Pound of Bread)

Remember the good old Osmushka, eighth of a
pound
Of black bread with orache and straw mixed in?
Gloomy and angry, the regular 'man in the street'
Considered it a cursed blight from on high.

In those days villains had us hemmed in tight,
The hangmen of the workers, peasants' foes.
They drew the noose of hunger round our weakened
necks,
As typhus' dark hurricane swept people away.

Unheated factories and homes were blackened
By death and disease. Our destiny seemed the grave.
But hearts burned on, with an unyielding faith,
Determined to achieve a feat of valour.

Lenin put out the call: 'Crusade against the kulaks!'
With iron hand he pointed the way forward.
We overcame the foe. He had to bow
His bloody, beaten, predatory head.

Back then Osmushka saved us from destruction.
Lenin kept close watch over every load
Of grain arriving in Moscow.
The phone and telegraph steadily kept him informed.

The enemy teased us, waving a loaf of white bread
Before our starving eyes, saying 'Down on your
knees!'
The people answered the Whites, prancing in their
'Eden':
'You take your hateful power and go to hell.'

The workers would not sell for a mess of pottage
All of what they had won, their sacred birthright.
Not just a loaf of white bread or jar of herring
Was what they won defending their native land.

Now labour's springs have flowed in great
abundance,
And well-fed life's in flower all around.
The years of starving, strenuous exertion,
The clash of stubborn battles—all were justified.
And now when skies are shining we remember
Amid the blossoms of a cloudless life

That old Osmushka of those hungry times.
Eighth of a pound, it fed our folk just fine.

(night, early hours of 19 September 1937)

[*NOTE: During the hardest days of the Russian Civil War, 1918–1921, the *Vosmushka*, one-eighth of a pound of bread per day, was the ration for city dwellers in the Bolshevik-controlled central parts of Russia. In everyday talk, the initial *V* was dropped; hence the notorious nickname for the bread ration, *Osmushka*.—G. S.]

Zhanna,* Faithful and True

The enemies' ships rode at anchor,
The ominous, mighty Entente.
Against us they brought their armies,
Their punitive landing parties.

Ship towers were visible out at sea
And long, grey artillery barrels.
The cabins were jammed with foreign troops
Intended for dark reprisals.

French soldiers trooped in squadrons smart,
Galivanting both night and day.
Their sabres glittered. And at street corners
Machine-gun fire kept barking away.

In Zhanna's soul rose an outburst of wrath,
Of sacred sorrow and anger.
Hardly breathing, she said to herself

She would fight this to the death.
A foreign land was now her home,
A mighty land, now dear to her,
And France's deeds seemed blacker, fouler
Than bloody butchers' in darkest night.

She glided swan-like to the soldiers—
Just like a swan, a lily-white swan—
Befriended them, taught them, and shamed them,
Appealed to them boldly, 'Revolt!'

But Zhanna fell into enemy hands,
Caught in a villainous web,
Court-martialled on a green meadow,
And sentenced to perish at dawn.

An eagle, she stood before the grim court,
Our daring, high-spirited Zhanna,
Though waiting for her, round the corner,
Was a bath of destruction and blood.

A shot rang out, short, crisp and dry.
No longer with us in this world,
She lay in a pool of thickening blood,
In the cold embraces of death.

The soldiers revolted, the regiments turned
Their guns against French commanders.
This was the great work of Zhanna's hands,
Though dead from an enemy bullet.

Time's fleeting pace has long since healed
Those bloody wounds of long ago,
But still there shines in our sunlit age
The heroic death of faithful Jeanneot.

(night, early hours of 19 September 1937)

[*NOTE: Zhanna is the Russian form of a French woman's name, Jeanne.—G. S.]

Earthquake

> And lo, the sorceress History has her whole
> cauldron bubbling.
>
> —Karl Marx

1

Upon the earth's rough, blackened breast
All mixed together are men and cannon,
Bayonet and shell, blood and fire,
An airplane, a tank, a horse . . .
Everything here is whirling, shaking.
And no one dares venture to say
What tomorrow will bring, or a year.

In Russia the people have risen,
Crushing the old without regret.
The masses have lost all patience.
Reliable rifles are in their hands.
Everywhere are soldiers' skills

And people's unrest is everywhere,
A spirit of anger, assertion of will.

The vampire of war has torn our flesh
And all the earth is sweating blood.
Poverty's growing everywhere,
And everywhere discussion's heard

Of hunger, death and rising prices,
About the necessary changes,
The battlefront, monarchs and the war,
Speculators, our country's fate.
Discussion's everywhere, on streetcars,
In city squares, over cups of tea
In restaurants, in gardens:
'Living like this—can't bear it any more!'

The masses of Europe are in ferment:
On battlefields are mounds of bones.
The soldiers' rage is ominous, furious.
The whirlwind's been sown in the factories too.
And on the sharp-nosed battleships
The sailors are in mutiny.
The air is full of the tension and strain
Of a destructive hurricane

2
Kaiser Wilhelm's army's beaten.
His cursed horse's hoof is cracked.
The silent anger's broken out

Into a flaming thunderstorm.
Berlin rose up with guns in hand.
In panic the Kaiser took himself off,
Crossed the border to Nether-Netherland.
No one could any longer hold
The wheel of revolution back,
Neither the Pope nor Almighty God.

The crown of old has flown away,
The despot is toppled from blood's throne,
And at the gates of history
A maelstrom's bubbling with foam.
The helm of state's slipped from their hands,
The earthly monarchs all a-tremble,
Afraid they'll lose their powers, their laurels
And at the same time, maybe, their heads.
They're picturing a dreadful scene:
The gleaming blade—the guillotine.
And in their hearts sheer terror reigns
Among the rich, among the kings.

The Hapsburg crown has now flown off
Into the whirlwind like an old crow
Flown from the half-destructed nest,
And trains speed on to cross the border
With the monarch's family and entourage.
In his hurry he forgot his Plutarch.

What fear's laid hold of the bourgeoisie!
In Bavaria there's Soviet power,

And in Hungary—hey, eat your fill
Budapest now has workers' councils,
They're governing the entire country
Everything's new now under the sun!

3

The interventionists are all alarmed.
They've got to flee. Their efforts were in vain.
And all the robbers, all the speculators
Are begging, pleading, down upon their knees.
To the grey-haired Whiteguard generals
They moan and groan, they curse and beg:
'Please stay. Please don't go away.'
'Don't take your troops out of here.'
Meanwhile the Reds are coming close,
Not letting the enemy out of their sights,
Thrashing him thoroughly, place after place.
The great court of history's been convened.
The hangmen-butchers are on trial
With their troops (hands washed in blood)
And their haughty officer corps,
A cursed, vicious flock of vultures.

And now from all of Europe comes
News of rebellions and of protests
By working folk against the war,
The sons of international
Solidarity. Their voices rise
Ascending loudly to the skies.

Mutiny has made its nest
Among the intervention's troops.
They pull their soldiers out, on tiptoe.
No longer will these blackguard men
Turn their machine guns on the crowds,
On sons of our awakened land.

The bosses lose interest in profits now:
'Heck with the gravy! Stay alive is what counts.'
The bosses want their feet to carry them off,
And to the Allies they'll say fond farewell
For the last time, and then forevermore
They'll leave our country, never to return.

4

Among the turbulent masses of Russia
The course of revolution revealed
Reserves of new, enormous energy.
They're reinforced enthusiastically
By the stormy movement in Europe,
The awakening of the working class,
An earthquake all around the world,
Tempestuous feast of revolution.

Crossing our borders from all directions,
Workers fly in from other countries,
Like birds in springtime's early days,
Participants in mighty battles,
And with passionate love they kiss

The blood-soaked soil of our land.
New words in Russia flourish now.
Where earlier 'knout' and 'vodka' were best known
The echoes bounce to these new shouts:
'Lenin', 'Bolshevik', 'Soviets'.
Moscow's become the capital of the earth.
No longer does the porphyry of tsardom
Betoken Moscow's power to the world.
The scarlet banner of the Comintern
Now flutters over greying Kremlin walls
And makes its name known over all the globe.

5

Europe's volcano is not extinct,
And to all the curses of old women,
The rich, the noble, the distinguished,
To the threats and angry swearing
Of savage greedy hangmen-butchers
And the dark rattling of sabres,
Our country listens closely, warningly.
No longer is it just a little child,
And anyone who takes up arms against us
Will get what's coming to him, get it good.

The payment for our suffering will be
The worldwide earthquake in a new explosion.

(night, early hours of 20 September 1937)

The Latvian Rifles

You Latvian riflemen!
Honour to you! And glorious memory!
Ah, your well-ordered regiments, where are they now?
The vigorous lava flow of your iron ranks?

Upon the field of battle you laid down
Your heads so proud, yes, almost every one.
But with your crimson blood you helped disperse
And pulverize the cruel Whiteguard hordes.

You Latvian proletarians, urban and rural,
You had a steel-hard chain of discipline.
When you pressed forward, enemies quickly fled
As combat turned the flatlands all to blood.

The whiteness of your bones shows everywhere.
Your unknown graves are scattered far and wide,

A country church's graveyard, vast, immense,
But you live on in memory without end.
Valiantly you gave your lives for others,
For a heroic and a glorious cause.
You live in great events of life today
Though long ago your bodies met decay.

(night, early hours of 21 September 1937)

For Bread!

> *Le pain est le droit du people.*
> ('It is the people's right to have bread.')
>
> —Saint-Just

Hunger is choking the cities,
The blood barely stirs in the veins,
Hunger's bony black hand, tenacious,
Has fastened its grip on their throat.

Proletarian detachments
Together with poor peasant folk
Are sent to the village for help,
For the requisition of grain.

The kulak beasts are greedy:
'No grain, no flour,' they say.
Deep pits they've dug to hide it
Beneath the hut and the barn.

Hatred is choking the kulaks.
Against the poor, the shirtless,
They've organized plots and intrigues.

Subtle sermons on the difference
Between the town and the country
Are given by the priest at mass.
The tavern-keeper runs to the woods
With a sawed-off gun in his hands
To set an example with lead,
A model for the kulak crowd
Against the poor, the down and out.

Wolves silently prowl in the forest
And walk round the village by night.
Their eyes are burning with anger,
Sowing hatred all about
Against workers' food detachments.
In darkness they creep through the garden
And fall on the sleeping men.
They put the sleepers to death
And flee like so many badgers
Across the ravine by the stream.

* * *

'Don't let them break our will, boys!
Don't let them weaken our hand!'
With the workers in command

The poor folk do what they have to
To cope with the bandit gang.

The iron-strong detachments
Dig up the wolves' hidden pits,
The pitch-black magpies' nests,
And take the supplies of grain
Stored away by the evildoers.

To the poor they give a share.
Up on the bridge they're loading
Supply carts full of grain
To the secret threats and curses
Of the kulaks hiding out
In the ravine by the stream.

(night, early hours of 21 September 1937)

Yudenich Marches on Petrograd*

Tu ne cede malis
Sed contra audentior ito
('Do not give in to evil
But march ever more boldly against it')
—from Virgil's *Aeneid*

Ou allez vous, monsieur l'abbé?
Vous allez vous casser le nez!
('Where are you going, M'sieur Abbot?
You're going off to break your neck!')

Yudenich's bandits had already reached
Fair Petrograd's outskirts, the key to the city.
A black sepulchral cloud, they marched
And brought with them rain, a hail of metal.

Yudenich, old villain, celebrated victory
Over this seat of eternal grandeur.
He hanged a few people for fun on the way,
Taking pleasure from the last cry of pain.

Bayonets glinted beneath a cold sun
And so did the golden epaulettes.
The priests with wonder-working icons
Shook holy dew on the regiments.

The general took up his field glasses fine
And gazed at the fair face of the city:
'Tomorrow reliable convoys will stand
By the Summer Palace's famous gardens.'

'Hey you fine fellows, march on! More lively!
May the Orthodox God be with you!
March on, you mighty Whiteguard host!
And squash the Bolsheviks in their nests!'

'By tomorrow I want Petrograd to be mine!
Go all out, men! Don't spare the cartridges!
There'll be heaping piles of rewards for you!
You can beat up the rabble all you want!'

* * *

The Petrograd factory whistles blow
And the wail of the sirens is long.
The cast-iron rollers with frenzied will
Valiantly ram the trench walls solid.
They're digging trenches everywhere,
Men and women, old folks and children.
There's dark fire burning in everyone's eyes
Under the glimmering light of the moon.

All around is heard the shovel's steady clunk
And the hurried swish of the pickaxe.
Persistent hands have already built
Huge silent mountains of barricades.

Our country stands under a giant question mark,
Besieged as it is on every side
By the Whiteguard hordes, the bloody dogs.

The whole city's dug up in a pattern of trenches.
Deep connecting ones wind around.
They're laid out sternly, in multiple rings,
Like dark and ominous serpents' coils.

The city's fighters have vowed to do battle
At every corner and every alley.
The deeper the bandits' wounds, the better!
Let them pay well for the spree they've gone on!

The general couldn't take 'Piter' by storm.
The bandit venture went astray.
The people rose up and roared like a lion
And came out to meet this evil foe.

They went on the attack. The elite,
The crack units of the capital,
Took the offensive against the White hordes
And crumpled them up. They chased off the wolves,
Turned their predator snouts right around.

And raising their banners high in the air,

The Bolshevik cohorts march forward.
The bandit canaille are already in flight,
All covered with blood and with mud.

The swift blow broke them and knocked them to bits,
The distinguished riff-raff of the Whites.
The famous general, sweating to escape,
Violently lashes the sides of his horse.

The staff and officials, the priests and valets,
They're all full of fear, heels flashing in panic,
Making signs of the cross on repulsive foreheads
As they scram away, hell bent for leather.

Their total rout is the battle's outcome.
They got their full reward.
To the sound of music, Petrograd's hero-sons
March back to their working-class home.

(night, early hours of 21 September 1937)

[*NOTE: In October 1919, the White General Yudenich led
his counter-revolutionary forces, 25,000 strong, based in
Estonia, in an assault on Petrograd, the cradle of the Russ-
ian revolution with a population of about one million.
Although this is not mentioned in Bukharin's poem, the
head of the Red Army, Leon Trotsky, personally went to
Petrograd and took leadership of the defense effort, stress-
ing particularly the mobilization of the city's working-class

men and women. As the poem describes, Yudenich's attack was thoroughly routed. See the chapter 'Defense of Petrograd' in Trotsky's autobiography, *My Life*; see also William Henry Chamberlin, *The Russian Revolution, 1917–1921* (Princeton University Press, 1987), VOL. 2, pp. 272–5. —G. S.]

Perekop

The Soviet land has been swept clean
Of greedy hordes, black-hearted Whites.
Everywhere bold armies' banners,
Loyal to Moscow's Kremlin, wave.

Only Crimea remains under hateful White rule,
And like a dismal gravestone
The granite wall at Perekop
Stands with its ugly maw, teeth bared.
On this narrow neck of land stand powerful forts.
More cannon than you can count.
Death yawns from the hollow roundness of their barrels
Waiting to wreak a furious vengeance.
Like a sentry, the wall stands high, ever guarding Crimea,

Guarding the keys, the entranceway into
The last remaining Whiteguard bastion,
Covered with blood and the black smoke of death.
The ruler is Baron Wrangel, man of bloody deeds
Paid for by the Entente's gold,
And there the knout, the lash, the aiguillette and
money
Represent the law of God.

* * *

In marching step, precise and orderly,
Working-class regiments head for the fortress.
One vigorous assault will end the reptile:
'Catch him on the points of our bayonets.'

Infantry, cannon and sabres, and banners from
famous battles.
What reigns here is courage and mind.
The sun turns Frunze's eyes dark blue; Budyonny
stands by.
Behind them are untold numbers
Of long-considered thoughts for storming the
fortress
And many sleepless nights that Stalin spent
And the bottomless depth of Lenin's mind,
Which leads the people to battle.
One thought flies up above all others, a spark
That glitters and has wings:

To crush the enemy with a lightning blow,
Blast him like thunder!
Our whole great land is holding its breath
Waiting for news from the front,
For the will of its valiant sons
To wipe the Whites from the face of the earth.

* * *

With madness of the brave, huge numbers rush to
battle.
In desperation our people
Wade through the shallow bay, Sivash,
To the whine of grapeshot and rumble of
cannonades.
Everything's covered with fire, smoke and stench.
Firing roars all around.
The land has become a blasted, blackened hell.
The thunder of heavy guns
Is growling and mowing down bodies without end.
Machine guns stutter.
From the fortress gates
Tons of death-dealing metal come belching forth.
Here shattered bodies fall in heaping mounds
With screams of dying horses.
Terrible are the wounds, the torn and broken flesh,
And the red pools of blood.

* * *

The whine and chuckle of flying shells,
Explosions, thunderclaps,
A fountain spray of earth and stones,
Outbreaks of blood-red lighting and a hellish din,
The rat-a-tat of a drum,
As clouds of smoke twist violently to heaven,
And bayonets are streaked with blood.
The storming of the fort is continuous, strong,
The irresistible wave of a river of steel.
Through blood and over the bodies of dead and
wounded
Over a bridge of corpses
With a hurricane howl they break into enemy lines
And start hand-to-hand fighting.
'Hurrah!'—the thunderous yell of thousands of
voices.
In the gunpowder smoke
Eyes flash and glitter with joyful, mighty fire.
An end to them!
An end to the last redoubt
Of the White aristocrats!
An end to every last baron!
In the Kremlin the news of Red victory reaches
Our leader, father, beloved Lenin!

(21 September 1937)

NATURE—MOTHER OF ALL

[Bukharin gave the above title to the 32 poems that he des-
ignated as 'series IV'.—G. S.]

Nature—Mother of All
(*Prámater—Priróda*)

Across two continents our land spreads out,
All seething with volcanic energy,
And proudly lifts its head—up high,
Wreathed with unprecedented glory.

The patterned foam of ocean's tide rolls up
Against the shores of our free fatherland.
Above the strict arrangement of earth's wrinkles
Snow diamonds rise: eternal cold and ice.

The heat of deserts there,
But here the North Pole's muted realm.
There luxurious brilliance, tropic valleys,
A feast of sounds, the jewelled wealth of flowers.

Almighty rivers, flowing oceanward,
Propel their way through forests, trackless, endless,
And from remote, extraordinary worlds
A silver caravan of stars gleams, mindless.

(night, early hours of 26 June 1937)

Journey by Air

A hop . . . Another . . . One more . . . Two . . .
And lo, we've broken free of terra firma.
We're hanging in midair . . .
And the mind
Rushes to start analysing.
How strange!
Nothing solid under us.
With no let-up the motor is rattling
Our vessel's steely concentration.

Villages, a mill, gullies, a river—
Have all retreated far away beneath us.
No evidence of movement in them reaches us.
Everything's made of glass, as in some ancient
Saga of enchanted kingdoms.

Tail ends
Of cloud are floating under us.

And already running past us,
Like female visitors from heaven,
Trembling and flowing
Back across the airplane's wings,
Are countless droplets of rain.
They tear themselves loose
And rush eagerly down to continue their flight.

The machine
Is stubbornly gaining altitude,
And suddenly, on the fly, the picture changes,
Just like a fairy tale.

Now the sun's burning to the point of pain.
You scrunch up your eyes against your will.
Dragons and serpents coil and curl beneath us,
Made of golden light and darkest blue.
Towers and crowns of mother-of-pearl,
Tender, milky colours.

A fairy-tale sea
Attired in pale yellow and lilac
Spreads negligently
Across the sky's expanse

And my little self
Is sunk completely in the waves of being,
In diamond-pure transparencies.

Here there's no gloomy, earthly vale of tears,
No passions, worries or alarms
In the great highways of the sky.

Just then some passions start to seethe
And thoughts fly forward, on and on,
To the stars, the moon, to carefree existence,
A bold and daring wave of dreams,
Nourished by human creative power,
Beckoning us to horizons full of promise.

* * *

Downward we dive
Through a dark blue window.
A ray of sunshine
Cut off a cornice from the clouds.
The earth looks like a map
Or the stage set of a giant theatre.

Looming before us in a haze of blue
Is an enormous, dappled dinner plate.

We drop lower
And see the smoking summits
Of blue hills.
The huge expanse of sky
Has vanished.

The warm breathing of the Earth
Is already upon us. In the distance—

A motionless ribbon of emerald, the sea,
The pattern of foam made by the breakers
Encased peculiarly in calm.

Ever lower,
Ever closer to the Earth,
We're flying over fields of crops,
Over forests and meadows,
The mirrors of the lakes are shining
Like little moons,
The rivers are winding
Like little threads of silver.

Already our eyes can make out
Human forms.

All at once
People are shading their eyes
To look at us,
Trying to figure out where that fly is
That they've heard buzzing.
Their little heads are the size of nuts.
The fields now lie in broad swathes.
The little plots of land, the scraps of poverty,
Have disappeared.
Now like green carpets of velvet
The meadows extend all along the river.
Then we're over a mass of rock and iron.

Circling, tilting on its side, the airplane has suddenly
Cut off a slice of space.
The Earth has turned
Up on its end,
Like a monstrous chunk of pie,
Its filling about to spill out.

At the airfield
They greet us
They shake our hands
We are back home.

(10 July 1937)

Blue Ferganá

Blue mountains' far horizons
Drowse in the hazy air,
Wrapped in a blue veil
In gentle half-sleep.

The blue sky
Wavers, grows still.

In sultry heat a bluebird
Flaps and flaps its wings.

The waters of the rivers
Give off a play of turquoise,
The azure wave
Of joyful nature.
Blue rocks shimmer
In the hot sun,

Their walls embroidered
In dark blue patterns.

O, land both hot and gentle,
Emerald-blue Ferganá.

(29 July 1937)

White Nights

In speechlessness of White Sea mirrors
The white nights, silently,
Reflect in water the grim grimaces—
If there's no surf and foam—
Of northern cliffsides, stern and grey and bare,
Unspeaking endlessness of calm.

The trunks of spruce like gloomy masts
Rise into pale white sky.
Somewhere far off, seals splash by rocks,
Beyond extended spits of land.

Unlimited white serenity
And silence.
Transparent depth of waters,
Coldly crystal clear.

O world! I am yours!

(29 July 1937)

Autumn Gold

V bagréts y zóloto odétiye lesá
('In purplish-red and gold the woods are
clothed')

—Pushkin

Enchanted are the woods of red and gold,
No stirring of a twig on any branch.
The bark from birch tree trunks stands out,
White circle strips torn from the heart.
The golden waving leaves extend
Like fans beneath the tents of sky.
Patches of cold dark blue break through
Embroidered patterns of amber light.
Coal-black tree twigs, etched distinctly,
Form a slender, exhausted array.
Coral red aspens are all aflame
Against a silkscreen of blue and gold.

Through fallen leaves a brook runs on,
Still finding familiar paths of old.
A damp breeze blows. The only disruption's
The vehement chatter of jabbering magpies.

(29 July 1937)

Crystal Kingdom
(On the Summits of Tien Shan)

Around me ice fields of a crystal kingdom,
Triumphant temple filled with frozen silence,
Great peaks' immeasurable grandeur gleaming,
And diamond cupolas that sparkle under sun.
Vast lengths of space extend to blue horizons.
Huge crystal blocks are overhung with snow,
Grimly they lean over depths unfathomable.
The floods of sky-blue ice have frozen still
That once flowed down to stony valleys,
A granite sea of black chains tightly knotted
Amidst an avalanche's thunderous din.
Then silence reigns again in Crystal Kingdom,
The icy heights' triumphal music plays,
The endlessness of space, a silver sound.
The mountain breathes. The winds blow free.

(30 July 1937)

Black Sea

Magnificent raw element of constant change,
Today you roar with darkening menace
And roll your storm-ignited waves
With their white manes of roaring froth.
Your waters, rearing up with hurricane strength,
Threaten to wipe man from the earth's fair face
With all the burnt-out cinders of his hearth.

Next day you barely plash upon the shore
With lazy rhythm, like a patterned ribbon,
And leave behind a covering of seaweed
Over a pebbled ridge with shellfish scuttling.

Within your depths of azure-aquamarine
The underwater plants wave back and forth.
Outlines of watery creatures can be seen
Moving about as in a dream of green.

Sometimes you gleam dark blue; you're almost black.
At other times you glint like fiery lava.
At times you're spread out negligent, a milky shroud,
Then you impersonate a sea of blood.

Sometimes you modulate into mother-of-pearl,
The inexpressible charm of misty mornings,
Or yet with glaring whiteness you dazzle the sun,
Or you're a smooth turquoise, and frozen still.

You thing of greatness, azure and alive,
O wondrous sea, O wondrous sea of blue!

(30 July 1937)

Out on the Steppe

Broad is the sunlit breast of the steppe, free and
easy,
Wide open are her carefree vast expanses.
Out of the blue enamel of shining sky
The gentle breezes find it good to blow here.

The heated steppe land breathes with listless
sweetness.
A soft breeze barely stirring, like fine mesh,
Fluctuates over grass in silken waves.
Speaking in modest unobtrusive whispers,
The subtle, burning stream of breeze flows on,
Drunk on bitter wormwood, fragrant grasses,
Spicy, intoxicating meads of flowers,
Astringent, aromatic sun and spring.

Wastelands of sky stretch out in all directions,
With towers of clouds, white-breasted, running free.
The blue of their distances pale, or bottomless dark,
Recalls ancient masters' lush lapis-lazuli.

Wide-winged and vigilant, a black golden eagle
In circles smooth is soaring up on high,
Swift watchman of the heavens' distant spheres,
He never seems to move his mighty wings.

Still quietly the clouds keep passing by,
Blue shadows slipping over waves of grass.

(31 July 1937)

In the Taiga

In mystery's half-light, shadows everywhere,
Chaotic criss-cross weave of bough and branch,
Mouldering rotted stumps, interpenetrating grasses,
Soft mosses overlay mould-covered bark.
A windfall, a hollow from which there's no escaping,
Pillows of flowering moss and black abysses,
Covered for months with emerald carpets of grass,
And next to that the ripples on a mire.

Here spruce trees stand, all overgrown with moss
With shaggy beards of dead moss hanging down.
Long-needled cedars rustle—they're such beauties!—
They scrape their heavy, full-branched trunks together.
Patterns of lichen on the rocks and bark.
Grass growing in vast and intricate designs.
In water holes of small rust-coloured marshes
Mosquito larvae hold their circle dances.

A black woodpecker somewhere now gives out
With his sharp, penetrating, shrieking cry,
Followed by a rotten bough's rough fall.

Amidst this savage, many-stemmed greenery
Are patches of red, the flowers of stone bramble
And hanging coral clusters of rowanberry.

A chipmunk whistles out his standard greeting.
He's bringing cedar nuts for winter storage.

(31 July 1937)

Stars Above Ice

Est via sublimis, caelo manifesta sereno;
Lactea nomen habet.

—Ovidius Naso*

These are the last of the mountains' spruce tree-
giants.
Beyond them lies a grey moraine of boulders.

They droop their shaggy paws—their branches
forming knotted chains,
Black lace in moonlight's cobwebbed silver.

The sky's a blue-black velvet tent, all stretched out
wide and free,
And in it shine enormous stars, miraculously bright.

Millions of lamps, sky's candles, spill their mysteri-
ous light
On the carpet of the mindlessly distant earth.

Among the peaks reclines a giant, a gently sloping
glacier,
Lustrous with emerald-phosphorous light, like the
moon.

An ocean of diamond fragments, light blue and ten-
der green,
Music of eternal cold, high over ardent summer's
song.

Amidst the velvet black of sky, the endless sky's
expanse,
A frozen fire sparkles in the blocks of snow and ice.

With myriads of starry eyes, with all the Milky Way,
The cosmos watches earthly life in its fast-fleeting
course.

(31 July 1937)

[*NOTE: The Latin quotation is from Ovid's *Metamorphosis*,
BOOK 1, line 169. It means: 'There is a sublime pathway,
plainly visible in a clear sky, and it has the name Lactea.'
The term in English, 'Milky Way', is a translation from the
Latin, *via lactea*.—G. S.]

Altai Rapids*

We're riding a raft
Down the River Biya
Steersman at his post
Firm hand on the rudder
The waters flow smoothly
Between forested cliffs
But ahead there are rapids roaring
A whole pack of angry voices.
With their ridge of stormy foam
They're coming up quickly
We won't get through in one piece
We're sure to go to the bottom
The raft shoots like an arrow
Into frothing wild waters
A mad wave carries it
Onto the rocks

An unexpected sharp turn
Roaring, frothing, thundering, whooshing
Our raft flies edgewise
Into a whirlpool, a savage abyss
Then it rights itself
It's back up again
And then
We fall head first into a new abyss
All breathing stops
Sodom and Gomorra
Are all around
We've dived into a bawling, watery maw.
Then headlong
Swallowing icy spray
Water collecting in our boots
We pop up again like a cork
And again we're riding
Down the River Biya
The rudder is obedient
In the hands of man

(2 August 1937)

[*NOTE: As an experiment, minimum punctuation was
used in this translation.—G. S.]

Vultures

High in the Pamirs, along the caravan road,
Bare cliffs stand all around, no bush or shrub in
sight.
The caravans have passed, gone far ahead.
Some of the camels drag along behind.

They're huge, half-dead, rib cages sticking out,
Legs shaking as they slowly make their way.
Brass bells upon their necks give off a sound
As doleful as a funeral's hopeless knell.

Around the body of a fallen camel
A crowd of carrion-eaters has dropped down,
A predatory ring of vultures black.
Their haughty stare is piercing, cold, and dry.

On bare, repulsive necks there's not a feather.
Sharp is the steely beak, a villain's dagger,

And huge and powerful their iron claws,
Forged from a metal fraught with evil passion.

From the great Pamirs' inaccessible heights
They have flown down to have their feast of blood.
They gulp the carrion, greedy, shoving each other
Like a bazaar of squabbling peasant women.

With filth and stench on their beaks, and smeared
with guts
They have grown heavy 'midst the bloody fumes.
Like drunkards they hop sideways, awkwardly,
Galumphing, foolish, unsteady, over the rocks,
Or having gorged themselves, sit gloomily
Glancing off to the side with lifeless eyes.

(2 August 1937)

Crab

The waters of the sea are see-through glass,
And on the bottom all is visible
Where the incline of cliffs has plummeted
Into the shadowy depths.

Rocked by the current,
A whole forest of hair is streaming,
The fresh-green tender braids
Of fantastical plant life.

By a hole in a porous block of stone
Where the sun's rays have weakened
As two large fish weave by
There sits an enormous crab.

He's motionless, half-hidden
By cosmoses of hair.

A smudge among pink smudges,
He's grown together with his rock.

But now he lifts a heavy claw
And moves it to the side.
Slowly, lazily he creeps
Under the intertwined mesh of grass.

Again his suit of armour's frozen stiff,
Like an outcropping of stone,
As though life's force did not exist
Beneath this crusty carapace.

But look! See how his eyes
On their little stems are roving
And by his mouth the breather-feelers
Flutter back and forth.

You leaned over to have a look,
And lo, in the wink of an eye
He disappeared—leaving the network of plant life
Empty and alone.

(2 August 1937)

At the Black Grouse Breeding Ground

It's frosty still. The moon is at the full.
It hangs against dark sky and adds its light.
Night's silence has spread out now, everywhere,
And ice bits crackle, fragile in the icy air.

In darkness still, a blue-green star's faint gleam
Shows through the branches of a hunter's shack.
Dry leaves of reeds, all frozen stuck as one,
Are rustling at a small stream's edge.

At once a ringing, shattering sound is heard,
A silver stallion's neighing clarion-call.
Another sound, a piercing whistle comes.
The male snipe's call! He's caught a mate's attention.
An answering sound is heard, a tap-tap-tap.

But hark! From gullies over by the woods
Something is giving off an ominous hiss.
Again. And yet again. A hissing and huffing.
Haven't a witch and goblin started tussling?

Suddenly some black lump comes fluttering down
And makes a gentle landing on the ground.
Another after it. A third. A fourth.
And there on frozen, yellow, last-year's grass,
Half blocked from view by morning whisps of mist,
The handsome blackguards start to strut their stuff.
They crane their necks and fan their tails out stiff.

It's quickly growing light, the mist's dispersing,
The sun's gold arrows soaring in and piercing.
Whole woods burst into song—grouse chiming in.
Their rumbling organs blend in eerie chorus,
As waves of wondrous music herald spring.

And on the ground the male grouse, fighting hard
To win the female, soon are drawing blood.
Their passions rage. They charge and leap about
And tear each other's fancy feathers out.

(3 August 1937)

Hawk Moth Carousers and Revellers

Twilight. It's getting dark. In flower beds
Seas of bright tints and colours have subsided:
Tobacco plant, verbena, heliotrope and petunia.
A tender river of fragrance starts to flow,
A veritable lake of perfumed clouds.
How good the evening coolness is.
The dew refreshes leaves on every tree.
The robin's roulade is faintly heard in bushes
In contrast to the nightingale's contralto.

Upon the flow of aromatic streams
There come flying in from all directions,
Quick on the wing like instants of pure flight,
Circling round the wreaths of evening flowers,
All trembling, with their wings so lightly humming—
The hawk-moth revellers, with stringy whiskers,

Inserting their long feeding tubes
Into the honeyed funnels of the flowers.
Be still! Don't make a move!
One move and the fragrant coronas sway free,
The hawk moth flies like a bullet up and away.

In the morning moths and butterflies sit in rows
On the curtain and ceiling of the terrace.
They modestly fold their wings into little roofs,
Dreaming their dreams in quiet and in peace.
Here is the vineyard hawk moth, little playboy,
All tender pink and olive-green and gold.
And the euphorbium moth, the troublemaker,
His wings are edged in green and black,
All patterned, all in fretwork,
A migrant dweller in the poplars here,
Among these lowly beasts, a lordly lion,
And lover of lilac bushes,
While over there, tucked in a humble corner,
Is pine-tree hawk moth. He's a modest grey.

All of them sleep peacefully and still
Until at eve, the buzz begins again,
Without the slightest effort it starts up—
The quick-as-lighting whirring of their wings.

(3 August 1937)

Birch Tree

O ordinary birch tree,
Dear simple friend of mine!
You're not prosaic, you're poetry,
And dearer than roses of Paradise.

There you stand all silvery,
Wearing a brocade of ice.
You're no mimosa of the south,
But what quietness you have!

Your snowy diamond pattern
Against the pale blue sky,
Sparkling and gently gleaming,
Gives off a silver shine.

Or after a springtime sprinkling,
When everything drips from the roof,

Your network of tiny, sticky leaves
Trembles tenuously green.

You overflow with birch sap,
And from your sturdy boughs—
Which radiate so verdantly!—
The cuckoo makes his call.

In summer your leaves are curly,
And like a slender candle
You stand and greet the poet.
He hears your joyful song.

And in the chilly autumn
Your candle lights up brightly.

Like scarlet-golden fire,
Your shawl of foliage blazing.

(3 August 1937)

On the Wild Boar's Track

In a tree I find myself a perch,
Press motionless against its limbs,
And try to imitate a lifeless beetle,
Just a human polyp, so to speak.

A bright blue titmouse flies up close to me,
Gives her head a twist and turn or two,
Then flutters lower from a branch up high,
Looks down at me, staring me right in the eye,
And suddenly alarmed, she flies away.

Above my head I hear the wind.
It came up quickly, carrying scents.
A flock of birds has landed, a huge gang.
But a falcon strikes quickly from ambush.
He's a young one, a real pirate
—I don't move a twig as I watch—

The falcon speeds off like an arrow,
His quarry in his talons.

* * *

It's getting dark faster and faster.
In the pale sky a star has caught fire.
The woods grow quieter, it's getting damper.
All Kabardá is lying down to sleep.

But hark, far off I hear the crackle
Of a broken branch.
Somewhere there's a stirring in the bushes.
My hand shakes, touching the gun.
There was a chuffing, an intake of breath,
Then silence reigns again.

A bat goes flitting by.
The moon shines through the trees.
A bass voice gives a grunt.
A boar is sniffing the air.

He's wondering if there's a hidden trap.
Isn't there someone concealed in ambush?
Again all sounds evaporate.
Muted silence reasserts itself.

But then, quite close, another grunt:
A boar moves through the reeds.
Then grunting, squeals and hubbub,

The drumming of numerous hooves.
The crackling of branches.
Limbs are breaking. There's squeaking and scraping,
All one great uproar,
Piglets playing, having fun.
A regiment of wild boar on the march,
An enormous tusked creature in the lead.
He knows his way around dangers.
With his humped back he cuts quite a figure.
He's gone behind a clump of aspen.
Others mince along after him.
Rubbing his bristles against a tree trunk,
He wrinkles the steepness of his sides.

Just then
The sound of an axe is heard
Thudding into a tree, giving off a loud boom,
And in an instant they're gone,
The whole herd—swallowed by the bushes.

(3 and 4 August 1937)

Mushrooms

'Ow-woo, ow-woo!' Then laughter through the
woods.
Among the leaves, on branches, there are nuts.
It's a bit damp, and there's a smell of mint,
Of mushrooms dank, and the decay of leaves.

Among bushes and grasses, where paws of spruce
hang down,
Some aspen mushroom cupolas appear—
Such sturdy fellows, chubby lads,
Such ruddy-headed rascals!

Parasol mushrooms squelch beneath our feet.
Snails sit on them and move their little horns.

'Are we picking agarics today?'
'Of course not! Forward march, let's go!'

'Look a whole slew of chanterelle.'
'Shall we skip them?' 'No, we've gotta pick them!'
(So many chanterelle poking from the ground,
You could fill a pond with them—no, *many* ponds!)

And there, in the moss, by a spruce's root
Some beautiful boletus makes its home:
Bright coloured caps on stubby, sturdy legs.
'Pass the bark basket over here!'

Off to the side, a bright crimson pattern:
Fly agaric puts on its insolent show.

And from a thicket, a cry of surprise,
'What a big one!' 'Size of a lifeboat!'
'But it's completely worm-eaten.'
'Oh sure . . .' A resentful look.

At the edge of the woods in a little clearing
A column of gnats is swarming,
Playing in a sunbeam.

An aspen glows brightly,
Dressed in its scarlet mantle.

And a spider web is wafted
By the soft, damp breeze
In the golden sun.

(4 August 1937)

In the Grass

Entire worlds live in the grass,
Upon the emerald greensward.

Flies and beetles, June bugs too,
And moths and the tiniest worms—
All bustle about under cover of grass,
Hastening to taste life's pleasures.

A leaf-miner beetle has crawled out
On the scrumptious leaf of a bush,
While inching up a blade of grass,
Stitching a path with his filament feet,
Is a geometrician, the measuring worm.

A swallow-tail butterfly lands
In a flutter upon a flower,
Taking its seat on its own pink throne.

An ant is dragging a beetle's corpse
Through a thick-branching, twiggy copse.
It fusses around a bit and drops it,
Then takes it again by the leg,
Stubbornly heaving and pulling
The black plate of its lifeless prey.

Under a leaf, half asleep,
Resting on a large stem,
Sits a grasshopper, totally green,
Silently waving antennae.

A bumblebee clings to its clover
As a fly lands on chamomile.

A grey honeybee is crawling
Into dark funnels of blue.

And a cricket, black as a Moor,
Hops off to the side from its burrow.

Fat as a priest of former times,
A ladybug from the fields
With its cap of many colours
Has turned up on my hand.

In the sweet-smelling grass I lie
Surrounded by a golden web
Of sunrays and by languages that
Remain forever unspoken.

(4 September 1937)

Flowers

Flowers! The joy of earth in spring,
Beauties of meadow, garden, field,
The eyes of nature, sweetness of summer,
Sunlit stream of every colour!

There's lily-of-valley, modest, tender.
In dewy shadow by water's edge,
It's worked into a cozy niche.

There's tender hue of mignonette,
Which when torn from its garden bed
Releases a subtle, fragrant perfume.

Forget-me-nots among moss in marshes
Look to the world like bits of turquoise
Or bright blue eyes of baby girls
With here and there some dew for tears.

Amid the vernal meadows, narcissus
Appears in the colour of white marble,
While raising up its head of violet
Is another early beauty, the iris.

Then there's verbena, varicoloured,
With its coronas of delicate petals,
And also bluebells, and Solomon's seal.

From under an arch of double-paired leaves
Flaming nasturtium faces gleam.

The crowns of crimson dahlias
And languid, fragrant paulownia—
All from a basket nod their heads.

In breezes flutter regal roses
Of every shade and every hue.
A scent is carried, with pollen dust,
Of the mimosa, golden, mute.

The funnels of slender, frail petunias,
Red, beautiful poppies in summer sun,
The blood-red lips of orchid flowers,
And heady scent of tobacco plant.

Then plain cornflowers amongst the rye,
The blue and violet heliotrope,
Our modest flowers of the field
In ditches, meadows, stacks of hay.
There's dandelion, and chamomile flower,
Cow wheat, and St John's wort.

And here are clover and wild asters.
How modestly their blossoms sway.

Wisteria with its clusters lush
Twines along the walls, hangs down.
Violet in colour, and dark-blue,
Its sweet scent fills the evening air.

The tulip stands up straight and proud
In full awareness of its grandeur.

That other poppy looks quite modest.
Nothing distinctive tells of its poison.

And quite unlike the Madonna poppy
Another poison is growing freely.
A drab plant, the nightshade belladonna,
It grows in the midst of enchanter's nightshade.

O, flowers of wood and flowers of field,
So many, many in the world,
More than I could count or keep track of,
With all your little bells and wreaths,
Blue and violet, yellow, scarlet
Gold or painted many colours,
Bright, sweet-smelling, big and small,
In the greenhouse or growing wild.

(28 September 1937)

Spring's Elemental Forces

O Erd, o Sonne,
O Glueck, o Lust . . .
O Leib, o Liebe
('O Earth, O Sun
O Happiness, O Pleasure . . .
O Body, O Love . . .')

—Goethe

The streams are flowing, the streams are roaring.
Their talk is a tongue-twisting patter.
The forests tumultuously turn green.
The hundred-voiced choir of the birds
Praises and nurtures and sings a lullaby.
Spring's elements are in their sacred eruption.
In the bushes everywhere there's rustling.
Languid sap's flowing in trunks and branches,
The tremulous note of the juices of spring.

And the bright rays of the sun give birth
To passionate gibberish and chatter.
There's drunken tipsiness in all things living
As shaggy Pan takes up his pipes
And plays forever in praise of Life.

The cradle rocks of Springtide fair,
Loud whistling, trilling, pouring forth.
The sun caresses the grass, earth's hair,
The wellsprings gush, reviving life,
And ardently drunk from the heat of the sun,
Lips seek out lips, press one to one.

The elements have lost their heads because of spring,
And people, too, with joyful soul,
Take to the paths of love and longing.

(8 August 1937)

Rainbow's Arch

Far away beyond the hills,
Beyond the dark-blue spaciousness,
Far, far away—oh, ever so far,
High in the sky, oh, ever so high,
Driven by swiftly flying winds,
Coming by ways that bring it quickly,
A cliffside of thunderclouds speeds near
And pours its cargo down, the rain.

Brightly, clearly, Father Sun,
Ah, that gold and crimson one,
Takes a peek and looks about
And makes a lunge with all rays shining
At the thunderstorm's steep sides.

The grass has turned all glittery, playful.
The silken meadow's grown greener still,

The wonderland of grass, the greensward,
Plaything for winds that sweep the steppeland.

There then spreads out over wet Mother Earth,
Glistening with lustrous diamond tears,
Pouring her dewdrop tears on the meadows,
Most marvellous of all—the Rainbow's Arch.

(8 August 1937)

Electron World

> The world, a oneness of everything, was not
> made by any gods or men, but was, is, and will
> be eternally living fire which regularly flames up
> and regularly dies down.
>
> —Heraclitus

All praise to Democritus' gifted insight
Divining what was hidden from our eyes,
What's now been won from nature for all time,
Laid bare by crafty instruments and by
The subtle skills of sciences exact,
The valiant penetrations of the mind
Fixed and set down in numbered formulas.

The bottomless abyss has now been plumbed.
The secret of the world stands naked now,
Captured in space's multiple dimensions
Amidst the cosmos' ornament and wealth.

All colours, sounds and smells inclusively
And all the pangs of human suffering
World without end, all have their firm foundation,
Their life and being's ageless, endless source,
In electricity's vast native land.

In the thumb of any human fool
As in the galaxies of distant stars
And in the convolutions of the brain,
In all things everywhere electrons spin,
The positrons and protons swing and swirl,
A circle dance of age-old symmetries.

As one thing passes into something else,
Changing its forms, shedding its substance-skin,
Nature's eternal motion comes to be.

'All is flux'

(night, early hours of 8 July 1937)

Biosphere

Life's everywhere—as are life's spheres.
There are, of living beings, countless myriads,
Teeming in every bit of atmosphere.
In golden motes of dust are flying monads,

Which we see only with the microscope.
Whole worlds enclosed in but a drop of rain,
Hidden away from us by nature's guile—
To them the microcosm bears its gifts.

The seas with plankton all are impregnated,
And mother ocean's every cubic metre
As if by law is fully saturated
With all the music of life's wondrous saga.

So too with every particle of soil.
Pick up a handful. In it you will find

Thousands of bits of life all moving, stirring.
Both near and far, in all things, everywhere
Are mobile aggregates of living matter.

O Earth! O Earth! You tiny planet fair,
Filled with the life of infusoria,
Unto the last descendant of Iapetos,*
Crash through the cosmos like Creation's wave!

(morning of 9 July 1937)

[*NOTE: In Greek mythology, Iapetos was a Titan, the father
of Prometheus, mankind's benefactor.—G. S.]

Opening of the Treasure Troves

Within the recesses of Mother Earth
Lie hidden like fine caskets of treasure
Magnificent and wondrous types of rock,
Magma that froze here in solid strata.

Metals lie here, and semiprecious stones,
Underground mountains of iron,
Entire Mont Blancs of coal,
The dead interment grounds
Of giant trees' extinguished lushness,
Lakes of greasy black petroleum,
The thick blood in the arteries of Earth,
Along with sparkling veins of gold
And salt hills' steep-sloped cupolas,
All of it hidden in underground gloom,
Dead treasure stored away for centuries.

But the hot flame of free and wilful labour
Has risen like Aurora Borealis
And with its fiery breath has wakened
The entire kingdom of sleeping treasure.
It's freed the elements from sleep's enchantment
Delivered them to serve new man and woman
In the transforming of Earth's ancient face.

(2 July 1937)

Swifts

The swifts are circling, flashing round,
Scanning the sky's familiar atlas,
Slicing the air.
Black crosses on a background of pale blue,
Zigzagging as they disappear.

After describing a circle out of sight
They're back again—wings whistling,
Emitting indescribably shrill cries
As piercing as the sharpest needle.

Headlong they shoot like arrows
In a frenzied downward swoop
And like bullets they've ricocheted
Around the building's edge.

The moral of this story? Speed!
And may we rush with even greater speed
Into new battles and new victories!

(19 July 1937)

Avalanche

A radiant sun shines in heaven this day
While coolness wafts from blue glacial sheets.
The air's pure and clear. The masses of snow
Are blotted with shadow beneath bright clouds.
A muteness, a silence embraces all nature.
Sealed are the mouths of the ice-cold springs.
They don't ask or answer. No one heeds them,
But their living streams still trickle unheard.

A sudden clap of thunder burst
Aloud from a thousand guns,
And all around,
From hills that had started to speak
There swiftly recoiled
A thousandfold echo,
Filling the valley all at once
With menacing laughter and chuckling sounds.

An avalanche is carried
With ever-increasing speed
Down the steep mountainside
While above it
With pearly dust going wild,
Clouds of snow,
Twisting and twirling,
Sweep madly upward.
The boisterous whirlwinds battle the sun,
Glittering with snowflake diamonds
And sparks of tiny fluff
Far up on high.

While boulders down below—
Like offspring of Satan,
Who has ripped them from an icy cradle
And hurled them down—
Go leaping, devilishly dancing,
Rumbling and roaring
Into the abyss.

And all at once the rebel thunder
Has passed out cold—
Again there's silence all around.

(22 September 1937)

Storm at Sea

The shaggy billows of incoming tide
Race shoreward, fiercely howling
And break apart against the walls
Of rocks on shore, foam hissing.

Their thudding blows drum heavily.
Like Janissaries, they rush to battle
Upon the backs of wild green steeds,
Crowns of foam on grey-haired horsemen.

Torn battle flags are splashing here,
Black raiment of many a warhorse streams,
And Boreas blows helter-skelter in fury
The white mane of each steed.

Sea giants grapple in fierce encounters
As drums tattoo a muffled pattern,

Swords are clanging, shields are clashing
In nighttime's black abyss of gloom

In all his fury the god of the sea
Strikes awe with the sound of his conch-shell horn,
And out of the clouds in the black of the sky
Fly mettlesome, fierce, majestic steeds,
The horses of the Valkyries.
Their armour shining, chain mail gleaming,
And warlike battle cries ring out,
Savage and ominously dark.

In the black heavens thunder rolls
While jagged bolts of lighting flare
And in the awesome clatter of battle
'Midst flashing swords of hammered steel,
Amidst the clashes, roaring, strident,
The awesome sea god, hoary-headed,
Shakes his heavy mace and trident.

(night, early hours of 23 September 1937)

Northern Lights

Marvellous streamers and bands of light,
Wavering, dancing in darkness of night.

Gold braiding, fiery, decorative,
Sparkling, flaring, playing about
Like miracles of flame.

Like rarest, lustrous gems they shine,
Like jewels glistening,
Serpents of fire coiling
In an iridescent brocade,
The golden necks of heavenly swans
Vibrantly twining in and out,
Floods and surges, plays of colour,
Pouring past in brilliant waves,
Twinkling enticingly
Like a rainbow, diamond-studded.

And the sparks play strange roulades
On the panpipes of the sky,
Trills of silver, silvery trilling,
In the still of hulking night.

And in that silent play of light
Magnificent chorales are heard.

Like a fiery mantle it hovers,
The entrance to heaven, to Valhalla.

(night, early hours of 23 September 1937)

Dust-Devil Whirlwinds

At the crossing of the roads
And over the sands of the valley,
Down from the mountain gorges to the lowlands
The horn of a furious windstorm is blowing.

Like columns of smoke, in rings and spirals
Dust-devils whirl and swirl and curl
And with mad speed in devil's dance whisk by,
Waving a shawl torn from a giant,
The dusty whirlwinds,
Hot and dry,
In fury flinging up the sand.

This sudden descent by demons of the air
Raises the sand
And lifts it to the heavens
To form an enormous elephant's trunk,

A dark constrictor flying through the air,
A serpent dragging its crazy tail behind it.
In haste
It flies.
Ramming its head into the sky, it wants
To cover the sun with its black gloom,
And from its greedy maw erupt
Clouds of dry sand.

Still flying,
Winding and twisting in free-flowing columns,
The ill-omened dust-devil flocks speed off,
Scattering sand on every pathway.

(night of 22 September, morning of 23 September, 1937)

Downpour

The blue expanse of heaven
                          is gaily shining.
Trees and plants open out,
                          displaying their costumes.
Hot as it is in the sun—
                          that's how cool it is in the shade
As the lovely day keeps playing
                          around with sunbeams.

But look, from an outlying edge of sky
Comes creeping—devouring space all around it—
An ominous, dark-blue cloud. Then thunder
Fires off its cannon with cast-iron shells.

Faster and faster the black cloud rushes on,
A giant piling-up of purple mounds.

It stretches out its hairy, hoary arms
As its ill-omened body blackly swells.

All nature has gone still, awaits unblinking
The lashing out, the striking of the storm.

Sullen cold wind has suddenly gusted,
Working its loud, swift-rushing wings.
And a whirlwind spins, sweeping dust and straw
High into the air, from the treetops tearing
A leaf that trembles in fear, despairing.
It's rushed off, pure innocent, into the sky.

Fighting the wind, hard-beating its wings,
A jackdaw, mute, speeds by in sidelong flight.
Cows moo and run for the safety of barnyards
And songbirds huddle in secret corners.

Already golden rays have disappeared
And gloom has overtaken skies of blue,
Covered them like a rug of darkened sea
And loosed the deafening thunder from its chain.

With piercing screech two herons hurry past.

Large scattered raindrops start to fall, then all
At once a hell of water gushes down,
And pellets of hail drum into new-formed pools . . .
The floods of water stream across the land,
Roaring and seething as though gone mad.

In the black sky there's a savage riot,
Roaring thunder, unrestrained violence.

The heavens really opened up this time.
Rain hammers its slanting, slender shafts,
Like nails into the ripples of puddles.
The stern and mighty thunder rumbles on . . .

(night, early hours of 24 September 1937)

Sunset

A symphony of colour has played out in the sky.
The eventide's aglow with precious stones.
There's swirling chaos too—swords, battle flags and helmets bronze,
And brilliant towers rising to the heavens,
Their summits still illumined by the sun,
The steep and golden peaks of giant mountains.

Bonfires flood onward like an ocean tide of light.
There's emerald, coral red, porphyry, ruby.
A purple river, in its bloody broth,
Is bearing dark blue monsters' mighty backbones off.
And everything is churning, more violent grow the flames,
As the ruddy ball of fire sinks, expiring.

(night of 1 October 1937)

HERITAGE

[Bukharin gave the above title to the 28 poems he designated as 'series V'.—G. S.]

Heritage

Through the dogma of centuries, the mists of time,
Epochs when crosses were planted
On earth's roads and mountain passes,
Amidst deeds performed by giants,
Battles of whole nations, titanic labours,
By the efforts of millions of hands,
The rounded compass of a great inheritance
Was formed for us.

There has piled up a Pamir Mountain range
From the childhood of humanity,
The childhood of all races, peoples, countries,
A Pamir of things, of thoughts and words,
The art of vanished centuries,
Their deeds of labour, the glory of their sages.

Philosophers of Hellas, in well-ordered ranks,
Go passing by with their majestic stride.
The voices of China and India reach us,
And dark mediaeval harmonies.
Then a new era shines with luminous spirit
Breaking from earlier generations:
Abstract thought and the microscope,
The symphony, the powerful machine,
The super-precision of science's telescope,
Architecture and painting,
The universal man, da Vinci,
Shakespeare, Goethe, Tolstoy,
The free-running Reason of Kant
And grand old Hegel's immortal works—
All of it's brought together in a giant crucible
And goes through ferment, turbulent, creative.
Insurgent fire burns off the rust of ages.
The metal of our times, forged Red and beautiful,
Before the world has now begun to sparkle.

(evening, 1 July 1937)

Europe and Asia

In the era of Europe's youth, there were streams of
brilliant light
That flowed in long, broad ribbons across the
Orient.
The Tigris and Euphrates, the valleys of Indus and
Ganges,
The channels of great China's rivers, Hwang Ho and
Yangtze Kiang,
All served as spacious beds for the culture of sages,
Who proudly raised their heads towards the summits
of Reason.

And there was Babylon, giant of ancient times;
And bloodthirsty Assyria,
Subjugating all around with greedy, iron hand.
They first called forth to life the masters of skilled
calculation,

Artists and engineers, astrologists and sculptors.
There was Elam and Iran,
And the Phoenicians, a race of daring traders,
Who sowed their purple seeds in distant lands and
colonies.
They made their way from Borneo's shores to the
Germans' sea,
Fighting with wind and wave, in search of precious
amber,
Bringing culture to barbarians' wild lands,
Sticking their needles of knowledge in Europe's
sons.

In yet another epoch, of mediaeval twilight,
The Arab culture flourished from Cordova to
Samarkand.

But the cycle of life in the world took a sharp and
cutting turn.
The fruits of all that labour, the peaceful work of
centuries,
Was burned up in wars.

With a shrill whistle the spirals of new epochs
unravelled.
New tablets appeared, new actions, people, ideas.
Asia's greying kingdoms drowsed sadly, sluggishly.

In Europe a violent god, Lord Capital, roared out in
triumph.

Its science, machinery, art, commodities, powder
and cannon
Surrounded and burned all laggards like stacks of
dried-up hay.

But once again the pendulum swung back.
Amidst the blood of emperors the half-mad beast
expired,
And after it went flying, into the ages' deep abyss,
All that the modern slave owners had lived by.

Across the space of two enormous continents
Arose a new power, free from profit and interest.
This mighty power's a unifier of nations.

Socialism has kneaded new dough from ages past,
Grown fruits of new cultures, new gardens and
orchards,
And lovingly nurtured new vegetables, grains and
flowers.

All of the West's technology, calculus, science and
art,
It took into its smelter, recreating with thought and
deed.

But precious to it as well are the emerald-azure
waters
Of thought and feeling from the ancient East.
All nations' culture-rivers run into one ocean,

Directing the course of their flow through giant filters,
Where shoots of illness, decay will be cleaned away.
A united front, New East–New West, will march ahead!

(24 July 1937)

Hellas

The sea wave splashed, light blue,
Beneath caressing azure skies.
The free man's life was bright and full
And blessed by Phoebus Apollo.

Temples arose of wondrous harmony
With rows of lilting colonnades.
Poetic daydreams flourished, rejoicing,
'Midst brightly envisioned naiads and gods.

On the agora, the tribunes held forth
Among talkative Athenian crowds.
From sacred heights of Mount Olympus
The gods leaned down to hear those words.

Hellas, the pearl of this secular world,
Gave it the most profound of thinkers,
Creators with a thousand faces,
Not only poets, but geometricians.

Aristotle, Plato, Democritus,
All still alive in our worldwide culture,
And fresh offshoots keep growing from
The thought of Heraclitus and Epicurus.

Long since have Homer's hoary narratives
Been echoing in new, inspired song.
The Golden Fleece of tragedy and drama
Keeps shining like the Spirit's torch, undimmed.

Euripides, Aeschylus, Sophocles,
Still, pincer-like, they tear at our hearts,
And Aristophanes' acid humour
Has found a home in European minds.

Euclid teaches geometry to this day
With mathematic mind, severe and clear.
Thucydides, father of history,
Exemplifies the art of exposition.

Their marvellous statues still shine in our eyes,
Those bodies of noble marble.
Praxiteles and Phidias richly serve
As models for sculpture in ages to come.

Their deathless works are magical as dreams,
Beauty herself sings out to us from them,
And solidly ensconced upon that throne,
She reaches out to us her august hand.

(10 September 1937)

Land Under a Spell (India)

Far off, beside a dark blue sea,
There lies a land of miracles
With snow-topped mountains for a headdress
Under an azure span of sky.

Crushed and abased, downtrodden
By those lately arrived from London,
The land trembles, all in blood,
At its new proprietors' feet.

The ancient temples of deities
Are overgrown by jungle.
Liana vines wind all around
The statues of epic heroes.

Enchantment of the ages
Spreads its perfume about,

And ancient Vedic tradition
Lures people with its verse.

The architecture of ruins
Is unbearably luxuriant.

Imagination's wildest thoughts
Are hidden in these sculptured forms.

Here all the world of nature
Is live, personified.
As at a feast, it's painted and
Adorned with vivid colours.

All strewn about are large-eyed peacock feathers,
And vivid necklaces of precious stones.

Poets, servants of the palace,
And ancient fathers of religions
Accumulated secret wisdom,
Knew how to skilfully control
The breath, the beating of the heart,
Defeat the wanderings of the mind
With the hermit secret of hypnosis.

Works by the learned stargazers,
The summits of mathematics
Of medicine and of poetics—
All frozen now in petrified ruins.

The ancient sages' teachings
Are covered over with burdocks,

Rich sources of thought, where the most diverse lie
hidden
In deep recesses, philosophy's storage chests.

The carnival of decay holds court here now,
With bare teeth grinning up at greatness past,
The tomb magnificent is broken, cracked,
Like someone half-alive, unseeing, deaf.

But in the end this country will throw off
The foreign yoke, the ugly yoke of Cain.
Already it has risen from its sleep.
With sacred wrath it now is breaking from
The shameful fetters of its ancient castes.
The tide will soon come in.
The rivers of Great India will flow
Down channels where World Labour's at the helm.

(15 August 1937)

Behind the Great Wall (China)

Grey-headed, ancient China, with your mighty
rivers,
The Ways of Heaven passing through the Middle
Kingdom,
Behind your walls of stone you hid from everyone,
But on a path of gold the foreigner broke through.

Your giant-sized canals brought all the waters
together.
In your people there blossomed the labour of
centuries.
You grew famous for your silks, your delicate white
porcelain,
The skill of your expert hands, your artistry superb.

You loved the land and its roughness. Your labour
knew no bounds.

You brought explosive powder to life, and also the
printed page.
The compass with magic needle—that too was your
invention.
Patience and art were embodied in the fineness of
your carvings.

And in philosophy's ocean, together with stern
Meng-tze,
There floats, in the mists of time, the ever-so-gentle
Lao Tzu.

(7 September 1937)

Voice of the Buried Sun
(Aztec, Inca, Maya)

> The Europeans fully deserved the appellation
> given them by one of the tribes of North
> America—*Ewie Daetlini* (those who drag death
> behind them).
> —Jean Jacques Élisée Reclus, *Man and the Earth,*
> (Russian edition, 6 VOLS, St Petersburg,
> 1906–1909), VOL. 5, p. 333

Where are you, lost lands of the Sun,
Of its feathered golden rays,
Wearing a crown, surrounded by halo,
Lands of the fabled winged Serpent?

Where are Tenochtitlan's
Fair temples and palaces?
The gold frames and decorations
And brightly embroidered patterns?

The Zapotecs clove through entire mountaintops,
A miracle of construction,
And the Aztecs built huge terraces
All covered with gardens and flowers.

There among the tribes of the Sun
Where Quetzalcoatl ruled
Among the many famous clans
Was that of Toltecatl.
The meaning of that word was 'artist',
And through their efforts they covered
Whole palaces and cliff sides
With a wordless painted record.

Where are the works of the ancient Maya
With their miraculous culture?
The doors to sunny paradise
Decorated with sculpture?

And the Tawantinsuyo of Peru,
Land of the four directions of light,
It sank into the dead of night
When the comet arose.

Aqueducts and roads,
Pyramids and halls,
Inca, Maya, Aztec.
The greed of vile Europeans
Drowned all in a sea of blood.

But a day will come when the misery
Of maimed and mutilated Indians
Will have passed forever.

(15 August 1937)

Gothic Cathedral
(Mediaeval Europe)

> It was bound to become the Bastille of the
> Soul.
>
> —Heine

It soars with well-shaped shafts of wood
Towards a broad expanse of blue,
A thing of lace, severely piercing
The sky—the Gothic cathedral.

Against sky-blue patterns there's gloomy singing,
The gargoyle's chimerical grimace,
Steep steps, pointed arches, and
Well-proportioned masses of stone.

Through the rubies of stained-glass windows,
Light filters from on high, blood-red,
While greens and dark blues symbolize
The discoloured wounds of Christ.

In the semi-dark are sepulchers
And ceremonious funeral music
As lowered eyelids sadly flutter.
The sobbing of souls in torment,
Crushed here below in chains,
Flies upward in search of salvation,
Exhausted by eternal patience
And tired of living as slaves.

The burden of their prayers
Reaches the hearing of no one.
It stands there, a solid wall of stone,
The Bastille of the Soul.

(night, early hours of 10 September 1937)

The Renaissance

It was the greatest progressive revolution that
mankind had so far experienced, a time which
called for giants and produced giants . . .
— Engels, in his 'Introduction' to *Dialectics of
Nature*

The black vampires of the church,
Who from the flesh sucked out the blood,
Erecting graven images
To the workings of evil spirit.
Black monks in their monkish robes
Burned heretics in God's name,
Put everyone's head on the block
Whose thinking dared rise above wretched.

The monks suffered a big defeat
To the cheerful strumming of
The teachings of a new world,

A world that shone with colour,
Yes, colours of living emotion,
Of bold and powerful thought,
Of art that was full-blooded,
And scornful laughter at
The foul and stinking, bloody, wrathful
Dismal dictatorship of the church
And at the toad-like, sleuth-hound
Figure cut by the Inquisition.

The gods of joyful Hellas were
Restored at one stroke from oblivion,
Its seething creative energy,
The colonnades of its marvellous temples,
Its poets and philosophers,
Its marble statues' fine physiques,
The rocket's glare of flaming thought,
All were reborn and began to sing.

Giants were born in the world
With sword belts round their waists,
With brilliant, searching minds,
Titans of thought, and giants of the heart.

They discovered new worlds,
Revealed the earth's rotation,
Created magnificent art
To express life's joyful song,
The joy of this creation,

Rebirth of youthful flesh,
A springtime of regal spirit,
Impetuous flowering of life.

From far off, it still shines for us
With brilliant words and deeds
And summons to new victories
Over the ages of decay.

(7 August 1937)

Schools of Painting

The Flemish world of painting,
The masterful work sung by Verhaeren,*
The mounds of pink bodies, luxurious plumpness,
And at this feast of plumpness the triumph
Of ardent natural urges of the flesh.
Here freely reigns Divine desire.
Among the elements of breathing flesh,
Perspiring bodies, and hot-burning cheeks,
Amidst an abundant store
Of fish and fowl and all the fruits of earth,
The steam of strong intoxicating wine.
In this aromatic mix of pungent vapours,
The mighty spirit of Rubens radiates.

But every country has its unique ways.
Under a sky forever luminous
Italy's offspring were awakened.

Under the Quattrocento's famous aegis
The twin stars of Venus and Phryne
Began to scintillate with wondrous beauty,
The elegance of naked healthy bodies,
Raphael's beautiful Fornarini
And the goddesses of Titian
Who blithely tossed her garments off, dumbfounding
The envious stares of prudish hypocrites.

(8 September 1937)

[*NOTE: The Belgian writer Emile Verhaeren (1855–1916), whose poetry also seems to have influenced Bukharin, published books about Rembrandt (in 1904) and Rubens (in 1910).]

Voices of the Past

I look at you, the portraits
Of kings long since decayed
In armour of bronze or all dressed up
In extravagant velvet costumes.

With proud gaze you survey your world,
With eyes both arrogant and cruel,
And with the secret hidden shame
Of life caught up in sensual vices.

You look around as though alive,
Blue veins visible in your hands.
At any moment you'll start to shout,
And for the slaves new torments will begin.

But your sword has long been covered
With red rust, as though by a crust,

And your skeleton's come apart
Beneath the stone of your tomb.

I look at the mummies of the Pharaohs
Dried up long ago, turned black,
Once occupants of fearsome thrones
While countless slaves bowed down to them.

In a sarcophagus, gilded over,
Swaddled in ceremonial cloths
And covered with hieroglyphic writing,
You have been lying beneath the mound
Of the sacred pyramids.
I see the gilding on your death mask
And hear your dry skin rustling.
I see the work of countless priests,
And we read your sacred hymns,
We read your songs, your thoughts and dreams,
Which once hung over the heads of slaves
Like so much dreaded black ash.

But you're lying speechless now,
There in your enormous tombs.
Immodest eyes peer at you intently
Yet, mystery, you hold your tongue.

I look on busts of pallid marble,
The heads of Caesars long since gone.
An age of bronze bequeathed them to us,
Bequeathed by Rome, both great and harsh.

Here's Caius Julius, warrior bald,
And here Augustus, and Tiberius.
Their age was the recipient
Of unique mysteries of time.

And I see angry, evil eyes,
Lips twisted in perfidious sneer,
In the half-dark of southern night
See rusted chains and tortured bodies.

And I look on baked-clay tablets,
Hammurabi's famous code.
Tablets unearthed from fertile plains
Where Babylon, the great, once stood.

Hear sounds from underground, the voices
Of ancient times long since gone by,
Of life that's disappeared forever,
An anthem praiseful of itself.

I look at the faces of lovely women
In paintings from the Quattrocento.
I see the dance of their lustrous eyes.
I see their ribbons and their lace.

They existed. They were living.
Their glances were aflame with passion,
But now beneath the earth their bodies
And dresses are dust. That's the new fashion.

And yet *alive* those eyes are looking
Of maidens once here in this world,
Eyes as black as wings of night,
Portraits of women who've now vanished.

And I look at the folios
And alphabet letters in ancient scripts.
All the Platos, Hobbeses, Kants
Arise before me in the gloom.

That which has been embraced by death
And buried away for centuries
Is now reborn before our eyes
Thanks to the spadework of our minds.

(9 September 1937)

Makers of Machines

The machine system with its huge bulk
Erupted in the hum and drone of metal
With a steady thump and clatter,
The signal of modern times,
The thousand-handed mechanism,
The dance of the factory's hell.

Drill bits, wheels and cylinders,
Amplifications of brain and muscle,
With steely grasp seized nature by the throat
Despite all her turbulent elements.

All of them, James Watt, Arkwright,
Newton and Stephenson,
The Newcombs and the Cartrights,
The Diesels and Edisons.

The engineers and the workers,
The genius of counting, measuring,
Thought, and labour were harnessed together
In the hot belly of Capital.

They laid the laws of nature bare
And sowed a crop of new ideas.
They've given a mighty forward shove
To world history's chariot wheel.

The sky's lit up already, in the distance,
With lighting flashes—coming revolutions.

(night, early hours of 9 September 1937)

Science

Intelligence's cold blue fire,
Well-ordered, triumphal science,
The churning of tireless labour's victories—
These are the legacy of humanity's sages.
It's not a Fata Morgana flitting before us,
Showing the pale blue light of phantom smoke.
It's fruit that's fallen round Nature's paradise-gates,
The product of cognition's stubborn striving.

Chromosomes and genes, the spectrum of light,
Dimensions of stars, the rushing round of bits of
matter,
Electrons; the universal paths of the planets—
Science has learned how to find all these.

And Reason's great power leads ever onward
To solving the riddles of ever-new sphinxes

From the tiniest particles on 'sinful' Earth
To realms of interplanetary dust.

Bacon, Newton, Maxwell, Galileo,
Darwin, Pavlov, Helmholz, Faraday,
Hundreds of other great and noble minds
Uncovered secrets of entire worlds.
Labouring over 'inert' earthly matter,
Encompassing all of Nature with the mind,
People have tamed the fury of violent forces,
Whose onslaught now is serving humanity.
Through *praxis*, through the mighty roar of factories,
Man has subdued the substances of Nature.

(morning, 13 July 1937)

The Master
(Leonardo da Vinci)

Mighty master of all times,
Elegant multiple thinker,
Amidst the many columns of bright genius
A universal mind.

Devoted to precision instruments
And carefully thought-out experiments,
Artist and engineer,
With a flight of genius he blended
The mathematics of curving lines,
The calculations of optics,
And cross-sections of golden light
With an interplay of tones and colours,
Shadows and half-light,
In the frescoes and portraits produced

By his demigod talents.
He played with everything, created anything.
Well known to his creative genius were
Computations concerning the heavenly bodies,
The wings of flight,
The impact of hard chisel blows
On marble.
He built fortresses and palaces
As well as city walls
And sent his thoughts to all the ends
Of our mysterious universe.

In his creative work he sought
Paths that were not well worn.
He was inventive and observant,
Drafted models, measured closely,
And tormented nature's substance
With fire and iron.
He loved to study peculiar things:
The patterns made by mould
And oddly deformed creatures.
From all the wells of knowledge he drank deep.

To us across the centuries
He directs his curious gaze,
And quietly he talks with us
Wearing La Giaconda's smile.

(night, early hours of 15 July 1937)

The Great Unknown
(William Shakespeare)

Who are you, William the Unknown?
The one called William Shakespeare?
Are you Bacon? Or another
Famous idol of the times?
This secret will remain through all the ages.

Regardless of who might have given you birth,
A genius of infinite power emerged.
Who built Cyclopean temples if not you?
Instead of stilts and wigs and affectations,
Scholasticism's chains of yesterday,
You viewed the whole vast smorgasbord of passions,
Spoke with the richness of the people's language,
Revealed the murky perfidy of kings,
The masses' turbulent will to self-expression.
You looked at pride, love, fear and jealousy

And heard the liberty-loving voice of the street
While on the stage floor there lay clotted blood.
What range and power! O what an artist's brush!
An age of sensibility's living breath
Is wafted by the breezes of your times.

We hear the bells of ancient towers ring
Above the clash and clang of heavy shields,
The bustle of cities, the plowman's song,
The husband's shout, the prattle of wives,
The shriek of a murderer, out of his mind,
And weighty words, the product of deep reflection,
The spirit's outraged groan, torn from the heart,
And the foul sword that pierces many a body.

We march to the worldwide festival of art.
The crown goes to you, William the Unknown!

(night, early hours of 14 July 1937)

The Lord Chancellor Philosopher
(Francis Bacon)

Vetustas cessit, ratio vicit.
('The old is giving way; reason is winning.')
—Francis Bacon

To him natural philosophy is the only true phi-
losophy, and physics based on the experience of
the senses is the chief part of natural philoso-
phy . . . All science is based on experience.
—Karl Marx*

Elegant and gallant,
Sharp in his use of words,
Wise, understanding,
And quick to take action.
That's how he lived his life
In brilliancy, Lord Bacon.

He thundered against authority
And trampled down false wisdom.

From the prism of scholasticism
He extracted priestly dogmatism
And slashed it with thrusts of his rapier
Of biting and pointed satire.

He applied the levers of science
And turned his eyes to the earth,
Leaving the heavens to the monks,
Made experiment thought's basis,
Taking instruments in hand,
Sang the praise of proof through practice,
And boldly raised the art of invention
To the level of pearl of creation.

He understood that knowledge is power,
The balance beam of human endeavour,
That discovery of a law of nature
Means unlocking impediments to action.

He marked a brilliant beginning for science
In capitalism's early day.
Youth is shining in his eyes
And strength is in his eager hands!

(13 August 1937)

[*NOTE: The Marx quotation is from *The Holy Family* (1845). Cf. Marx and Engels, *Collected Works* (New York: International Publishers, 1975), VOL. 4, p. 128.—G. S.]

*Amor Dei intellectualis**
(Baruch Spinoza)

The quiet flame
Of his glowing dark eyes.
The deep soul's voice,
Full worthy of greatness.

His mathematical, crystal-clear mind
Aspired to mountainous heights.
He destroyed the grey blocks of false belief
With his high-ranging thought's resplendent logic.

He revealed that Substance is one
In the multiplicity of things,
Reconciling Spirit and Matter
To benefit future generations.

The sharpened daggers of his thought
Still glitter brightly to this day,

Gifts of true genius that scraped
Away the scabs of superstition.

Hounded he was from every side
By the dogs of synagogue and church.
Still with his pale and slender hands
He kept to his work of grinding lenses.
To live, to think, to go on fighting—
He's not about to let them crush his thoughts.

In solitude proud he ended his days,
Still master of his spiritual forces.
His spirit, clear-eyed and majestic,
Stands covered with quiet glory.

(13 August 1937)

[*NOTE: The Intellect's Love of God.—G. S.]

Phalanx of Sword-Bearers
(The Encyclopaedists)

An immortal phalanx
Of combative minds,
From the centre and the flanks
They crushed the armies of the gods!

They were familiar with
Weapons of every sort
And never forgot or left at home
The hunter's horns they counted on.

Everything was fit for their use,
Condemnation by ridicule,
Pamphlets, scholarly essays,
Analysis, investigation,
And science's rigorous court of law.

The warriors La Mettrie and d'Holbach
Sharpened their swords well
And marched into battle,
Diderot himself at their side.

The clear mind of d'Alembert
Set the example for all.

Their thought was as unstoppable
As a bonfire's tongues of flame.
Godlessly they brought Spirit
Down from the sky to solid ground,
Reduced it to an attribute of body
That ends with death and doesn't go on.

They restored the rights of passion,
So wrongly vilified,
And undermined the foundations
Of every monarchical power.

They erected a wholly new canon,
The laws of Nature and Reason.

(13–14 August 1937)

Worlds in Formulas
(Isaac Newton)

Among the geniuses of the past
He stands encircled by
Entire seas of ideas,
Newton the divine—ineffable Newton.

The flow and movement of eternal
Matter.
He revealed its hidden laws.

He discovered
The fall of worlds through the curves of orbits,
Set a universal symbol for gravity (G),
Explained the roads and paths
That the planets travel,
The laws of swift-winged light,
And the flaring of the solar corona.

With Leibniz he had the honour
Of deciphering the book of nature's
Infinitesimal reductions,
A new world—the magnitudes of calculus.

Granted that science's later course
Has taken us much farther forward,
Always leaving more to do.
Still it's true that, yes,
Newton lives here too!

(14 August 1937)

'The Colossal Old Fellow'* (Hegel)

Old fellow of immense, unequalled erudition
Whose powers excelled his peers'
A hundredfold, a man who was truly great,
A gigantic snowy peak above plain mountain ranges.

With his all-encompassing conception
Of Nature's being and of Spirit's nature,
In the cosmos' concrete building blocks
He found the universal, and the transition
From nonexistence to essential being (which is,
becoming),
Eternal motion, built-in contradiction,
All things being born and passing away,
The interpenetration of opposites,
The roaring play of all of these
At the cosmos' multicoloured feast.

He first revealed with godlike profundity
The universal laws of relation and connection,
And he spread wide the cloak of necessity
To cover also the accidental,
The small change of particular occasions.

But deeply immersed in the epic of the Spirit,
He made of Spirit the central principle.
He traced the world's beginnings back to it,
And in his philosophic symphony
Raised it to the rank of dominant chord.

He crucified the boundless cosmos, turning it upside
down,
Assigning priority to ideas and concepts,
Inserting every object made of matter,
Into idealism's jar of abstractions.

But Marx with his colossal mind corrected him.
Once more the world could dance on its own legs.
Yet as we walk the riddle-strewn paths of knowledge
Hegel will long be dear to us. We'll hold him in our
hearts.

(14 August 1937)

[*NOTE: A phrase used by Friedrich Engels in a letter to
Karl Marx, calling Hegel *der kolossale alte Kerl* ('the colossal
old fellow'), serves as the title for this poem. Early in their
lives Marx and Engels had been Left Hegelians.—G. S.]

The Eyes of Zeus
(Goethe)

An eagle's gaze, the eyes of Zeus,
The sweep and thrust of fiery thought,
A golden light of greatness
Above the world's secrets and human vanity.

All Nature's rhythms he understood:
The rolling of wave upon wave,
The trembling of trees, the breathing of mountains,
The expanse and scope of the turbulent wind,
Star signals from bottomless darkness,
The blood-red coral of evening twilight.

His contemplation covered the Universe, the Whole,
Searched out its iron laws,
The elements, the primal forms of grass and leaves,
And Nature's amusing oddities.

The stern and sweeping course of human life
In ages remote—he investigated that,
The changing patterns of great cultures
And the gods that humans created.

The luminous force of his genius
Subjected all to magical creation.

He reconstructed the paths of nations' destinies,
Composed an epic in honour of struggle,
And on his tablets chiselled messages
That will survive through all of time.

A giant, he stands on the border of ages,
A peer to the gods of Olympus,
A Sun immense among the lesser planets,
Man of Learning, Thinker, Poet.

(16 July 1937)

Temple of Human Glory
(Ludwig van Beethoven)

> Yesterday, Zmeskall, with your sermons you
> drove me into terrible depression. Devil take
> you, I don't need your moralizing. Strength,
> energy—that is the morality of people who
> stand out from ordinary mortals. That is my
> morality.
>
> —from one of Beethoven's letters*

The head
Of a lion
Lips compressed
Teeth clenched with will and energy
The deaf titan
Of sound

Commander of thunder
A giant

Breaking his way into Fate's abode
Battering ram of awesome power
Against the tragic walls of Destiny

Menacing volcano
Singer of change
Of iron strides forward
Great victories
And joyful years
Turbulent
Breaker of chains
Tempestuous flame of passion
Rock of hardness
Many-stringed, many-streamed
Cascade of creativity
Golden stars' waterfall
Heavenly planets' chorale

A hymn majestic he composed
An immortal Temple of Glory
To worldwide love
Declaring all men brothers
Melting with fiery lava the links
That hold Freedom in chains
Let thunders of music roll forth!
Let lightning flash and break!

Flow onward,
Floods of lava!

Enter, O people,
Into the Temple of Human Glory!

(16 July 1937)

[*NOTE: The epigraph is a somewhat adapted Russian version of a passage in a letter written in German by Beethoven in Vienna in 1798 to a fellow musician, Baron Nikolaus von Zmeskall von Domanovecz (1759–1833), a young Hungarian aristocrat who, in Vienna in the 1790s and early 1800s, became a close friend and confidant of Beethoven, and sometimes his benefactor. Compare the translation in Emily Anderson (ed.), *Letters of Beethoven*, VOL. 1 (London: Macmillan, 1961), p. 32. The original German text may be found in *Ludwig van Beethovens sämtliche Briefe* (Tutzing, Germany: Hans Schneider, 1975).—G. S.]

The Lyre of Irony
(Heinrich Heine)

> Your most amusing raillery
> Is wiser than a learned lecture.
> —Boileau, *Stances à M. de Molière sur sa comédie de*
> *l'Ecole des Femmes*

In and of itself, wit has no value. I recognize its worth only when it rests on a serious foundation . . . The ordinary joke is only the intellect sneezing, a hunting dog chasing its own shadow, an ape in a red camisole admiring itself between two mirrors, the mongrel child of reason and madness, whose birth is the result of a chance encounter on the road.

—Heine, in a letter to Moser

King of nightingales and poets,
Singer of magic fairylands,
And Lover of the Lorelei,
Among the stars, a golden comet.

* * *

The strings of his lyre resound
In a world of fantastic dreams
He sings at the feet of fair Lady Luck
Amidst roses and laurel and myrtle.

* * *

Here are the bold exploits of knights
And night and love and the moon
And the whisper of lips grown mute
By a humble dwelling's window.

* * *

But in the voluptuous languor,
The sweet-salt tears of lovers,
The inroads of wicked irony
Rip petals from tender roses.

* * *

And merciless laughter echoes.
It's teasing and combative.
A twitch of annoyance alters
The lips that curve in a smile.

* * *

The next day sarcasm's arrows
Fly in droves in glorious battle.

Before us, courageous and bold
Is a fighter, a dashing drummer.

* * *

The summons of his brass bugle
Loudly resounds in the valley.
His sharp sword gleams in the hollow
Between the woods and the fields.

* * *

With heavy blows that hit the mark
He slashes at Teutonic asses.
The heads go flying in a swarm
From shoulders of priests and kings.

* * *

A mattress of suffering became your grave.
Your flashing spirit was laid to rest.
But always you will be dear to us
With your great power of irony.
You posed a riddle to the gods:
Where are you, what are you up to?
You chuckle with a subtle smile
At them and at yourself.

(night, early hours of 14 July 1937)

The Brightness of Joy
(Alexander Pushkin)

Pushkin, the brightness of joy,
Elemental native force,
Eternal youth,
The glory of Russia,
Art's radiant, beaming sun,
Yours is the purest music!

You were like a child,
But wise to the ways of the world,
Suffering and joking,
Cursing and loving.

Friend to the tense strain of contemporary thought,
You were our Apollo,
But you lived pinned down
To a wolfish existence.

The Emperor's throne,
Insatiably thirsting for blood—
It turned
The law of its evil life
Against you, wise one.
It hounded
The singer in his gaiety and freedom.
It shed his sacred blood.

Among us you are still alive.
You sing the sweetness of freedom,
Forever young, the friend of life,
Pushkin, the brightness of joy.

(15 July 1937)

The Count in Peasant's Bast Slippers
(Leo Tolstoy)

> . . . with the sharp glance of his eyes . . . I felt
> that I had been pierced by a bullet.
> —Stanislavsky, *My Life in Art*

Grey-headed, short. With a spade-shaped beard.
Nose like a potato, big and broad.
It seems he's about to start mumbling, 'Um, ah, yeah,'
And shuffle off to church on the day of the Lord.

But stop and look, what a sharp eye is piercing
From under brows hanging like flax fibre.
And what a head! The bumps on his skull,
Like huts on a silent Caucasus hillside.
They speak of life itself.

One of the world's great geniuses. Simple in
appearance,

But in fact enormously complex.
He reigns over that complex simplicity
To which a stormy, troubled spirit gave birth.
The life of our epoch, both hugely strong and
weakly pitiful—
He seized it like an eagle with the talons of art.
At the same time he kept a sharp eye on the jackdaw
Beating its wings in struggle against the wind.

Fearless, he went down into the soul's hiding places,
Having thoroughly explored the surface of things,
And with a sidelong glance of his burning eye
He penetrated past the broken shell to the yolk!

An empty, thoughtless life was torture to him.
How vividly he denounced that kind of life,
Painting with a steady hand
Those who lived high and those they lived upon!

His peasant's faith was quite naïve.
The burden of his song was misdirected.

The tragedy of his end was tragic beyond compare,
A sheer disaster. He was not to blame.

His death was such a simple one, and yet so pitiful.
A great soul, said the people, softly sobbing.

(15 August 1937)

The Secret of the Human Species
(Charles Darwin)

I have a grand body of facts & I think I can
draw some sound conclusions.
    —Darwin (letter to Leonard Jenyns, October
                                    1844)*

Calm and patient, a rigorous thinker,
An elder with wrinkled furrows in a noble brow,
Immortal guide for generations, centuries of science,
Revealing the secret of human origins in this 'sinful'
world.

Thousand and thousands of observations he made
In fields, gardens, villages, among grasses and flowers,
And among creations of human art, of livestock
breeding,
Sheep and horses, doves and pigeons, pigs, cows,
oxen . . .

With persistent, attentive gaze he explored
The colour of feathers, the number of petals, the
shapes of legs,
Differing weights, marks on skin, capricious patterns
on wings,
Things that, according to ancient tradition, God
gave to the world.
Tireless, he made observations of nature in the wild,
Of countless living species, of their struggle for
existence,
Extinction of some varieties, survival of others.

His stubborn, curious mind also thrust under-
ground,
Comparing skeletons, leg bones, ribs and skulls
Preserved in sandstone or in black masses of coal
Or where old burial mounds had covered graves.

Around the world he travelled, driven by thirst for
knowledge,
Voyaging on *The Beagle*, whose name lives for all
pioneers,
Five years, from summer to winter, and from a new
winter to summer.

He carefully steered the powerful flight of his
thoughts,
Keeping strict track of his Mont Blanc of data,
Double-checking himself at every step.

His genius arrived at conclusions filled with grandeur,
Confirming Reason's motto: 'I *can* gain knowledge.'
His mind demystified a grand old mystery
At its very foundation—the origin of species.

Humanity now has seen the laws of nature at work,
And calmly can chase the gods from its thoughts
and reflections.

(14 August 1937)

[*NOTE: The letter to Jenyns is quoted, in the form given
above, in David Quammen, *The Reluctant Mr. Darwin* (New
York: Norton, 2006), p. 80.—G. S.]

Mad Prophet
(Friedrich Nietzsche)

Prophet in thrall to the mania dark
Behind King Capital's gilded crown,
How perfidious it is that Fate
Made madness your primal principle.

From under hanging, bushy brows
With gloomy look at us you glare,
Your forehead filled with wrinkled bridges
As though death sentences lurked there.

Your sanguinary delirium
About the 'will to power',
Morality of the master caste,
The blonde menagerie
That subjugates the people;
About smoke and blood and bonfires,

About wars without end;
And the Dionysian orgies
Of the predatory beasts.

Your ravings about the 'Superman',
About the slaves, 'the herd'
Of those who under him will kiss
The dust from aeon to aeon.

All Zarathustra's aphorisms,
The virgin soil of paradox,
Are elegant, subtle sophisms
Turning everything to blood.

And it's no accident that now
War, robbery and every vice
In your high pride are blessed by you,
Prophet of the Lunatic Asylum.

(13 July 1937)

Swamps of Decay

The only thing left that can save property is
theft; religion, apostasy; the family, adultery; the
existing order, disorder.

—Karl Marx

Lilies that fester smell far worse than weeds.

—Shakespeare

Among the world's corrupted swamps
Amidst black smoke and adversaries' trenches
The mindless orgies of a drunken satyr—
Foul harvest for the worms—
The singing of Verlaine's frail violin,
With its deathly aroma of decay,
Mystical illuminations that speak
Of 'Carrion' a la Baudelaire,
The strange exoticism of Rimbaud,
And Merezhkovsky's devil, so sincere,

The nightmares of Poe, refined, precise—
These are the plague spots of a dread disease,
Luxuriant fungus on a rotting stump.

They're sipping poison at the feast of fate,
And all around are harlequins and clowns
And phalanxes of saucy acrobats,
The panderers and whores of soullessness,
Sucking golden-ducat juice from everywhere.

And not far off, a crowd of well-drained brains,
Of academic mummies turned to stone,
A puffed-up, self-important coterie,
Mindless vainglory's true embodiment.

Everywhere there's rot and the slime of rot,
The art of the salon and the alcove,
Lumped together with brothel and tavern
In the impotence of sickly feeling.

Yet now the fascist hero comes along,
With his empty pumpkin head,
As elementary as a log,
Bringing with him the promise of change.
Chewing his cud like an ox,
He drains the swamp
And refills it with blood.

(20 July 1937)

Twilight of the Gods

Universal anarchy, worldwide chicanery—
plainly, the intervention of the Lord.
                              —Heinrich Heine, in a letter

A grey-haired brigand, a giant
Whose crimson age was a caravan of crimes,
Is now in the throes of paralysis at death's door,
Covered in blood, but on a brocade of gold.

Mountains of riches he has accumulated.
All lands were plowed and furrowed by his hands.
His chains have bound and hampered people's lives
Like the tough braids of underwater plants.

Some of his parts have now been seized with fever,
The factories are dark and at a standstill.
The quagmires of joblessness run deep.

The common people's rebel bands have risen,
And blood is flowing in a river wide.
To choke on its scarlet wave is terrible.
The previous triumphant faith has gone.
There's only smoke, the foul-smelling stench of
sulphur.
Strange is the decline, made rosy with rouge,
Of the regal gilded gates of Capital.

An ice-cold twilight filled with torment
Has doused the lantern of the last good mind.
The augers, tools of the brain, have been broken.
Flowers and grass in terror have turned grey.
The healthy flow of blood has now dried up.
Vice and depravity are everywhere.
A flood has come, of lustful mysticism,
Fortune-tellers' secret dens, and horoscopes.

Only the poor—they listen to a different tune,
A different ending to the world's disaster.
Another dawn is glowing bright for them,
A dawn of crimson in a sea of amber.

(26 July 1937)

WAR OF WORLDS

[Bukharin gave this title to the group of 28 poems that he
designated as 'series VI'.]

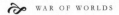

War of Worlds

Wer über den Parteien sich wähnt mit stolzen Mienen,/
Der steht zumeist vielmehr beträchtlich unter ihnen.
—Gottfried Keller*

Where all the world's roads intersect
The people of two worlds stand armed
On the eve of great battles of steel,
The threshold of an immeasurable future.

The pinpoint of contradictions is stripped to the core.
The world of large-mouthed predatory spiders
Is saying its rosary, counting its beads of skulls
And weapons of fire, poison and metal.

They bear the black and tattered banner of death,
Asphyxiation of all forms of life.
From human bones they have devised a crown,
An axe, a sword, a swastika, a knout.

The fascist chefs are villainous and thieving,
Ready to tear scalps from the whole world's head.
Long has their drunken soldiers' lyre been wheezing:
'It's time! It's long past time! It's time to start!'

To them the other world replies with calm:
'We're ready for you—go ahead and shoot.'
While in the sky there flies a countless flock
Of eagles brave, the Soviet aviators.

Here labour's blood-red banners proudly rise.
The forests of ideas have here grown high,
Inspiring the sons of valour strongly forward
To final conflict, for human happiness.

And breaking through the fire and smoke of battles
From dark abysses rising ever upward
Up from the land emerges a dauntless giant
With thousands, thousands of arms, thousands of
heads.

(17 August 1937)

[*NOTE: The quotation is from a poem, *Parteileben* (Party
Life), dating from the 1840s. In it the Swiss writer Gottfried
Keller (1819–90) argued that the poet or writer ought to
take a political position and be involved in the struggles of
his or her time. The meaning of the two lines is roughly,
'Whoever proudly imagines he stands *above* parties/ Most
often ends up being considerably *beneath* them.'—G. S.]

The Masses

Together with the increased soundness of the
action of history, there will be an increase in the
scope of participation by the masses, for the ac-
tion of history is nothing other than the work
of the masses.

—Karl Marx

The masses of workers,
Architect builders of a new world,
The working people, millions strong,
Bear victory's banners with joyful song.

In worm-eaten centuries, ground down by pain,
They had been nothing,
Meaningless fodder for cruel history,
The source of crushed rebellion's groans and cries.

But now in the abyss of roaring disaster,
On the world arena where gods are dying,
The roll of victory's thunder can be heard.

Many-headed, many-handed, many-faced,
Great in outbursts of action,
All of one will
In the fight against evil fate,
The people,
Long victim to grave misfortunes,
Have burned out the plague once for all
And put an end to years of misery.

The whole stage of history
Has been taken over
By the 'dark masses'.
Raging and storming,
They did it rejoicing.

They seized the world's arena
In their firm hands,
The hands of liberated slaves
Now freed
From the cruel law codes of an endless time.

We hear the rhythm of their iron tread,
The pounding of hammers,
The singing of millions of happy voices
In praise of the Great Transformation.

(26–27 July 1937)

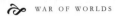

Adversaries

One stands with haughty gaze,
Wearing armour, bearing a sword,
Labour's hangman, worldwide thief,
But there's a bad cut on his shoulder.
He has behind him a solid record,
Whole centuries of evil plunder.
Trembling with demonic malice,
He stands there, gloomy and foreboding.

The other wears a steel-starred hauberk.
He's bold and cheerful, young and brave,
Playfully ripples his powerful muscles,
Unyielding as a boulder great.
Stern years of battle he has known
And bears the scars of heavy wounds.
Our epoch awarded him a medal.
It honours the triumphs of labour, the hero.

(7 August 1937)

Ideal Types

> Murder and robbery, sanctified by law
> —Goebbels

There he stands: the feudal robber baron,
Stern warrior, with his horse and armour.
He's been crowned by God Himself, he says,
To plunder the impoverished huts of serfs.

He's loyal to his forebears, honours his ancestry,
The pride and arrogance, lush splendour of the castle.
To him the people's a monster and a freak,
The peasants are animals, both male and female.

He has refined respect, though, for his lady,
Dignifies her with the name Madonna,
But like a bandit, with his hairy hand,
He fastens iron round her sacred belly.

For him the master swordsman, executioner,
Wine, love and blood all stand under one cross,
And this dark dog, this sombre hound of hell,
Proudly salutes his family coat of arms.

Then there's the plump, well-satisfied bourgeois,
Hero of the office, bank and dress shoe,
Stingy, calculating, but he's peaceful
As long as no one's reaching for his profits.

Litigious, voracious, insolent and thieving,
He buys and sells, for commerce is his trade.
If there's disaster, famine, thousands dying,
He'll skin each starving person three times over.

For him the only god is ready money.
All else is drowned in crafty calculation.
His son's a blowhard and a *bon vivant*,
Knows nothing of work, and could care less about it.

But history has deprived them of bright days.
No more idyllic times shall these swine know.
Their craftiness, their perfidy, their mercenary minds,
Their placid kingdom—history's brought to an end.

Then there's the fascist—bastard offspring of two
worlds—
Defender of god and gold and noble lineage,
Of all heraldic ancient coats of arms
With sword in hand, but worry in his eyes.

Under his well-forged iron soldier's boot
He tramples all that's human in the world.
With battle-axe and pole-axe he has made
The blood of nations flow like festive wine.

'Race' he has placed up high on a pedestal,
Along with a large-fanged breed, the blonde-haired
beast.
He's insolently broken culture's thread,
Turned everything into a murder-machine.

(night, early hours of 1 July 1937)

Greed

A skinny, repulsive old hag
With bracelets and rings on her hands,
And from her ears hang precious stones
Set in heavy gold earrings.
Her gleaming predatory eye
Is the hungry eye of the carrion-eater,
With frenzied, insatiable maw.

Instead of reason she has calculation, cold and
crafty.
She's ready to pick over the whole world,
Avidly digging with covetous hands,
And to flay the fresh skin from every back
Of ever-new victims, in chains held fast.

At the sight of gold she starts to tremble,
Flushes with pleasure, gets numb and blocked-up,

Cracks and crunches her bony fingers,
And sweat starts pouring from every wrinkle.

* * *

All skinflints and misers are under her power,
And filthy usurers, with their paper hearts.

On every side, and all around, they're ornamented
With pearls— made from people's burning tears.

Her most recent lovers are the bankers,
The Krupps and Rothschilds, Rockefellers and
Morgans.
To gratify their passions the world keeps opening,
Ever anew, the bleeding wounds of misfortune.

Those seized by furious greed are blinded
By the wave of gold washing over them.
They have ignited a worldwide bonfire
And are whipping the human herd to the slaughter-
house.

Also torn by the talons of avarice
Are fathers who lead their daughters to the altar,
Trading in people's hearts and feelings,
Exchanging them for gold chains' ringing sound.

Teeming everywhere are the small fry of this base
passion,
Bureaucrats, rentiers, philistines,
Shamelessly folding their hands into grasping fists.

In their impure cupidity all are equal—
Whether Buddhists, Muslims, Christians,
Or the worshippers of Sinai's Jehovah.

An impoverished beggar stands at the gates of a
prison.
Greed takes the very last fragment from his mouth.

(5 August 1937)

Brutality

Bestial fangs on a well-groomed face
Where hangs the sign of hidden vices.
O, how many like that there are
On the back steps of every epoch,
Both well remembered and forgotten!

The Assyrian kings were famous for
Mountains of severed heads and arms.
Rome too was proud, as Carthage had been,
Of slaves crucified along well-travelled roads.

And the Persian lords tore the living skin
From the body of Mani, wise prophet of Iran,
Blew it full of air and outside the palace
Hung it to delight the beasts and fools.

And Caracalla, 'Cosmocrat' of Rome,
Was thrilled by murder and the sight of blood.

While his woman ogled the coral jewels,
He waited, smiling, for the wheeze of the dying.

For the Berserkers, the god of the gallows
Was their One God, their cruel lord and master.

Also, the emperors and popes
Through the whole of mediaeval times
Were dipping their hairy paws in blood,
Taking malicious pleasure when
The Iron Maiden's spike entered the brain
Or the dreadful odour of burning flesh swirled
around
The bodies of heretics, or of swineherds.

The passion for brutality, a cannibal passion,
With fangs bared and eyes all bloodshot,
Harking back to fathers' and forefathers' cruelty—
It's been implanted in gorillas armed with poison gas.
Here is the source of the bloody fascist orgies,
Here death's decay and sadists' black insanity.

(5 August 1937)

Selfishness

A petty personality, a heart shrunk down to
wrinkles,
A teeny excuse for a soul, cowardice unlimited,
Constant trepidation over one's foul self-interest,
A dry self, crusted over, the size of a bread crumb.
Sidelong glances, cunning calculations,
Petty concerns exclusively self-centred,
Weighted down by the burden of property-owning.
Horizons no wider than one's little finger.
The seed of stinginess has grown into the burdock
of envy.
This ugly little 'soul' could fit in a cockleshell.
What does this selfish person care about others?
But driven to frenzy, the shopkeeper fascist is
dangerous.
In violence he's frantic, insane; he thirsts for blood.

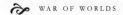

So rise up, warriors of universal brotherhood,
Go into battle and let
The resounding clash of victory ring out!

(7 August 1937)

Jealousy

O! beware, my lord, of jealousy;
It is the green-eyed monster that doth mock
The meat it feeds on.
                    —Shakespeare, *Othello*, Act III, Scene 3

Jealousy has a savage fury
Whose roots are deeply hidden.
It branches out of nature's ancient soil.
Ah, jealousy—what great strength it has,
Reinforced by power and property!
We human beasts grew up, and proclaimed
In the name of noble honour
The right of reprisal, base and foul!

Jealousy wanders,
Jealousy strolls,
Through village and city,

Driving men out of their minds,
Sowing evil among the houses.

A serpent of blind rage,
It creeps into men's hearts,
Inflames the frenzied sowing
Of deadly dragon's teeth.
It makes men blind
And violent.
Drives them to the dagger,
To poisons.
It is the pricking of bloody revenge,
Stubbornly calling on men
To take up the gifts of the Devil.

Desdemona, most tender of beauties,
It strangled with the beast-like hand
Of Othello gone mad. And subject to jealousy's law
Was the whole, vile Karamazov clan.

But sometimes the accursed fury lurks
Behind the curtains of the soul, out of sight around
the corner,
Then suddenly flares up and makes its savage rush,
Burning with blood and fire!

(7 August 1937)

Paris, Light of Wing

Aux armes, citoyens,
Formez vos bataillons!
('To arms, citizens,
Form your battalions')

—from the *Marseillaise*

Insatiable Vampire, l'eternelle Luxure
*Sur la Grand Cité convoite sa pâture.**
('Insatiable Vampire, eternal Lust broods
Over the Great City, thirsting for its food')

Paris is a world of passion and art,
Of feeling and sensibility, and of vice,
Of mighty deeds and fiery ideas
Of labour and luxury, real people and petty traders.

The handsome city has spread its wings out wide,
Wings as light and airy as a dream.
Under clear skies its beauty still conceals
Some effort made, but lightly done, pastel.

The Champs Élysées—what an avenue of grandeur!
How magical the Louvre, the statues and fountains,
The bright green of the boulevards and poplars,
And splendid ancient chestnut trees in bloom!

The buildings speak of proud majestic power,
Each street and square its sacred legend keeps,
Marat's old wretched hovel, the Panthéon,
Workers' quarters, where battles were fought,
Napoleon's tomb.
And the back alleys, where from heaps of paving
stones
There once arose barricades of the Commune.

The ribbon of the Seine flows slowly, triumphantly,
And beauty trapped in stone—beyond the sphere of
dividends—
An amazing composition that pierces the sky,
The giant arched cathedral whose praise was sung
by Victor Hugo!

But the odour of vice and depravity's right there too
A kingdom of women, mere playthings for the males,
Debauchery, orgies, plain drunken benightedness,
Eunuchs of parliament brazenly for sale,
Deception and vulgarity, muddied waters,
The carousel of greedy property-owners,
Obtuse, complacent fools, in an endless row,
One scoundrel after another playing the panpipes.

But beyond the warped, enticing luxury,
Covered with powder, ribbons and perfume,
Beyond the banks and swampy mires of commerce,
Stands working-class Paris, with its sturdy arms,
There'll come a day when a mighty voice rings out:
'Now, Paris, you are mine!'

(5 August 1937)

[*NOTE: This was a caption on a famous engraving by
Charles Meryon (1821–68), an associate of Baudelaire. The
wording is Meryon's. A reproduction of the engraving with
its caption may be found on the Internet and in James An-
derson Hiddleston, *Baudelaire and the Art of Memory* (Ox-
ford: Oxford University Press, 1999), p. 198.—G. S.]

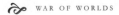

Berlin Barracks

The streets are straight as nightsticks.
The squares, for parade-ground use, strictly.
Stubborn, energetic expressions on faces,
And piles of primitive-looking buildings.
In the spirit of Fritz's Spitzrute*
The barracks smell spreads all around.

Meanwhile, fluff from the poplar trees
Sails through the air and onto the pond.

To the rat-a-tat of the drum rolls
The soldiers are marching in step.
In the restaurants good times are rolling
To drown out the angst of the Volk.

Stretched out as though on a cable
Stand the Kaisers of Siegesallee.**

A cripple lies on his side,
Begging alms in a shy, timid way.

Down well-paved streets, all spic-and-span,
Rolls the sleek enamel of luxury cars.
And a haughty, contemptuous shout
Rings out from a greatcoated Nazi.

The workers' quarters are dismal.
Karl's grave has been desecrated.***
The Swastika's grim power
Is darker than autumn night.

Thaelmann is languishing somewhere
Behind locked doors of a prison,
But already a menacing knock is heard
On the door of Germany's madhouse.

Berlin was once a beautiful red
And we'll restore that colour yet.
We'll put an end to the vile, ignoble,
And dangerous fascist foe!

But for now what holds sway in Berlin,
Like a fortress of mediaeval times,
Covered with the blood of workers,
Is the Moabit torture chamber.****

(6 August 1937)

[*NOTE: Spitzrute—literally, 'sharp or pointed rod'; figuratively, 'stinging switch'; in the tradition of Prussian military discipline, a symbol of corporal punishment as used on common soldiers as well as children.

[**NOTE: Kaisers of Siegesallee—In 1895 and after, by order of Kaiser Wilhelm II, the Siegesallee ('Avenue of Victory') was lined with statues of the Kaiser's forebears, previous rulers of Prussia.

[***NOTE: Karl's grave—probably a reference to Karl Liebknecht.

[****NOTE: The term Moabit was commonly used for the central criminal court, located in the Moabit district in the centre of Berlin.—G. S.]

Octopus London

Low to the ground, spread out, soot-laden
Heavy, solid and enormous,
Along the Thames lies the Octopus City.
Its monstrous tentacles are sucking
The juices, gold and bloody, of half the world.
It has extended foul extremities
Across the earth, and climbed on the pedestal
As 'most far-reaching empire centre yet'.
The metal of its guns has not grown rusty.

To it there flows, driven by lust for profit,
Iron and gold, pineapples and bananas,
Cotton and diamonds, meat and rubber,
And precious treasures from the Pyramids,
Held in the British Museum's dusky depths.

London took shape over centuries,
Constructed out of slabs of heavy stone.
It's solid just like thick-soled English boots,
From its Parliament walls to its cunning science.

Covered with smoke and soot of centuries,
The walls of its majestic buildings,
The grim London Tower, the dial of Big Ben,
Have seen great changes wrought by Destiny,
But it still stands on sea legs, as before,
Thickset, strong-rooted ruler of colonies.
In London all traditions are preserved,
The laws of pirates, highway robbery.

Mighty heart of finance, The City beats.
The stock-exchange church is full of supplicants.

And yet the wavy mound of powdered wig
Shakes on the Speaker of Parliament's head,
And carefully shaven pink cheeks burn
On the crafty diplomats of Downing Street.

The sparkling store windows are resplendent,
The lights on Piccadilly and in its shops,
But on Hyde Park there's harsh green stubble,
And on the leaden Thames a panorama of waves.

Out of view are the neighbourhoods of the poor,
Dark cellars, Lilliputian kennels,
The hotbeds of disease and poverty,

The dark obstructions of misery.
Whitechapel's children also have dreams.
Those dreams are the halos of poverty.

Class hatred has its residence here,
A vital force in history.
Here the Molly gang's not forgotten, and even
The paving stones cry out to heaven, and here
The Demon of Revolution will spread its wings!

(6 August 1937)

New York, with Its Towers

Hubbub and racket,
Thunder and clatter.
A sea of light,
Fiery serpents
Spraying electricity.
The whistling and screeching
Of subways
And els.
The dance of advertising
On the sidewalks
And above the clouds,
On buildings and boulevards.
On Wall Street—look!—
The cars are moving
At a slow pace
Alongside and between

High ridges,
Rows of tower-buildings.
The city has thrust its cliffs,
Great tall ones, with a hundred stories each,
Up into the sky
Ever so high

* * *

They walk by
Chewing gum
Whites and Negroes
Swedes, Hungarians
Italians and Finns
Ukrainians from the steppes.

Flashing in the windows
With lights playing over them
Are candies and belt buckles,
Perfume and suspenders,
Books and appliances,
Lobster and tires.
The offices of banks
Have sturdy window blinds
And plate glass,
Irreproachably clean.

* * *

On Riverside Drive things are different—
Residential realm of the wealthy,
Well furnished with villas and gardens—
Here peace and quiet reign.

To try and take off some weight,
With his dog on a leash,
With a neck like a bull's,
One of the super-rich
Is out for a stroll with his daughter.
It's a cleanly atmosphere,
The idyllic family sphere.

The bingeing is under way
The drinking bouts in the fancy restaurants
With air-conditioning machinery,
A clamour of voices, refined quality,
With expensive delights shipped in from every
country
And fabulous orchid flowers
Of exotic beauty.

* * *

But in the dirty, rundown neighbourhoods
We find the frills of filthy streets,
Scraps of paper everywhere,
Rags, eggshells, cigarette butts.
From every little nook and cranny
Flows the river of the poor.

* * *

A district with dens of Chinamen,
The opium poison quarter,
Offering joy to unfortunate cripples
Despite the raids by men of the law.

* * *

The hovels of Jewish tailors.
The nests where Negro workers live.
Excessive workloads' terrible strain.

* * *

The stars on the flag are dollars.
The Depression's pinch is relentless.
Millions of jobless stand at the gates.
A whiff of Red rebellion's in the air:
'Tomorrow whose turn will it be?'

* * *

The buildings have spiralled so high,
With hundreds of floors,
They've risen like so many towers
Crowded with businessmen.

On the banks of the great Hudson River,
Where the Statue of Liberty stands.

Gleaming in the light of the sun,
Is New York, the many-faced Giant.

But when winds grow more boisterous
There will strike a hurricane,
And the Kingdom of Money will sink
Beneath Oceanus' mighty wave.

(5 August 1937)

The Colonies

All dressed in white, the whites live high,
Fanning themselves with pale-white fans,
They kick the backsides of the blacks,
Then head for cool rooms to have a tall glass.

Hot rays are shining from white skies,
Striking dark bodies with stinging pain.
Work must be done from early morn
On craggy height and hill and plain.

Colonial slaves—they number millions—
Black, yellow, red and coffee-tan.
For heavy labour great fanfare's made,
When with poor scraps of grain they're paid!

Black people's backs bend to the task
As heavy sweat rolls down those backs.

The white man threatens still to strike
With hardened India rubber stick.

Bananas, rubber, lemons, limes,
Iron, cotton, copper, gold,
Cocoa, coffee, on and on—
The blood-red money-juice from slaves

Is sucked out so the life of wealth
Can keep on blooming like orchid flowers,
So uppercrust whites can hold their sway,
So the necks of slaves stay forever bent—
Until there comes the day of reckoning.

(25 September 1937)

Path of Thorns
(Soviet China)

E pur si muove.
('In spite of everything, it's moving.')

—Galileo

We made the Long March barefoot, thousands of
miles.
We found our way over mountain paths
And across burning sandy deserts.
We swam through stormy river waves,
Scorched by the sun and drenched by downpours.
Often we had not a handful of rice,
Wounds, blood and dust covered our legs.
We marched through the belly of ancient China.
Chiang Kaishek's machine guns watched for us,
The pilots of Von Seeckt were bombing us,
The Japanese devil set out nooses for us,

But our regiments would not surrender,
Our glorious regiments,
City coolies, village peasants!

They tortured our prisoners with hot irons,
Bloodily ripped out their tongues,
Fastened boards to their necks.
They cut off our women's breasts,
And our men they buried alive.
That's what those 'cultured judges' were like, the
dogs!
Still they could not trap or encircle us,
Disarm us or smash us,
Inexhaustible,
Uncatchable.

We sift our way through villages,
We crawl up over mountains,
And once we've regrouped
We suddenly make a raid
And grappling with the foe,
We destroy him.

* * *

All the doors of village huts are open to us.
Each poor peasant greets us as a brother,
Brings us water and gives us rice,
Even though, poor man, he's barely alive.

Everywhere we set up peasant Soviets
And everywhere punch rich folks in the mouth.
There are millions of us, millions . . .

And soon, crowns will fall from rich men's heads,
The Japanese dragon we'll burn to a crisp,
And the throne of the Devil himself will topple!

(22 July 1937)

Economic Crisis

Motionless stand the giant factories.
The dance of the machines has died away.
They've boarded up the exits and entrances.
The fathers and the sons—all are left jobless.
And useful goods are rotting on the shelves.
People in poverty cannot buy them.
The flames of warehouse fires lick at them.
Or else they're shipped away and dumped at sea.
The owners of big money won't deliver
Such goods to starving people free of charge.
Far sooner they'd see fire destroy them
Than hand them over to the poor.

Millions of people are jobless.
Stark poverty has come to stay.
The dark clouds of worry impend

And water has flooded the cellars.
Misery's also stalking the village.
Belongings go under the auctioneer's hammer.
In churches, whether Catholic or Protestant,
The praying and appealing are in vain.

The ruined farmer with his sack or satchel,
Dragging his wife and children after him,
Leaving behind the old, familiar places,
Heads off towards the city, cold and distant.
There he wanders, a feeble shadow,
Starving, without a crust of bread,
And dying in delirium sees
Nothing but dark days ahead . . .

Disaster has licked at others too:
White-collar workers—their turn comes
To sell their clothes to earn their keep.
Out on the pavement—that's their place,
Out on the sidewalks, crowding around.
No cheerful pipe-playing then is heard
In honour of the Golden Calf.

In cellars and hovels where workers live
Hearts are beginning to boil with rage
And fire is starting to glow in their eyes:
'We're not gonna sit here and take this forever!'

After all, there exists in the world
Another country, a land of labour,

That does not have these evil crises,
One that has wiped out joblessness.
We have to follow that example
And put an end to all of this.
Life then will be immeasurably full.
Both fathers and sons will be free of care!

(night of 29 September 1937)

Blood-soaked Spain

O, you proud land,
Land of olives and rocky cliffs,
You lie there soaked in blood,
The Escurial surrounded by fire.

* * *

The Spain of old once gleamed
In all its mighty power,
Subduing half the world
With commerce and the dagger.
Young Isabella's eyes
Were dark and shining bright
As the caravels of Columbus
Like thunderstorms rushed off.
The round of days at court

Were dismal, full of blood,
And life was deemed a dream
By a great man, Calderon.

* * *

The priests and monks and kings
Devoured all the land,
Waging war against the peasants
For entire centuries.
The smoky bonfires guttered
Where heretics were burned.
Around the fires the monks
Sang *Te Deum laudamus*.

* * *

Then for the first time in centuries
The people rose against the throne.
With warlike rounds of grapeshot
The *padrones* fired at their heads—
The landowner, the Jesuit
Wearing Loyola's mantle,
The sybarite and the cocotte,
And the monkish locust swarm.
Fierce and savage and cruel
Are their Mussolini hordes,
And their Teutonic regiments
Have the ugly mugs of hangmen.

* * *

Madrid's in a ring of fire.
The smoke curls upward like
Ill-omened sinister serpents,
And yes, Madrid is burning.
Blood's scarlet sheen
Is on the pavement,
And buildings are shaking
From cannonade thunder.
Things are decomposing underfoot.
Facades are listing here and there.
Demolished houses, cinder hulks,
Yawn like black holes, like greedy maws.

* * *

But there are sturdy fighters in Madrid.
They're short of sleep but unfatigued,
Young men and women, old folks too.
They fire from the windows.
Here every house is a fortress.
Each city block's a battlefield.
Sometimes the city committee
Doesn't sleep for weeks.
In the air and on the ground
The enemy keeps sending
More and more new forces,
More enemy cannon fodder.

But our gallant fighters are bold
And steady is their hand,
And fighters of the air
Are knocking the enemy dead.
The great heart of the city
Beats loudly amidst the smoke.
Yes, in the enemy's forehead
A deadly crater we'll blast!

(22 July 1937)

Prometheus and the Red Cap of Liberty (A Joking Fairy-Tale Medley from Various Lands and Times)

Wotan thundered furiously
With his enormous gold-plated hammer
Against bronze plate.
He summoned his Vikings to war,
Bellowed and drunkenly cursed
In triumphant voice.

The mighty rebel Prometheus
Had been freed of his chains:
The two-headed eagle, his cruel tormentor,
He'd strangled long since
And tossed out the window.
In place of the chains' heavy weight
He smushed down as headgear on top of his curls
The Red Cap of Liberty
And went around wearing that cap, just so.

Meanwhile in the East, an evil, sideways-coiling
Dragon
Frightening the fearful crows
Dancing a harakiri dance
Began to imitate Wotan,
Playing insinuatingly on his warlike lyre.
(The Dragon's mother was an Aryan.)

Just then the ancient She-Wolf
That suckled the twins, the founders of Rome,
Referring to forefathers' behests
Thought to add her loud howl to theirs.
(That She-Wolf was a real *Lupa*.)*

Thereupon our Prometheus,
Started mobilizing people,
The Titans, who would not go to Canossa,
But famously piled Helion on Ossa.
They'd known how to do that
As a way of taunting the gods.
To his banner he also called Daedalus and Icarus
(Who had earlier suffered foolish punishment)
And supplied them with aluminum wings.
He'd been taught this art by Vulcan.
And he put up a Tower of Babel
(With Gilgamesh's diligent help)
And invited the Chinese Medea
To join in, as an expert on Dragons.

There flashed the lightning bolts of Wotan
And threatening thunders started to rumble.

Fenrir the Wolf, held captive by Wotan,
Was known to be his fierce enemy.
By a chain he was fastened
And ever so tightly shackled.
But with one blow Prometheus
Freed him from all his chains.

Firing came from the tower,
Icarus flew over the plowlands,
Daedalus flew across the seas,
Fenrir began gnawing on Wotan,
That savage, drunken fire-eater,
While Medea went all the way to Osaka,
And there the Dragon expired.
That's where he breathed his last.

Meanwhile that super-hysteric and blowhard,
Wotan, died in a pool of his blood.
And, lo, five-sixths of the globe was now
Wearing the Red Cap of Freedom.

(22 July 1937)

[*HANDWRITTEN NOTE BY BUKHARIN: *Lupa* in ancient Latin meant both 'she-wolf' and 'bitch'. According to legend, Romulus and Remus were raised by a she-wolf.]

Leningrad

On marshland black, on bones of white,
They raised up a city of granite,
Prim and shapely, hiding the lusty sweep
Of an empire monolithic.

Riverbanks were dressed in eternal stone,
By the waters of Nevá majestic.
And sternly the hand of Peter suppressed
The lava of people's rebellion.*

On blood the gardens and palaces grew,
The avenues, bridges, canals,
Feasts rang out and songs were sung.
Bright lights in ballrooms shone.

While, clattering, galloped the Horseman of Bronze,
Creation of old Falconetti.

The pedestal of the tsars stood high
Illumined by sinister searchlights.

In well-ordered rows stretched official chambers
And luxury's palace facades.
The sun as it set brought carved fretwork to life
And diamonds that sparkled in crowns.

Triumphantly gilded by sunset as well
Were the Peter-Paul spires on the skyline.
In shackles there languished the flower of Russia
Behind blood-reddened fortress walls.**

In outlying districts, once peopled by strangers,***
New factory whistles were being heard.
In the workers' kennels, in cellars and attics,
New forces were growing and speaking their word.

More than once did the thunder of workers' revolt
Shake this capital's fortresses grim,
And winding around the palaces' turrets
Rebellion was flashing its lightning wings.

A great wall of water rose up, wall of fate,
Over the ancient imperial seat.
The huge, heavy wave crashed down on their heads,
Crushed all in the rich people's mansions.

By night and by day the streets were seething,
Every palace was flooded with masses,
And rushing by, pale-faced, beset with fears,
Were the cashbox-proprietor bankers.

Bayonets gleamed and anthems were sung.
The people prepared for new battles.
With iron tread marched the Bolsheviks
With the wisdom of Lenin before them.

In combat fierce with the officer caste,
With the bourgeoisie and the Whiteguards,
The workers and soldiers with rifles well aimed
And strong plebeian arms prevailed.

This giant city became the great heart
Of our fearsome revolution.
Speculator, industrialist trembled before it
Like men without clothes in night's frost.

The fight was horrific, a fight to the death
Across immense stretches of country.
The spirited ring of a trumpet of brass
Resounded, the summons, the war cry.

This great city's sons then were found everywhere
At the forefront of battle, unfailing.
The old order's leaders ferociously cursed them
While saying their foul-smelling prayers.

Petrograd has won fame for all ages and times.
Its name became City of Lenin.
The heroic impulse he gave has not died.
His enormous star burns in our heaven.

His city grew up, ardent labour has raised it,
And all of it gleams with new life.

It has severed villainous poverty's head.
Its renewal brilliantly shines.

Untiring, this giant creates and creates
The base for a worldwide Commune.
This valorous warrior awaits without fear
The menacing prospect of oncoming war.

(1 and 2 September 1937)

[*NOTE: The phrase 'people's rebellion' probably refers to
the mutinies of the Muscovite soldiery, the *streltsy*, and the
peasant-and-Cossack revolt headed by Bulavin in 1707–08
during the reign of Peter the Great (Tsar Peter I of the
Romanov dynasty).
[**NOTE: The Peter and Paul Fortress was St Petersburg's
equivalent of the 'Bastille'. It was notorious as the place
where, for many generations, thousands of Russian revolu-
tionaries were held prisoner under grim conditions and
where many perished.
[***NOTE: The phrase 'districts, once peopled by strangers'
probably refers to the *slobodá*, certain districts outside the
city to which visiting foreign merchants and traders were
formerly restricted.—G. S.]

The Bugler Plays Reveille

The small grey clouds are chased away
As the scarlet dawn arises
—Lermontov

From heaven's vault, light cannot be removed
The gleam of rising sun can't be concealed
With purple mantles or dark priestly robes
—N. Lenau*

You cannot take the sun out of the sky
Nor hide the glimmerings of coming dawn
Beneath dark robes of priests or kingly purple.
Arise, dear friends! Enough of sleeping!
Tarantara Tarantara

Dawn has broken. Sun is shining.
Who in the world does not perceive it?
His beams give off the heat of life,
Bestow the sacred gift of Reason.
Tarantara Tarantara

See how the heavenly body burns,
How the force of life is flaming.
New human beings have grown up,
And boldly they will fly to battle.
                    Tarantara Tarantara

Clouds visible on the horizon
Creep like serpents, sprouting wings,
And icy winds, dark as the grave,
Have cedars bent against the rocks.
                    Tarantara Tarantara

Arise, all fighters for the Sun.
Fly up, you youthful messengers, fly!
Prepare the ranks for battles fierce!
Don't let the clouds engulf our Sun!
                    Tarantara Tarantara

The bugler plays. New winds burst forth.
The brass's ringing sound is carried far.

(24 July 1937)

[*NOTE: Nikolaus Lenau (1802–50), Austrian Romantic poet, considered the chief lyric poet of Austria.—G. S.]

Red Army Song

The sun shines over our native land,
Shines over our glorious country.
We're ready for battle as we march,
Sons of the field and factory.

The dawn has put on its rosy rouge
In a fine-embroidered scarlet sky.
Our enemies in foreign lands
Will soon learn how to bitterly cry.

We won't surrender the land of our birth
To be turned into ashes (they'd like to).
Our pilots—our eagles and falcons—
Are flying up high in the blue.

The accursed foe, if he comes against us,
Will long remember what it means to fight.

We've learned well how to throw our grenades
And to drop our bombs, don't forget.

We are the land of peace and labour.
We don't want someone else's things,
But we won't let ourselves be hacked
By the fascists' battle axe.

With awesome, unexampled power
We'll march against our enemies.
Under the sign of the bright Red Star
We'll smash them all to smithereens.

Over our country the sun is shining,
Over the glorious land of our birth.
Forward, all! Prepare for battle,
Sons of the factories and fields!

(3 September 1937)

Song of the Pilots (of the Red Air Force)

The falcons, dear little falcons, have flown off.
Proud flock has soared above the clouds, aloft,
Like whirlwinds rushing off into the blue.
Perfidious foe, beware our mighty host.

Our countless-numbered wings eclipse the sun.
The awesome power of this host's invincible.
Skies shudder from the roar of our machines.
Our well-aimed salvos will not miss their mark.

Far, far below us is our Mother Earth.
Our hands upon the wheel are firm and strong.
We've been to both the poles and over the seas.
Our planes keep flying swiftly through the skies.

When enemies encroach on our motherland
In darkness with thunder and lightning we will
smash them.

We'll blast them with a thunderstorm of fire.
We will destroy the cursed Axis swarm.

Our flock of falcons flies among the clouds,
Keeps watch along our borders for the foe.
Let him not set his highway robber's foot
On the merest edge of road of our dear land.

From the sky we greet the workers of our land.
We all remember Stalin's wise command:
'If the villain ever dares attack our country,
Smash him to pieces, and don't spare your lives!'

(3 September 1937)

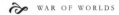

Red Sailors' Song

The angry wave—it seethes and roars,
The storm cloud hovers, black.
On swiftest wings the squall flies in,
But our strong will—it never goes slack.

We are the sons of the stormy sea,
Of the dangerous grey-haired gale,
Warriors of labour's sacred land,
The only one in the world.

We're watching over our sacred land
On the seas and underwater,
And we'll search out every enemy
Who threatens us with disaster.

Our fathers, for October's cause,
Fought hard all over our country.

Our memories hold the scars of their wounds
We were conceived in that fire.

We grew up in a rigorous school,
Our arms are strong and sturdy.
We can sight the enemy from afar,
And the blows we strike are unswerving.

To battle we go as though we were one.
There's a flame in our unyielding hearts.
In the world we'll plant the banner firm
Of our dear, beloved Commune!

(night, early hours of 4 September 1937)

Dance of the Gorillas

Hoarse shouting, clanking, screeching,
Rumbling, chuckling, drumming,
Thumping, swearing, the spraying of blood.
The gorilla cancan is roaring.
An enormous bonfire in their midst,
Crackling and hissing, the crunching of gristle.
Someone dark and someone evil
Brings firewood, a load of bones.
He throws books on, to fuel the fire.
Black fumes of smoke curl to the skies.
From the ground, bemired in blood,
Ominous exhalations rise.
The interlacing of hairy hands,
The stamping of feet and clinking of spurs,
Teeth grinding, lips smacking, nasal breathing,
And bits of lascivious conversation.

But now the stars have all burned out.
The bonfire's long since died away.
A rooster has begun to crow.
Perched on a corpse, it screeches 'Heil!'

(15 August 1937)

Berlin Zoo

Fear chills my blood if ever I may hear
A wolf or jackass sing the praise of freedom
Or when of love a serpent starts to coo
                    —Heinrich Heine

1. Crayfish

Devouring putrid, rotted offal,
The black-shelled crayfish crawl.
Ass backwards, moving forward,
Gaze fixed behind, not onward.
They hate the colour red.
For them it bodes no good.
In redness trouble's waiting,
For they turn red when dimly viewed
Through good hot boiling water
Prepared by a chef who's shrewd.

2. Hyenas

With stealthy footsteps soft they pad,
The venomous hyena brood.
Hot blood these beasts lap up with lust.
They have no taste for blander food.

They're eager on the battlefield
To feed upon the dead and dying.
Good, give them rope enough to use
To carry out their own self-hanging!

3. Wolf

Gaunt and at the same time huge,
Sinewy and never sated,
Voracious, greedy, and he hasn't
For a long time been defeated.

He looks to the right
For a lamb to be had.
To the left on the meadow
Isn't there a calf?
Some creature to slaughter,
Some being to destroy?
Who or what can he slash
With the steel of his teeth?

Wolf, your howling and prowling
Has set drums beating steady.
You've prepared your own trap.
Now fall in it already!

4. Buzzard

'Midst bloodied bits of meat
He sits on a limb befouled,
This cruel chief ataman
Of a highway robbers' band.

Now he's stuck in a sturdy iron cage,
A model for all of buzzard make,
The buzzard-men, we'll call them.
And that's just the way things ought to be.
Isn't that right, kids? Okay!

5. Crocodile

Remarkable terrarium
With palms and araucaria,
As though this were the sacred Nile,
And there reclines the crocodile.

Pharaoh is what he brings to mind,
The glory of the priestly throne.
It seems that what he dreamed to be
Has come true in reality.

He loves to chew a bit of meat.
He'll eat the father and the son.
His favourites are the Semites and
Curly-haired Blacks, smooth-skinned.

But there's such grumpy folk these days
Who don't like crocodilian ways,

Who won't submit to being chewed.
This signal honour they've eschewed.

Man-eater, your feasting days are past
And soon you'll die from your long fast!

6. Polecat

You're unremarkable yourself,
So small and inconspicuous.
Yet you're a dreadful grumpy creature,
Scoundrelly polecat that you are.

Under a roof of canvas here,
Your lair stinks worse than garlic.
You're snobby and you're stuck-up too,
And on top of that, a cowardly varlet.

7. Wild Asses (*Kulany*)*

What muscular fellows,
These long-eared *kulany*,
Teutoburg asses,
No goat beards among them.
Their faces clean-shaven
By the new safety razor.
(Hurrah for collective security.)

Always braying 'Eee-Ja!'
(Instead of 'Heehaw'),
'Heil!' with triumph they roar,

And they applaud splendidly, as behooves,
With their heavy, solid hooves.

(3 October 1937)

[*NOTE: The Russian term *kulan* (plural, *kulany*) refers to a species of Eurasian wild donkey (*Equus hemionus*) that was once widespread in desert and semi-desert regions of the Near East, Middle East, Central Asia, Ukraine and the Caucasus. In English, the term *kiang* or *kiyang*, of Tibetan origin, is also used for this species, which is likewise called 'Mongolian wild ass'; also, 'onager'. Some scientists have classified the different varieties of this creature, found in various and diverse localities, as separate species. See the drawing of a *kulan* in the *Bolshaya sovetskaya entsiklopediya* (Great Soviet Encyclopaedia), VOL. 13 (Moscow, 1973), p. 581.—G. S.]

Lament of Shame

What has become of the land of old,
Of poets and philosophers?
The land where Beethoven and Goethe
Rose up like mountains, and Heinrich Heine
Like a rocket fizzed and sparkled,
Wearing his crown of gold,

Where Kant and Hegel richly flourished
And Feuerbach did his work as well,
Where for the long view, for coming ages,
A mighty genius issued the call.
Those burning words of Marx are now
Leading the worldwide people's war.

Land where exactitude of science
In laboratories, and in thought's silence,
So greatly lengthened our hands' reach
And gave food also for the soul.

All of us, all looked to this land,
Sang praises to its thinkers grand.
But now it has been taken captive
By a bloody gang of bigots,
Its body pecked from every side
By drunk adherents of 'olden times'.

Germany, the police-state land,
Germany, land of the barracks.

The spirit of science bows its head,
A muzzle fastened over its mouth.
Books of wisdom blaze in bonfires.

A Nazi trooper in drunken stupor
Stomps on them, swimming in smoke
And clapping his buddy on the rump.

Foolish cartoon caricatures
Of German masters, Bismarck and Stein,
Have torn up all flowers by the roots
Driving out Haber, expelling Einstein,
And jailing under lock and key
Any who even dare to think.

Mediaeval curse of bigotry.
The hoarse and husky Landsknecht shouts.
Blood's principle, blood's brutality.
The savage face of the Übermensch.
The summons to war, vendetta, revenge,
And a limitless ocean of flattery.

Here Reason's totally cancelled out
It's too old-fashioned for these Volk
It's been replaced with cries for blood
And the lechery of violent ranting,
Reigned over by the old god Wotan,
Furious, menacing and drunk

Hangmen of the working masses
Sing songs that take the movement backward,
Sharpening swords and battle axes
For ready use at every moment
And preaching, preaching constantly
Of barbarism with graveyard spades.

An evil spirit rules the land,
Teutonic wild insanity,
Savage Hessian-type mercenaries
Destroying bluntly, unreflecting
The tender blooms of human culture
In fits of black obscurity.

But days of reckoning will come!
Chainmail of Dark Age robber baron
Will not be reigning here forever
Nor torrents of blood forever flow
In a land where men's black hands
Are more like beasts' cruel claws!

(night of 2 October 1937)

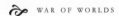

Conversation Between Two Worlds

> And if nothing else remains for you than to
> commence the last great war dance—that won't
> start us weeping.
>
> —Friedrich Engels

When at dawn the sun began
To shine one fine November
And when the Russian people grand
Overthrew the entire breed
Of princes, tsars and boyars,
Factory owners and dignitaries,
All the ravens then flew up
All the buzzards began to squawk,
All the jackals and hyenas,
The dogs and wolves, all bared their teeth.
All the hangmen and the butchers,
All the gravediggers of life,

Started to hoarsely bay and howl,
Reviling this bright sun of ours.

How're you gonna hold your power?
You're only gonna fall apart!
Within a month you'll all go flying.
You have no firm seat in the saddle!

We didn't go flying. We held on,
We Bolsheviks. We showed ourselves
To be a firm and sturdy power—
We were Lenin's good apprentices.

How're you gonna cope with the troops
That the Entente will send with gunships?
That enemy has heavy weapons.
You'll be left with nothing to eat.
They'll need only their bare hands
To capture you on the battlefield.

But look, they didn't capture us.
They fell apart, took to their heels.
And as for all the Whiteguard bandits,
We beat every one of them to shreds.
The last of them, a little baron,
We drove him into the sea.
(To your sorrow and woe!)

In the country, though, the peasants will eat you up.
Among you they are famously barbaric.

You wouldn't let them do their trading.
Now they'll show you what's what, really!
They'll raise you on the points of pitchforks.
They have the strength to do that!

Wise Lenin introduced the NEP,
And trade revived in our country.
Firm stands the House of the Soviets
In a solid bloc with the *serednyak*
(The middle-income peasant).
But what's going on with you, Messieurs?
Hasn't disaster shaken you up?
Everything's burning under your feet
And in your head, there's a buzz.
Something's coming your way, wait and see.
But history judges us favourably.

Still, for sure, you'll be done in soon!
You're playing a mouse's game with the cat.
No matter what, the cat will win.
It'll eat you with one gulp, after playing.
How can you compete in commerce?
How take up problems of production?
In your land everything's in ruins,
All backward, dark and ignorant.
In large-scale global competition
You'll really have your head bashed in!

How frightening! You're scaring us!
True, we haven't fought those battles,

But we're building up resources,
Developing our industry,
And we've walled our country off
With a foreign-trade monopoly.
We have learned skilfully and well
To engage in peaceful struggle.
And that's the way things are!

Still and all, you're gonna fall.
You live like wild barbarians.
No literacy among the people,
They're just savages by nature!
All they live on is canned herring.
White lightning eats away at their brains.
'They just ain't got no kulchah.'
The whole world's closed to them.

Don't you worry about all that!
We know your kind too well.
We're raising our level of education.
And in spite of all your malice,
Our people are growing hour by hour
Like the fairy-tale giant child.
But make no mistake, you're on the threshold
Of a terrible economic crash.
We'll see, but things look bad for you,
And that will be a gain for us!

Sounds like you've gone off your rocker.
Take this Five-Year Plan of yours,

Why, it's sick, fantastic nonsense,
Delirium of backward Asia,
There's no real measuring or accounting.
It's all falsehood and fancy gilding!

Hey, cool down your hostile ardour!
Has your heat affected your head?
Don't you see factories and canals?
The caps of brand-new mineshafts?
The countless new collective farms,
Tractors, machines and state farms?

Yeah, but that's barely a beginning.
The kulak soon will show his sting.
Just take a look around your land.
What you've got is Sodom, that's all!

What's Your Grace trying to tell us now?
That there is no decay where you are?
Hasn't the downturn grabbed your throat?
It's choking you, and your big gun barrels
Will not help you deal with that.
You're decaying hour by hour,
But in our country, we've won.
We have solved the kulak problem.
With cheerful stride forever onward
The toiling folk are marching!

Yes, it's true that you have factories
And machine tools, quite a big pool,

'Cause you imported a lot of our stuff.
But you can't make porridge with machine tools,
And you don't know how to use them.
You're breaking the machinery.
You don't know how to work with it.
Your ignorant men and women
Don't know anything about it.
They don't understand a thing.
A shameful downfall awaits you,
The finale for all of history!

So that's what you say? That's nice!
But look, try to see a bit farther.
Our people now have education.
They're breathing happy and free.
The clavichords have begun to play,
And we'll be setting world records
Of labour, compared to you,
And to your sorrow and woe!

Okay, then, we'll turn the voice
Of our cannon against you.
We will crush you. Better watch out!
Don't tell me you're not afraid!

So that's how it is! Well, we'll see.
But the disaster won't be ours.
We're ready for that combat.
We're terribly strong, we warn you.

A host of heroes has been born
In our consecrated land.
As for you, you've just returned
To where you started from.
The only hope that you have
Is to smash us with your guns.
But things will turn out better for us.
History will judge us with its favour.
And let us tell you this once more:
You'll get what's coming to you, but good!

(night, early hours of 26 September 1937)

An Old Prejudice Shaken

The portly philosophers allow themselves to say
The outer world's but the fruit of imagination.
At the same time they're cudgeling our brains
With the assertion that capitalism's eternal.
The winds of history are blowing hard
And chains of stubborn foolishness are breaking,
But what can you do if under the edge of a curtain
They glimpse volcanic lava and think it's stove ash?
Reality's considered an illusion.
Illusions and mirages are thought real.
Still, a colossal earthquake's under way.
It can't be covered over just with stove ash.

(18 July 1937)

Birth of Humanity

The world today stands at a turning point
And fate's decisions now will be colossal.
A quarter hour is all that's left for Capital.
Thus toll the bells in towers of oblivion.

Mighty generations were consumed
In bloody warfare time and time again.
The smell of conflagrations and decay
Is carried down to us through all the ages.

Babylon was destroyed, its grandeur turned to ashes,
And mighty Carthage was despoiled by Rome.
Tyre and Nineveh, Sidon and Susa—
Were all wiped out in savage, bloody war.
Sooner or later all the giants perished,
All the giants of blood and deception.
The haughty Pax Romana fell apart,

As did the half-world ruled by Alexander,
And the domain of the Tatar Tamerlane,
And all the conquests of Great Cyrus of Persia,
The ancient iron crown of Charlemagne too,
And Napoleon's empire with its rod and staff.
The sages of olden times—in vain they dreamed
Of brighter days, precursors of humanism,
The Stoics and the early Christian fathers.
Their dream was drowned in blood and tumult of
battle.

Peacemakers' speeches now, and cosmopolitans,
Faced with the devil of putrefaction, fascism,
Are like the bleating of sheep at a rampaging wolf.
Only a well-steeled sword will stop the beast.

The fascist onslaught, bestial and black,
We'll meet with heavy cannon and with grapeshot.
A shameful and a deadly end awaits them.
Victory's laurels will rest on workers' brows.

The gods of black and gold will meet their twilight.
The final conflict history will see,
Marking at last the birth of humanity,
A single family united.

(12 July 1937)

LYRICAL INTERMEZZO

[Bukharin gave the above title to the group of 29 poems that he designated as 'series VII'. They are mainly poems of love and loss, especially those for or about his beautiful young wife, Anna Larina.—G. S.]

Tristia

Per me si va ne la città dolente
Per me si va ne l'etterno dolore
Per me si va tra la perduta gente

—Dante*

You are not here, my lovely, gentle friend, my dearest.
Into thin air, all that we had has vanished.
Alone I'm grieving, sick at heart and sunk in gloom.
Sorrow weighs on my soul.

Through mist the autumn rains come down in
filaments
And drum upon the roof.
Burdensome reflections, thoughts of cruel fate—
They torture me.

Monotonous the steady tap-tap-tapping on the roof,
The drip of icy tears.

The dismal wind has taken a wet maple leaf
Up higher, higher, higher.

Two bare, misshapen tree trunks scrape their limbs
together
Sadly, mournfully.
They are two skeletons, and their dead bones
Are rubbing, grinding, grating.

I call out an appeal to you: 'Beloved, dearest,
Quick as you can, come, come!'
My suffering knows no limit and no end.
Sit beside me. Comfort me.

(24 August 1937)

[*NOTE: The quotation from Dante is significant. These are
the first three lines of Book III in Dante's *Inferno*, begin-
ning the famous seven-line inscription over the Gates of
Hell that ends: 'Abandon hope all ye who enter here.'
[These first three lines of the inscription in Italian might
be translated as: 'Through me you go into the city of sor-
row/ Through me you go into eternal pain/ Through me
you go among souls of the damned.'
[Like many others, Bukharin experienced Stalin's prison sys-
tem as an entering into Hell.—G. S.]

Remembrance

Do you remember the pale blue night,
The walkway among thick lilacs,
And the light rays' golden dance,
The light-hearted sport of elves?
The mists were making loops, playing.
From the fields wafted subtle perfume.
From beyond the river, behind a hill,
Came accordions' loud pizzicato.

From the village the singing reached us,
A woman's high voice, tremolo,
As though the torments of passion
Were bursting from some lonely soul.

Your dress was softly rustling
With the whisper of raw silk,

And you fell into my embrace
On the edge of a steep precipice.

(night, early hours of 24 August 1937)

White Snows

Happiness gleamed with light,
The snow on the pond shone brightly,
The sun radiated its welcome
In the bittercold early morning.

And you, with flushed cheeks, were shining,
Soft as the breath of morning.
Enchantment caressed your eyes,
Your dearly beloved blue eyes.

You were luminous, fully, with joy,
And tremulous was your hand.
All of nature was covered now
With the counterpane of our love.

And our spirits joyfully sang
A song of the sea so blissful.

The snow shone serenely white
Over silvery fields of freedom.

(24 August 1937)

Eyes

> With dark eyes never fall in love
> Dark eyes are dangerous
> Fall in love with eyes of blue
> They're the loveliest
> —Russian folk song

I've known you well, O dark eyes' scorching fire,
Lightning's fracture,
Love's thunder,
With raging passion turning my soul to ashes.

Then there's the frenzied cry of eyes of brown,
Endlessly turbulent,
A face gone insane,
Cheeks burning, and savage passion shouting.

But I prefer the gleam of the deep waters
Of azure eyes,

Shoulders' soft sigh,
The tender tremor of your caressing breast.

I find you everywhere,
Gentle, kind spirit, kindred soul.
As at death's hour I disappear forever,
Into those eyes I'll stare.

(24 August 1937)

Together

Among blue mountains
And snowy ridges,
Through valleys wet with waters wide,
You and I kept riding ahead.

The noisy rivers' waterfalls
With waves aplenty, churning black,
And the sheer drop of deep abysses
All ran past us in their turn.

Earlier, splashing of ocean tides
With arabesques of lacy foam
Playing, swirling round our knees—
They too had sung to us their song

And drunk we were with happiness
And the twilights so intense

Being born and dying out
In that happy land remote.

Glory to the beauteous bride.
We alone, you by my side.
And what within your hand you held
Was always, always mine, my hand.

And thus we lived and thus we loved
Our cup ran over; we drank its pleasure.
No knowledge ours in that fair Eden
Of pain and torment's prick and sting.

(24 August 1937)

To a Hittite Maiden

> . . . Heaven bless thee!
> Thou hast the sweetest face I ever looked on.
> —Shakespeare (*King Henry VIII*, Act IV, Scene I)

Have you ever seen my love's
Proud gaze,
Reproach ineffable
In azure eyes?

She's lovely as the chamois that leaps
On cliffsides stern.
Love's coral gives her crimson lips
A scarlet turn.

And her black brows, like two
Slim snakes,
Make arches over two blue waves—
her eyes.

Heavy black braids form rings above
A forehead proud.
Her speech—the tinkling of little bells,
The sweetest sound.

Her nose, a finely chiselled line,
Is sharp and aquiline.
And from her wondrous almond eyes
Piercing looks shine.

Eyelashes form black shadows dense,
And they conceal,
Just like the wings of nesting birds,
Blue eggs of eyes.

Her thoughtful, tender countenance
Is filled with love.
The proud disdain that beauty knows—
It's in her blood.

Like marble slightly warm and pink,
The colour of her cheek's
Preserved forever by the radiant
Eros, god of youth.

Blood of the East flows through her veins
And shows in all her ways.
The enigma of her Hittite eyes
Works sorceries.

(24 August 1937)

Nymph

Gurgling and playing,
Over rocks sparkling,
All silvery breaking
Through mountainous hulks.

The stream of the mountain,
Collecting its rivulets,
Taking flight stormily,
Pours down its bed.

Cheerfully light specks,
Weightless, many-sided,
Bright lances of sun,
Are thrusting point-blank.

A nymph all naked,
From the sun all golden,

Laughs loudly, throwing
Her clothes on the bank.

There now she has scattered
What covered her curls,
And with her hand splashes
The silver of water.

She's frisking and giggling,
Like a whirlwind she's skimming,
To deep pools she's rushing
As light as a feather.

Like a fish she's splashing,
Her back freely flexing,
She bends with a smile on
Her dear little lips.

She dabs at her temples,
Then laughs again loudly,
Already she's chirring
Somewhere in the bushes.

(night of 25 August 1937)

Parting

I am to go far, far away
And it may be forever.
With thee, beloved, azure-eyed,
The time has come to sever.
I know that you will weep and weep
In quiet times, recalling me,
And on the white sheets of our bed
Your tears will fall unceasingly.
But you won't let the people see,
Within your soul, the yearning,
And hotly to your bosom press
The child of our dear union.
My darling, till we meet again,
Farewell, forgive me all!
Land of our birth, may you prosper,
And don't despair, dear, don't despair!

(25 August 1937)

Universal Love

Voice of nature, dance of heavenly bodies,
Woodland whispers, murmurs of the wind,
The stamping feet of giant storms,
Thunderous, awesome forces singing,
The mutter of rivers, streaming floods,
Resounding mountains, whirlwinds chasing
Clouds along from distant places,
Oceans seething with bottomless chasms,
Churning up emerald-gleaming waves
Till giant arms lie prostrate on the shore.

Everything sings of turbulent life,
Everything flames with fiery passion,
And the rainbow wants to tell us
Something of multicoloured joy.

Green, the little blades of grass,
Wise saga-singers of the meadow,

Bejewelled teardrops of the dew
Transmuted into sunlit steam.

Under the sunrays' warmth the grape's
Curled whiskers are more tightly twisted.

The sky's red sphere at sunset
Is agonized and turns to blood
As violent bonfires light the sky.

Earth is all a-bloom with flowers,
Its countless multicoloured eyes,
The dazzling eyes of maidens fair,
Gazing into heavens far.

And from the beat of Earth's strong heart
Impassioned torment radiates.

Songs of birds, the forest's chorus,
The voices of all living things,
The sweet aroma of the flowers,
And the wild wind's fluttering wings—
It's all the wondrous, miraculous turning,
Turning of the golden wheel.

We sail among the Cosmos' waves
Upon the Universe's ocean,
Driven by our love and passion,
As particles of cosmic being,
As stardust from a life remote,
Benevolent, and all-embracing.

Our little, swiftly sailing boat
Flies through the fogs to infinity.

(29 August 1937)

Beginnings

> It was long, long ago—long ago, long ago—
> In a kingdom, a land by the sea.
> —Konstantin Balmont

It *was* long ago, truly long, long ago
In a kingdom far south by the sea.
You came and you found in the gold motes of
light
My abode by the shores of that sea.

The sea was a-quiver with untroubled waves,
The incoming tide softly sighing,
And we swam towards a steep-rising mountain of
gold,
All flooded with sunrays' bright shining.

A cavern was there 'midst a jumble of rocks
With schools of fish playfully swirling.

In the vertical mirror-like watery depths
There were dark-blue harmonies stirring.

Between the cliffs the shade breathed cool
And a brook ran gurgling down.
We sat in the dampness, the secretive shadow,
You and I—together, alone.

You said to me trembling as if in a dream
'How peaceful it is here, my darling!'
And my soul was abashed as, with mystery's breath,
You reached out your dear hand towards me.

A furious squall in a rush swept down on us,
In darkness we had to swim back.
Dark watery walls played around us and bellowed
White manes on their curving black necks.

Pounding wild all the while in our hearts was joy's
voice
In that fateful and danger-filled hour.
Our spirits just laughed, they had started to soar—
Oh, how good those moments were!

(night of 30 August 1937)

Conception

A floor of clay in a little room.
The chaos of nights camping out.
A mountain goat tied nearby
Is leaping against its rope.

An eagle-owl with injured wing,
A tumbled heap of wildfowl,
The worthy shotgun in its case,
Cartridges, leftovers, dishes.

The moon shines through the windowpanes,
Pale eye of the mountain sky.
On the shaky chair near the window
A thick slice of black bread still lies.

You sleep by the wall, on the floor,
Having loosened your braids of black hair.

Exhaustion looks out from a corner
With the ashes of dropped cigarettes.

Your eyes are closed. There's stillness.
Your chest's even rise and fall.
I gaze at my beloved's face
And cannot sleep—so strong is love.

What if I kiss the marble brow
Of my dear, exhausted one?
Would I waken my beloved
If I kissed her lips of scarlet? . . .

On that night, in the bleak desert foothills,
Alongside the great high mountains
Where the wing of the eagle stretched out
You first gave life to our son.

(30 August 1937)

Moonlight Sonata

Strings of pearls, lunar strings on an instrument,
Whispers, and rustlings, and shadows quite ancient.
The murmur of boughs, the moonlight glimmering,
A cobweb fabric of lace, all silver.

All of it weightless, all unfamiliar,
Incomprehensible, strangely uncertain,
Drawing eternally towards sweet mystery,
Luminous, sad and dearly beloved.

A brook bubbles over its pebbles and stones,
Its silver waves tinkle like tiniest bells.
Sudden changes of course, as though in alarm,
A timorous beastie that flees from the sun.

In the sleepy air, blue shadows lurk,
Patches of fog, reflections of moon.

In the sky, giant steps lead towards the stars,
To the Milky Way with its many-stringed beams.

The waves in my heart rise higher and higher
All overflowing with sweetness of passion.
The waves now subside, growing quieter, quieter
To the silent sound of the moonlight's singing.

Over the keyboard your hands are in flight
Like ivory birds over dark blue sea
And I am tenderly wrapped in a veil
Of enchanted rays by the Queen of Night.

(30 August 1937)

Glory to Life

Glory to life unbounded,
And to the sun in the sky,
Which shines upon us, then crouches
In hills at sunset time.

Glory to the stars, the birds,
To every tree and flower,
To fiery chariots of the dawn,
To grasses, seas and rivers.

Glory to the breath of breezes,
Glory to people on earth,
To the trembling of tender bosoms,
The half-dreaming sighs of passion.

Glory to human creations,
Glory to clear-eyed labour,

Glory to courage tremendous,
Glory to intellect proud.

Glory to mothers and children
Glory to youthful beauty!
We celebrate every hero,
All those of valiant spirit!

Glory to our country's new years,
Glory to a party of fighters,
Glory to Life, to the Sun,
Glory to hearts aflame!

(2 September 1937)

Anthem to the Sun

Light-Giver to life on earth,
Gigantic, you circle the sky.
We greet your life-creating force
With a triumphant anthem.

The source of radiant light rays,
You pour forth streams of warmth.
A force elemental of fertile fire
Has been lodged in your inmost core.

As your golden wheel revolves
It breathes an ocean of flame.
The sky's blue cheerfulness burns
With the smoldering of your rays.

You sing your song in spirits,
In animals, flowers and epics,

On the ocean and on dry land
In specks of dust, in human plasma.

You've given birth to terrestrial life.
You blossom in raindrops and crystals.
Your brilliance lights up the rainbow
And the scarlet-purple sunsets.

Father of fire, in curls of light,
With your crown of golden hair,
You ride your horse, the colour of fire,
With saddle blanket of rubies rare.

O you luminous light of day,
Sailing across deep blue of sky,
You gave the earth the gift of joy,
We give you back a hymn of praise!

(6 September 1937)

Idol

> Make not unto thyself any graven image
> > —The Bible

> To make a poet of himself, a man must either
> fall in love or live in calamity
> > —attributed to Lord Byron*

Don't make an idol for yourself,
No idol should you make!
Thus twangs divinity's holy lyre
And thus the priests insist.

These voices—they are idle voices,
Voices of an idol that wants
To be the world's sole, one and only
Miracle-working idol.

But I don't need a miracle-idol.
There are no miracles

And there's no idol that can spare
The world from mortal woes.

Of you, dear friend, my golden lyre sings,
My lyre luminous,
Luminous as lyres at the feast of life itself,
Or as willows by the water.

At the feast of life when the lyre resounds
There may be many tears.
And after joyful spring, life's lyre
May play the sounds of frost.

But after winter comes summer again
And summer lives in us.
And in that luminous summer, my dear,
The songs of spring rejoice.

(22 September 1937)

[*NOTE: The epigraph attributed to Byron is a literal trans-
lation of the version provided in Russian by Bukharin. The
original English wording (sure to be different from this
back-translation) remains to be found.—G. S.]

Young Woman's Song

Flowers, grasses curly-headed,
Where are you, dear, sweet, little flowers?
Without you there's no love, no fun.
Where in the world is my dear one?

I am suffering and I'm sobbing,
Longing for you, my sweet darling,
And I, poor peasant girl, don't know
What in the world has become of me.

Trouble and longing devour me,
Teardrops are falling from my eyes.
Mad woman, I, by the palisade,
For an entire hour was standing.

Why I stood there, I don't know.
You weren't there. You aren't coming.

Again I start to weep and sob.
A sharp, keen knife is in my heart.

Can it be that you don't love me?
Can it be that you've forgotten?
You know I'll be destroyed forever
If you've fallen for another.

I don't believe it. Do you remember?
You swore that you were mine completely.
That was in the oak grove dark
Where oak leaves rustled overhead
And at our feet the flowers bloomed.
How fine they were, the little flowers!

Can it be those lovely days
For me are gone away forever?
On the bare field snow is lying.
The blizzard's howling now, and moaning.
In my heart there's woe and longing.
Can it be? Summer's not coming?
Can it be the sun won't shine
And nightingales will not be singing?
The oak grove will not welcome us?
And the moon won't rise again?

Suddenly the sun is shining!
I hear singing! Flowers are blooming!
I've just taken a look out the window
And there outside the window you're standing.

The dear, little flowers for us *will* bloom!
Ah, they're so fine, the dear, sweet flowers.
The lovely days of summer *will* come!
And in the oak grove, leaves are greening!

(night, early hours of 24 September 1937)

Car Chase*

Madly we raced on, you and I,
In that sorry little Ford,
And you yelled at me 'Watch out!'
As I drove at a dangerous clip.

The glacial peaks surrounding us
Looked sternly down into a vale
Of dark and dusky sands, far down.
But wings—that was what we were on.

Swiftly we flew on, like eagles
Over gloomy deserts below.
A long-bodied locust on the fly
Struck a shotgun barrel and died
As we rushed uphill, gravel spurting.

And firmly you held on to me,
So I wouldn't fly out, accidentally.

And music was playing,
The music of wind
In the gun-barrel holes,
Music whistling, whispering
Of those dark eyes of yours,
And summoning us to new life . . .

Desert antelopes rushed wildly,
Like wind blowing free in the fields,
And after them we came speeding.
Such the heated dispute of our race.

You took me by the shoulder.
Your arm went round my waist.
Your breath was burning fire,
Your heart enlivened by the chase,
By sun and wind and me.

And speeding along with my darling,
I was with you heart and soul,
I was one with you, light-winged love.

(night, early hours of 24–25 September 1937)

[*NOTE: This was an unusual scene, a Bolshevik leader hot-rodding in the 1930s in a remote mountain region of the USSR, his young wife with him on a hunting expedition. —G. S.]

Sirin and Alkonost

Within my soul two fabled birds reside,
Magical birds, the birds of fairy tales,
And their enchanted songs mark out in me
The tracks and trails of joy, and misery.

Here rosy Sirin on a rose branch rides,
Bird with the features of a lovely maid,
With ruddy cheeks, bright curls and ruby lips
That sing out sweet, enchanting melodies.

And her song brings good cheer to my poor soul,
Miraculous birdsong with its golden tones.
Like joy of Paradise, celestial music flows,
Pouring emotion forth, stream upon stream.

The other bird is fabled Alkonost.
His handsome eyes are full of muted woe.

His feathered costume is a plain, dull black.
The pallor of his cheeks tears at my soul.

The choking sob of torment is his song.
His mournful lips sing of this harsh world's pain.
His wings funereal—they sway so woefully,
And from his dark eyes sorrow's teardrops rain.

The spell of melancholy fills the dungeon of my
soul.
I'm overcome by sorrow's fierce bewitchment.
Yet on and on he sings to me, he sings, this wizard
bird,
This angel sad of weeping and bereavement.

(night, early hours of 25 September 1937)

Rádunitsa*

ZashuMELi   v leSAKH   vetry BUINiye
In woods, the winds began a noisy turbulence.

PonaDVINulis   TOO-OOCHi   CHORNiye
Coming on were clouds, black and gloomy ones.

ZabliSTALa   kaLYONa   gromoVA strela
Then gleamed, white-hot, the mighty thunderbolt.

ZatruBILa   v veTROO   zoloTA truba
Then echoed in the wind a golden trumpet's note,

ZoloTAYa   truBA,   truba ZVONkaya.
A trumpet of pure gold, a trumpet ringing loud.

ZaiGRAL   yary GROM   po podneBESyu
In heaven Yary Grom,** the angry thunder, started
playing,

PereKATami   v TOOCHakh   greMOOCHimi
With rolling thunderclaps in clouds, with rumbling
claps,

ZastuCHAL on   gorYOO-OOCHim   MOLotom
And with his burning hammer he began to pound,

ZasverKAL   ogNYAmi   paLYOOCHimi
Began to flash with all his fires, scorching ones,

OgneVOI   parCHOI   grozOI-malonyci
Like fiery brocade, his thunder-lightning storm.

Kak uDARila   gromoVA   streLA
And as the mighty thunderbolt came striking down

I rasSELasa   groboVA-dosKA
Cracked open was the crypt, the vault, the grave,

RaspakhNOOLisa   BYELy SAvany
And parted were the shrouds, the whited funeral
shrouds,

OtvaLEELisa   ROO-OOki   BYELiye
And spilling out were hands and arms, pale white.

Ot toVO li   ot SERDtsa   ot MEELovo
Are they of the beloved, the departed one?

V ledyaNOI   moGEELe   v poLOOnochi
Still lying in the icy grave at midnight?

Iz moGEEL   mertveTSY   podyMAYootsa
Now from the graves the dead are rising up,

Ot TYOPloi   veSNY,   bouinoi RADosti
Thanks to the warmth of spring, its turbulent joy,

Ot veSELya   da KHMELya   YaREELova,
To Yarílo's good cheer, his merry tipsiness,

Ot veSENNevo   GROMa   greMOOCHevo
Thanks to his springtime thunder, roaring, rumbling.

Mat'-SyRA-zemLYA   prosyPAYetsa,
Now Mother Earth, the dewy one, awakens,

MoloDOOKHoi   zemLYA   prinaRYAZHena
Like a young bride, the Earth now is all decked out.

ZatsveLA   tsveTAMi   laZORevymi,
She's started to bloom with flowers, yes, with azure
ones.

GoloSAMi   zaPYELa   maLEENovymi.
With voices she's started to sing, with such melodi-
ous ones,

ZoloTOYe   bleSTEET   Solntse KRASnoye
And golden gleams the sun, all bright and beautiful.

SereBROM   plyVYOT   mesyats   PO-nebu
Like silver swims the moon across the firmament.

Svetyat s SEENikh neBYES chasti ZVYOZDochki
From dark-blue skies, shine tiny stars, thick-clustering

Ot veCHERnei zaRI i do UTRennei
From the evening twilight till the morning comes.

* * *

Brodit KHMEL*** po poLYAM, po troPEENochkam,
Stumbles the tipsy god through fields, down little paths,

Po looGAM, po leSAM, da po doROZHenkam
Over meadows, through forests, down this byway and that,

Po khoROMam, kleTYAM, da po LESTnitsam
Past the churches, past the sheds, and up the steps

Po svetLEETSam, gde SPYAT krasny DYEVitsy
To the rooms where pretty maids lie sleeping fast,

Da po EEZbam, gde SPYAT dobry MOLodtsy.
To peasant huts where goodly lads are sleeping too.

GoryaCHEET on im KROV moloDOO rudu,
He warms the blood up in their young and lusty veins

I zoVYOT- zazyVAYet pod YELnichek

And urges them, Come out beneath the spruce trees
young,

Da pod YE-Elnichek,   pod beRYOZnichek.
Yes, out beneath the spruce trees and the birch trees
young,

TseloVAT   miloVAT   DROOGa milovo,
To kiss and to caress the boyfriend well-beloved,

KhoroVODy   voDEET'   do poLOONochi
To dance the round dance right up to the midnight
hour,

ObniMAT'   doroGOOyu   poDROOZHenku.
And squeeze her tight, the girlfriend, the beloved
one.

[Vot I] GLYANet   YaREELo   na ZELen loog—
Lo, he glances, Yarílo, on the meadow green,

ZatsveTAYoot   tam TSVETiki   ALiye
And there the crimson flowers start to bloom.

[Vot i] GLYANet   YaREELo   v teMEN syr-bor—
Yarílo glances deep into the woodlands dark

ZashcheBECHoot   vse PTASHki   ot RADosti,
And all the birdies start to chirp from happiness.

[Vot i] GLYANet   na VODu—tam RYBochki
He glances at the water and the fishies there

ZableSTYAT   cheshooYOYoo seREBryanoi
Start showing off their silver scales, all shining
bright,

ZaiGRAYoot   veSYOLymi   PLYASKami
Start in to play with happy-splashing dances.

Stoopit v LES   soloVYI yivo   priVETyat
He takes a step into the woods—is greeted by

GoloSEEStiye   CHOODo—   soLOVushki . . .
The full-voiced, the miraculous, the nightingales . . .

* * *

A poMRYOT kak   YaREELo   v IVANov den'
But Yarílo will die on the day of St John.

ZamolKAYoot   pevTSY v toske-GOResti
Fall silent the singers in sorrow, in woe.

KhoroNYAT   YaREELo   veSYOLovo
They buryYarílo, the cheerful one.

MoloDOVo   YaREELo   veSENnevo
The youthful Yarílo, the springtime one.

(27 September 1937)

[*NOTE: An inscription in Bukharin's manuscript assigns this poem to the 'cycle: Lyrical Intemezzo'. It imitates or reflects the manner of some Russian folk songs, with chanting lines, unrhymed, and with three main stresses per line in the original Russian. We have given a transliterated version of the Russian, line by line, capitalizing the stressed syllables. Following the poem we have appended an explanatory note about Rádunitsa and the god Yarílo.—G. S.]

[**NOTE: The phrase *yary grom* literally means 'angry thunder'. Here it is personified into a god, apparently a form of the god Yarílo.—G. S.]

[***NOTE: 'Khmel', the term for 'tipsiness', is here personified, a kind of God of Tipsiness.—G. S.]

NOTE ON RÁDUNITSA AND YARÍLO

Rádunitsa, among the Eastern Slavs, was a pagan spring festival celebrated during the week after the first sun-worship day after the first full moon after the vernal equinox. Some sources say that it was related to ancestor worship, and even today families go to the graveyards of their relatives on Radunitsa, the Sunday after Easter. But the festival also has to do with sun worship (greeting the return of its warmth).

This is of course the time, after a long, hard winter (especially where Eastern Slavs lived), when the hours of sun and daylight began to be longer and stronger than the hours of night and cold.

The name is probably derived from the adjective *rad*, meaning 'happy, glad, joyous', or the noun *radost*—gladness, joy, good cheer, pleasure. Hence we might render the word Rádunitsa as 'Good Times Celebration'.

The festivity is probably akin to the maypole and Queen of the May festivals in old English folk culture—which, according to some sources, had their origins or parallels in the spring fertility festivals of ancient Egypt and India. But probably such seasonal celebrations took place almost everywhere in the Northern Hemisphere as the sun and warmer weather and the growing season returned.

(Compare the *Columbia Desk Encyclopedia*'s article on May Day, originally celebrated in honour of the Roman goddess of spring, Flora, whose festival was 28 April–3 May.)

Yarílo, in the mythology of the Eastern Slavs, was god of the sun, of springtime, fertility and love. In Bukharin's poem he is given attributes similar to those of the Greek god Dionysos.

As a survival of paganism, spring festivals (*prazdnestva*) in honour of Yarílo are accompanied by dancing and *khorovody* (which are round dances or circle dances, with chanting; these may have originated as pagan ritual dances).

And there is a symbolic killing (a sacrifice, or 'sacred doing'). Among the Hebrews, a lamb was killed and eaten. Among the Slavs, Yarílo had to die, but would be reborn.

In some parts of rural Russia, as late as the beginning of the twentieth-century, rituals, ceremonies or festivities in honour of Yarílo were still being held, according to the article 'Yarílo', in the 1978 volume of the *Bolshaya Sovetskaya Entsiklopediya* (Great Soviet Encyclopaedia).—G. S.

The Road

Bright sails the moon in a dark-blue sky
Above the wide, pale blue of a road.
In the sky there's no yearning or harshness,
No troubles, no sorrow, no fear.

From the fields in a gentle wave
The night breeze blows, perfumed and cool.
All is filled with muted stillness,
Filled with the trembling diamonds of dew.

The golden pins of the Milky Way
Are fastened against a curtain of blue,
And from the Pleiades light is shed
On the conflagrations of human woe.

Quietly over the meadows the spice
Of incense spreads in fragrant flow,

As honeyed purple clover gives
A toss of its head in the grass below.

It's good to be walking with you here,
On a silver-lit road through fields of corn.
Above the river, a falling star.
And rippling in waves, the moon's twin horns.

We walk in silence through summer night,
Surrounded by sweetness and sad delight.
Your dark-blue eyes, so dear to me,
Gleam with your soul's immensity.

(night, early hours of 28 September 1937)

'After Horace'

You and I together, on a bench were sitting.
'Twas the midnight hour, and the moon was shining
Out from behind dark woods, which stood on the
bank
Like a black mass.

You said to me, leaning forward, softy,
That long you had loved me, loved with all your
heart.
Everything in me seethed from what you said.
My blood was burning.

And I embraced you under a moon of silver,
And ardently and long I kissed your lips
And could not go away. I could not part
From my beloved, my dearest.

Extinguished were the gold pinpoints of stars,
Arose the dawn, chariot of Phoebus Apollo.
Floods of golden rays came spraying down
From sky to earth.

We, hand in hand, kept sitting side by side
As if in golden fog, as in a dream.
There shone in us, the same as in the sky,
A sacred sun!

(28 September 1937)

Spring
(In Imitation of Ausonius*)

The swallows, the quick ones, towards us
      direct now the flight of their wings.
Into village and hamlet they fly,
      the swallows, the quick ones, towards us.
They noisily chirp and they twitter,
      to their native penates returning,
And as their nests they are building,
      they noisily chirp and they twitter.

Woven are field and meadow
      with flowers bright in the grasses.
Like a carpet of many colours
      woven are field and meadow.

The bee flies in haste to the meadow,
      full ready to suck out the nectar.

To the tenderly perfumed flowers,
        the bee flies in haste to the meadow.

The woods roundabout have turned green, they're
        swaying their youthful branches.

Dressed in their newest attire,
        the woods roundabout have turned green.

A mirror of waters in silver
        is reflecting the azure of heaven,
And far in the distance there glitters
        a mirror of waters in silver.

The clouds are silently sailing
        through clear lapis-lazuli blue.
Like a flock of imperial swans,
        the clouds are silently sailing.

The ardent rays of the sun
        embrace the young beauty, the Earth.
They warm her and they caress her—
        the ardent rays of the sun.

Rascal Cupid is honing his weapons,
        light-wing arrows directed at people.
So their hearts may be sweetly transfixed,
        rascal Cupid is honing his weapons.

Born-of-Seafoam, towards us softly,
        approaches divine Aphrodite.**

She directs her light-as-air footsteps,
    Born-of-Seafoam, towards us softly.

                         (29 September 1937)

[*NOTE: Ausonius was a Latin poet of the fourth century AD who lived in Burdigalia (now Bordeaux).
[**NOTE: In Greek mythology, Aphrodite has the epithet Anadyomene (Born of, or Rising from, the Sea Foam).
—G. S.]

A Dream

I dreamed I was with you, my dear one,
I was with you again, my darling.
And everything shone with the springtime of youth,
And from somewhere we heard a brook singing.

The evening light came through the window,
The lindens thrust towards us their verdant boughs,
And the white kitty-cat was meowing,
Messing round with books piled on the floor.

We're again on our sofa, familiar,
Sun gilding Dutch tile by the stove.
You're wearing your multi-flowered robe,
Black ringlets of hair all dishevelled.

On your breast's caressing tenderness
I press my troubled head . . .

And awake all at once, filled with longing,
All alone in the rigours of winter.

(night of 30 September 1937)

Battle of Ideas
(A Sonnet)

I love the circle dances of clear thoughts.
They sparkle with the stars of many eyes
Amidst the heavy gloominess of night,
Like rows of fairies, delicate and wise.

But false ideas in thought's realm too may swarm.
Pitilessly strike them. Crush the worms.
They're black and foul and evil, snakes in grass
'Midst lovely roses' purple shapes and forms.

The dance of thought may not be innocent.
Beside clear waters, pools of mud may lurk,
And filthy scum can make its vile protrusions.
The world must be protected from this murk.

From blinded superstitions' ancient wheeze,
Black poison-blood in Evil's arteries.

(night of 30 September 1937)

Meditationes

> I despise the type of idealist philosophy that
> tears human beings apart from nature. I am in
> no way ashamed of my dependence on nature.
> —Ludwig Feuerbach

Speechless the sky, and the stars glitter.
All nature breathes of grandeur immense.
Like shadows, individuals flicker,
But mankind's footprint is firmly fixed.

The soul, meditating, merges with
The breathing of a vast, mighty chest.
Nature and world embrace, encompass us.
Like a wave, an ocean, age-old, multifarious.

We are, after all, her living creation,
Our human tribe with miraculous minds,
A precious florescence of planet earth
That sends up its soul-breath to heavenly climes.

And with our scarlet blood we feel
All of life's pulse, vast, universal.
With nature bound by subliminal love,
We feel the strain of her rhythms in us.

Submitting to her elemental force,
We bow to necessity's laws, objective,
And with those laws, we make her bow, in turn,
Before the wondrous-gleaming throne of Reason.

(1 October 1937)

To a Jewish Maiden

O sweet are dark-eyed Dora's glances,
Those darkling glances are the piercings
Of arrows flying into distance
To where, beside the sea—blue mountains!

The patterns of those darkling glances
Have seen their fill of grief, whole mountains,
Have known the heaps of dirty linen,
Heaps of squabbles, heaps of quarrels,
Bark of reproach, and ugly bluntness,
The idiot laugh of condemnation
And all the idiotic blaming
And shaming by bigoted old dames.

Those glances say, 'Time for using the brain,'
For shaking off the Torah's blinders,
The choirs of savage superstitions

(Which are hilariously funny),
For opening blinds of the Tabernacle,
Where the Lord, like a thieving impostor,
Has crept into the sanctum sanctorum.

(2 [or 4?] October 1937)

Ancient Landscape

So vast and great are you, my native land,
Spread out from sea to sea, so grand,
The silky rustling of your endless steppes,
The dreamland darkness of primeval woods,
Your southern desert's burning yellow sands,
Your snowy mountains' lofty white-capped heads,
The rushing of your rapid rivers deep!
Dear Mother Volga's broad and sweeping reach,
And of the Dnieper, and the quiet Don,
The hero Yenisei, and Lena-Mother!
Green do you grow, with grassy greensward lush,
Embroidered all about with azure flowers—
With azure flowers and with scarlet too,
On bushes large and small, and on your willows,
By bridges large and small, and on viburnum.

The bright red sun looks from the edge of sky.
Its hot rays light up, warm up everything.
With golden arrows sharp, how they can sting!

And in the heavens high, the cranes do fly
And with loud voice give vent to their deep cry
As though 'twere freedom they were trumpeting.
And soaring in the clouds are falcons bright,
And on the lakes and rivers snow-white swans
Are swimming with their little cygnet-babes.

And hiding in the woods are herbs and flowers:
The kind of plant our folk call 'devil-chase',
Monkshood and wolfsbane, purple loosestrife too,
And what the folk call orphan plant, which grows
Beside a greyish stone, combustible,
A kind of stone our people use for fuel.

But autumn weather now is setting in.
The birds fly off beyond the warmest seas,
Far off they go into the heavens' heights.
The fish drop down into the waters deep,
Down to the darkest canyon slopes and pools.
And through the trackless forests flee the beasts,
Retreat to thickets where they can't be reached.

Nor chirp nor twitter in the early hours
The sparrow birds that lived beneath the eaves.

Only the watchdog now is barking, howling,
And in the cornfield mooing stands the cow.

And rushing thunderstorms that bode no good,
Are rumbling in the skies the livelong day.
And downpours come, rainstorms unquenchable.
The earth is shrouded in white mists and fog.
And cold winds from the north begin to blow,
And winter comes in, grouchy, blizzardy.
On the bare fields the snow is gleaming bright,
And smoky snowstorms sweep all else away.
Siberia's *purgá* wraps all in white,
All paths and roads obliterated, sunk,
The paths that lead us to a friend's warm home.

(4 October 1937)

On a Bridge

The cold pallor of the mute heavens
Shows blue
The bridge abutments take the splash
Of the Nevá at full flood.

The wind gets fresh, and on the fly
Slaps our faces jauntily.
At your skirt and at my coat
The cheeky fellow tugs away.

Hold tight, my dear, hold onto your hat
Or else for sure it will get snatched.

Now put your little hand in mine!
What weather! What a ripping time!

The dark blue waves are swollen full.
The river's all in wrinkles.

The fishermen along the quay
Stand frozen in position.

With all its granite fortresses
Out on a sunny day's parade
Fair Leningrad has gone all out,
Fair Leningrad—does itself proud!

(5 October 1937)

Night

Far off a long and lonesome sound
As train or factory whistles blow
Somebody's pensive gaze is blurred
By the pain and yearning we all know

Against a sky of black the moon
Hangs like a prop in a theatre
At work beyond the window frame
Is silent night, the sorcerer

(18 November 1937)

EPOCH OF GREAT WORKS

[Bukharin gave the above title to the 23 poems that he designated as 'series VIII'.

[Some of these poems, with fulsome praise of Stalin, might better be placed in an Appendix, where they could be viewed as the false and rather unpoetic curiosities that they are.—G. S.]

Emancipation of Labour

A new epoch of world history has begun. Man is
freeing himself from the last form of slavery.
— Lenin, *The Third International and Its Place in
History*

Am Anfang war die Tat. ('In the beginning was
the deed.')
— Goethe

Beginning of all beginnings, life-creating,
Let triumphant chorales be sung to you!
In mud, in sweat, to the whistling of overseers'
whips
The slaves did labour for the kings and pharaohs,
With blister-covered hands built pyramids
And Semiramis' garden paradise,
Temples of marble and gold, entire cities,
Canals where water tinkled like crystal,

And prisons, underground pits, where languishing in
chains,
Convicts had nothing but foul-smelling dust to
swallow.
Wherever axes chopped down oaks in forests
Or where the Gothic cathedral
Lifted its arrow pattern to the heavens,
Everything was made by stubborn labour.
All the works of the Muses and Graces,
All the wonders of civilizations,
Flowed from one miraculous source,
One that will never run dry.

And this force suddenly grew,
With unexampled speed in the era of Capital.
Yet labour, as before, was plagued, tormented.
Here too the whistle of slavers' whips was heard.
The worn-out slaves of the machine
Still bent their backs to jobs that gave no joy,
The source of all, still poisoned by slavery's
corruption.
The very thought of work was under siege,
Held in contempt by rulers, philosophers, poets.
Work was the curse of only the peon or helot.
At first there were odes to spotless white hands,
Odes to the gods, to refined bits of fashion,
To porcelain, to the gold of palaces,
To the victorious ending of
Some bloody adventure of war,

Or to a ballerina's figure,
Or even—and this is no made-up story—
To someone's beloved borzoi hound.

The revolution's thunder knocked Moloch over.
Slave labour became a thing of the past forever!
Free, self-defining labour reigns in our land,
Waging holy war against all things old.
It's living and creating, and it's winning.
Continuously it's building
A grand and bright, well-ordered world.
The epoch's new feast
Is crowned by songs of triumphant glory,
A majestic hymn to immortal labour.
May our enemies perish!
And may heroic labour live forever!

(night, early hours and morning of 10 July 1937)

Stone Tablets of the Five-Year Plans

Once the dreaded lord of Sabbath
From the highest peak of Sinai,
In midst of thunders, gave to Moses
Stone tablets, the ticket to Paradise.

And with those tablets then the people
Went searching for the Promised Land.
Generations honoured those tablets,
While living the lives of accursed dogs.

New tablets of our modern times
Were given by neither Zeus nor Yahweh.
Petrograd and Moscow gave us
New law books, product of great labour,
Gigantic effort of the masses,
Toil's exertion, the flame of thought.

The workers gave these to the people,
Raising the sacred banner aloft.
No god it was that chiselled these tablets
With terrible thunder rumbling in heaven.

Thought flowing from the brain of Stalin
Has been condensed in rows of figures.
With his mighty iron hand,
Authoritative, strong and firm,
He led the people to new battles,
To conflict hard and dangerous,
And in that combat we've come out
Victorious all along the line,
Building a house of light-filled life
And on the horizon's the communist future.

Yet at the point where all roads cross
Our adversary, raven black,
Croaked of disaster. The workers broke free
Of all their chains. Brave and unstinting,
They smashed the fetters of poverty,
Swept away the old order's chaff,
The burdensome life and ignorance,
The hell of ancient prejudice.

'The plan—that's us,' our leader said.
In feverish toil, fighting the foe,
In rain and in fine weather too,
Exerting all their strength and might,

Our people built and entered boldly
Into the gates of a brand-new life.

Behind us are the ills of former times,
The song of victory has rung out clear.

(26 September 1937)

The Lever of Archimedes

The power of giant factories,
Machine tools in a shining row,
They've crumpled up, subdued the old,
Pressing it down forever
Beneath a weighty tombstone.

The lever of Archimedes
Has been applied.
How long is this arm's mighty reach!
Victory stands beside it,
Breathing her hot breath.
Blast furnace's belly of fire and heat,
Chaos of lighting, force of steam,
And metals furious—
Man's put the bridle on them all,
Weaving together monstrous machines,

Linking up fabulous devices,
Wheels, rollers, cutting tools coupled together . . .

To all the ends of our country
To wage the frenzied battle
We send out more—more new machines.
The moss of routine is scraped away.
The picture's not the same as before.
On a tractor instead of a horse
The flag of victory flaps in the wind.
The end has come for the wooden plow,
The separate strip worked by each peasant.

An end has come to accursed miseries.
We're at the glorious turning point,
The time of great change is here!

(morning, 5 July 1937)

Metamorphosis

Giddap and drag yourself along, grey mare!
—Koltsov

Scene One
Crooked little peasant huts.
Rowanberries under the window.
Skinny cattle grazing
At the edge of woods.
Bast sandals full of holes.
An old and worn-out sheepskin.
Nothing but trouble and longing
For every gnarled old soul.
In the middle of the village
Squats a tavern with its sign.
Here the whole world comes
To drown its sorrows:
Sotskiy and *uryadnik*,

Priest and *stanovoi*,
Kulak and *ispravnik*,
Judge and *ponyatoi*.*

Beyond the sleepy pond
On a hilltop steep
The columns of the local count
Give off a gleam of white.

'Pull the plow, grey mare!
Giddy-up, keep pullin'!
We've gotta patch our winter coat
Made from the fur of fishes.'**

Scene Two
'Comrade Pyotr, why're you lagging?
You know, the meeting's waiting for you.
You've got some nerve. Get moving! Run!'
Thus speaks Kegím, for Pyotr's edification.

The meeting's going on real loud,
The big room's echoing.
'We got enough tractors; they've arrived,
But Mitry's taken sick.
Very few combines been delivered.
There weren't enough for our province,
But there are peasant lads enough,
And plenty of trucks have come!
All right, let's draw up our plans!'

'What, have you gone crazy?
How are you counting?
What about the district?
Where's the law on the overall plan?'
'We've got to reorganize the stables,
Put in a water line to them,
Finish building the movie house . . .'
'But what about our workdays?'
'Ask Ivan about that
Or else Stepan Somov.'
'Is it true what they say
That next year
He's putting a piano in his hut?'

Meeting's over. They go their way.
Everyone's in a sweat.
They've dealt with matters and now
They're heading off to sleep
And some of them, to read.

(23 July 1937)

[*NOTE: In a four-line passage Bukharin lists some of the various types of tsarist officialdom in rural Russia who kept the semi-serf peasantry in line. *Sotsky* was the lowest rank in the rural police of pre-revolutionary Russia; an *uryadnik* was a village constable; a *stanovoi* was head of a police subdivision in a rural county; an *ispravnik* was 'police superintendent', or chief of police of the rural county; a *ponyatoi* was an official witness whose duty was to be present as an observer during police searches.

[**NOTE: In old Russia, the expression 'made of fish fur' (*na rybyem mekhu*) was used to describe a garment in such sorry condition that it could not keep out the cold.—G. S.]

The Land
(*Zemlyá*)*

The land! How much blood, how many salt tears,
Have been shed over you, dear land of our birth.
The blueblood landowner, a dangerous and
predatory foe,
Kept you held tightly in his imperious hand,
And the kulak kept you under his boot heel,
As did the monastery, gold cupola and all.

The peasants kept sweating away on land owned by
others
Or tilling a tiny scrap, a handkerchief's size,
Only tormented by a bright dream, a longing
For some black earth of their own. And the blood-
thirsty foe
Would hack their heads right off at any time
When peasants took up the axe to fight for land.

O how they dreamed of the land! O how they loved
it!
They worshipped it as Holy Mother Earth.**
And all the roots of that savage, lean existence
Were bound up with earth, the source of nourish-
ment.

Still, peasants kept persistent, stubborn faith
In the power of the earth, its strong black womb.

The peasant's little patch of native soil,
Unhappy, sorry handkerchief of land,
Was cut off from the booming life of machines,
From city life's enlightenment. All cares
And troubles were heaped together on his little plot.
The wooden plow, manure, a five-cent piece
Were all the world of this existence bare.
The evil seed of greed, of craftiness and grasping,
Many times led to breaking a neighbour's skull.

Today the fields stretch out, all velvet green,
And now the peasants' Holy Mother Earth
With all the mighty plenitude of nature
Has become the nation's common treasure.

The ancient lovers have converged for good,
Exchanged their vows of passion everlasting.
The peasant, once hunched over, scrounging in dust,
Has straightened up, proud owner of Mother Earth.

No longer knows he trouble, longing, woe.
Proudly he stands at the wheel of a machine,
At the helm of the Five-Year Plan.
He's weeded out the evil nettle of graspingness
With the fight for collective farming. Now a new
race
Has sprung up in the village, like mushrooms after
rain.
The country people have begun a new life.

Feeling ardent love for the fair young maid, the
Earth,
The peasant lad cares for her tenderly, builds her
strength,
And he will defend the land against all foes
And be in battle merciless and stern!

(early hours of 24 September 1937)

[*NOTE: In Russian, the word *zemlyá* means both 'land' and
'the Earth'.
[**NOTE: The Russian phrase is *mat' syrá-zemlyá*, literally
'mother damp-earth'.—G. S.]

Kulak Perdition

The collective farms marching!
Tractors moving, rumbling.
Stalin's leading the masses.
The kulak's gone kaput!

Some life it used to be,
Buying and selling.
Lending money at interest,
A life of golden opportunity!

It was fun to live that way,
Have know-how, be crafty, make profits,
Dupe people and cheat,
A lifetime of good living—knowing no grief.

But now, look around,
The shirtless ones have risen up.

They're pushing us kulaks back.
Don't even look at them!

Our house was full of everything.
They took it all for the kolkhoz,
A whole wagonload.
It's the time of Sodom again!

And the kulak picks up a gun,
And he shoots and he burns,
And expects from God
All kulak miracles.

The villagers are restless.
They start to rise to power.
The bloodthirsty monster
Bares wide his greedy maw.

But his whole back is broken
By the people in struggle.
His turn has come. Time for
The kulak to meet his fate.

He lives in penal camps
And his snout has been muzzled.
He's forever gone silent.
Else they'll chain him up.

The collective farms are flourishing.
The machinery's humming.

Peasant women having babies,
Freely singing, bringing in harvests.

Millions have found
A new life's comfort

They've got themselves shelter
And a life of brightness.

And free labour blossoms
On wide fields and plains,
Broad expanses of meadow
Where machinery reigns.

The whole land is prospering
And in it all are studying.
For both father and son
Life's become truly full!

An epic hero, a giant,
The people, strides forward,
The turbulent force of its battering ram
Knocks down every enemy wall.

Life has grown grand and good!
When the kulak is gone,
Then the peasant can live,
A lifetime of good living—knowing no grief!

(night, early hours of 22 September 1937)

Symphony of Cooperative Labour

Only he is the possessor of a free life who de-
votes his life to unceasing, arduous struggle.

—Goethe

People grow when their goals rise higher.

—Schiller

*O saeculum, o litterae! Juvat vivere, et si quiescere non-
dum juvat.*

—Ulrich von Hutten*

An epoch of great works was opened by victorious
socialism.
Giant wellsprings—limitless creative forces—
bubbled up.
Sculptors of human life, builders of towns and
villages,
Artists of plants and fields, of orchards and new
fruits,

Designers of clever machines, masters of science, poets,
Millions of worker-warriors, whose deeds were clothed in legend,
In their multidimensioned work, are constructing the new world's order,
A harmonious choir of labour, seeking new solutions to riddles.

At power plants, luminous temples of industry,
Covered with cold marble, at waterfalls,
At dams of the most enormous size,
Beside the cupolas of dynamos, by the vanes of turbines,
Or beside blinding white fires,
The super-hot craters of electric furnaces,
Beside the fiery lava pouring from monster-sized ladles—
Everywhere is the intense free labour of people.
Behold the incandescent depths of blast furnaces,
Whose sighs are like a Moloch that's been tamed.
And over there, the giant roller of a blooming mill
Is turning over fiery lengths of metal,
The heavy tons of an electric hammer fall,
A clang of flashing steel, 'midst clouds of stars,
The heat that's given off as casting moulds cool,
And the sharp cutting edges of monster scissors,
And jaws and snake-like arms, all made of steel
And mobile cranes, with long necks like giraffes,

Which quickly swing a pile of rails like tree limbs,
Like thoroughly dried-out wooden boughs.

* * *

In underground mineshafts, the Minotaur's
Labyrinth,
Coal-cutting machines are at work, like armoured
brontosauruses
Come back to life by some strange miracle
From the epoch when coal was still growing as lush
forest
Of giant club moss, *Lepidodendron* and *Sigillaria*,
Amidst Saturnalias of fire and madly flooding waters.

* * *

Over here are distillation columns
And towers like the craws of great, enormous birds.
Very high pressures
And tensions of electric current.
Gigantic retorts
And pipes forming aortas
Like the trunks of extinct Leviathans.
And burial mounds—huge tanks for holding natural
gas,
Like puffed-up, swollen bellies.
And flower-fountains of oil gushing skyward.
And infinite numbers of ingenious machine tools,

Products of calibration and the laws of mechanics—
They cut metal, saw it, press it, plane and shave it,
Sharpen it, round it off, grind and polish it.
For the spinning and weaving of textile fibres
Shuttles are on the move, quicker than lightning.

* * *

Into the fields from the yards, like tortoises,
Slowly crawl tractors from their storage parks,
And other machines, like fairy-tale giants
Full of weighty mystery, the combines,
Like ancient mastodons, which with their carcasses
and tusks
Have rested for centuries in icy graves.

* * *

And in the silence of laboratories,
Exquisitely clean, like mountain sanatoria,
Among the strange instruments and devices,
Science's amazing accessories,
Differentials
And integers,
Curves and equations—this is Thought come to life,
Components of the Deed, links in Action's chain.

* * *

Geologists and members of prospecting expeditions,
Experienced masters at handling
The most sensitive instruments of geophysics.
With the pointers on their dials, subtle feelers
Of the earth's many-powered energies,
They study the riches held beneath its crust,
And in the ebullience of their thought they hear
The singing of precious stones, rare minerals.

* * *

The divers of EPRON,**
Whose suits are strangely pop-eyed,
Reveal the wonders underneath the sea,
While our falcon pilots do trailblazing work,
Paving world-class highways in the skies.
The poles, both north and south, they've taken prisoner
And conquered vast and icy distances.

Canals have been dug—they're lengthy, serpentine.
The greedy mouths of excavating machines
Lay bare the bowels of the earth,
And the seas are extended in a ribbon of mirrors,
The earth is bestraddled with wrinkles
As though tectonic forces had
Revived the violence of primordial changes.

Along severely iced-up shores,
Bound by the frozen shackles of ocean,
A cluster of artificial hills has risen.
Here cities have grown up beside the sea
With mighty radio tower masts.
No distance any more is to be feared.

* * *

Throughout the country, where labour
Has been emancipated from rusty irons
The joyful back-and-forth calling of millions is
heard.
They are the future's source, key-holders of victory.
Flint-like and sturdy, they have thick-veined hands.
Their workdays too are swollen, full of life.
A great, heroic process has unfolded,
The heated chariot race of socialist emulation.

Statistical records, like obelisks of the era,
Gleam with victories on their solar disks.
The sons of textile and metal, blacksmiths and
poets,
Kolkhoz workers and miners, fathers and sons,
Factory technicians and land surveyors,
Science's strict creative workers, engineers and
conductors—
The energetic strength of women in the vanguard—
They've transformed life in its most everyday aspects,

And the selfless aspirations of hundreds of nations
Are laying the foundations for communism,
An edifice of universal joy,
A well-shaped structure, the fellowship of all.

In a harmonious commonwealth,
Powered by beautiful impulses,
Well-tempered against all disasters,
The people are composing a great Symphony of
Victories,
A titanic Chorus of Cooperative Labour, a chorus
of all the peoples,
And a sentence of death for the Thousand-Year
Evil.

(27–28 July 1937)

[*NOTE: Ulrich von Hutten's Latin phrase might be rendered in English as 'O world! O letters! It is a joy to be alive and, even more, not yet to be inactive.'
[**NOTE: EPRON—initials meaning 'Expedition of Special-Purpose Underwater Operations' (*Ekspeditsiya podvodnykh rabot osobogo naznacheniya*), a special branch of the GPU established in 1923, at first for retrieving sunken ships, and later for assisting vessels in distress. By 1932, all organizations in the USSR involved in such work were merged into EPRON. In 1941, when war with Nazi Germany began, EPRON became part of the Soviet navy, the branch of the navy concerned with salvage and rescue operations.—G. S.]

Shock Workers

We march onto the battlefield.
Sun shines for us through fog.
Like lava's headlong stream
We rush on towards glory.

To labour's thunderous drum we march,
Not scared by the enemy's ugly snout.
We're setting new records
With our stubborn strength of will
In the factories and the fields.

We know about storming fortresses.
We'll take them one and all!

In unison with iron tread
We break the back of every trench
Or obstacle across our path

So later we can join in battle.
The enemy will bow his head
To dauntless labour!

So all disasters will disappear
And happiness shine forth for all,
And gardens of a joyful life
Grow green all over our land.

And may our homeland flourish well
So as to repel the enemy thunder.
We work for the good of all the peoples,
And the valour of many storms endured
Has entered our muscles and veins.

More strength with every hour,
Growing like a rolling snowball,
We march!
We're the shock workers' brigade
From all the hulks of factories,
Collective farms and mines,
State farms and highways,
And when the thunder peals
We'll take up arms!

Joyful our spirits are---not sad
And mighty Stalin leads us.
We're his apprentices.
We're all now Bolsheviks.

 NIKOLAI BUKHARIN

We promise the Council of Commissars
That they will hear victory's thunder!

(night, early hours of 28 September 1937)

The Stalin Charter

How full of grandeur is this structure!
Included in it
Is the law of the epoch of world-creation,
The Law of Labour.
The balance sheet of victories won
Is here condensed,
And in it the new world's mansions
Are embodied.
This draws a line under our battles,
A line of victories.
The balance sheet of the years resounds,
Not as pleading or as prayer.
Here lie the concrete foundations
Of the stern and rough-hewn will
Of the worker masses.
A mighty stratum,

The social order of socialism,
One complete structure,
Triumphs here . . .

And the decline at the enemies' gates
Casts but a shadow on the greatness
Of these granite accomplishments,
The difference between today's two worlds,
Two epochs' separation.

The people has been consolidated.
Into one great unity.
The barbarism and swinishness of former times
Have disappeared.
Everyone's well fed, well shod, and happy.
That's how we're living.
Here the right of free labour
Is open to all,
To a job, to enlightenment, culture, knowledge,
To a peaceful life,
To education, to creativity,
A system of freedom!
Unfazed by the howling, threats and assaults
Of fascist dogs,
A creation is growing in the land of labour
Made by hands and minds.

The stone tablets of our Constitution
Are solid and reliable,

And there's a glow of sunny horizons
For the masses of the world!

(night, early hours of 1 October 1937)

Masters of Fate

Such is Fate, the accursed mighty giant.

—Hauptmann

Fate? Why, that's politics.

—Napoleon

In recent times we humans have grown wings,
But earlier the sense of impotence
In face of Nature's awesome elements,
Which have been known to crush unlucky nations,
In face of war and economic ruin,
Of flourishing countries' downfall and decay,
Created a mournful spectre, the phantom Fate,
A power to which the gods themselves submit.

Among the Romans the Fates were called Parcae.
For the Greeks, they were the Moerae,
Enforcing implacable law, called Ananka.

Among the Slavs, there was *rozhon*—
Against which you cannot go,
For otherwise you'll be struck down,
Whether in battle or in your home.

Greek tragedies singing about Fate's power,
The wailings of Israel's prophets foretelling
Inevitable doom and sure destruction,
Remorseless Destiny, immune to deterrence—
In the rotting fortresses of Gold
All these notions continue to live.

What fate, in fact, awaits us in the future?
Whatever fate's decided in the struggle!
Through struggle we have solved enormous
problems
And paid back enemies in their own coin.
Our people have become the Masters of Fate.
Like oak trees, young and strong, these generations
Of Health Personified are growing up.
Gone is the habit of letting things drift, blind and
aimless,
And with that has gone the idea of perfidious Fate.
The people determine what fate will be,
Creating whatever they desire.
The mass of the people with their hands and
thoughts,
Their muscles and nerves and brains,

Have replaced chaos with well-ordered planning.
Blind forces? Those nests they've destroyed forever.
The Fate that once seemed awesome, terrifying—
They're leading it around now on a leash.

(17 July 1937)

Capital of the World

Where is Moscow the golden-headed?
Moscow, bent at the knee?
Moscow of the merchants,
Moscow worn full of holes,
Prayed for by God's fool, the *yurodivy*?
Uncouth Moscow, the Moscow of taverns,
The Moscow of old rags and tatters?
The 'forty times forty' churches have disappeared
Along with the constant chiming of church bells,
The clar¹.ing of chains, the groaning of people in
fetters.

The narrow streets have passed away,
The little dead-ends and back-alleys,
The houses of charity,
The land-owning nobility,

The obscene guard posts,
The endless prayer services.

Moscow, the centre of worker rebellions,
Has flown up, a free bird in flight.
The worker's hand rose to avenge
Razin for being drawn and quartered,
Pugachov broken on the wheel,
For the harsh whip of the factory owner,
For the forced labour of slaves,
For the oppression of the peasant.

Moscow is now the capital of labour.
A row of splendid buildings has been built,
Making an elegant wall along the streets,
Which stretch out straight as arrows.
The wounds of harder times have long been healed,
Gone is the fog of years of cold and hunger
When in fever and delirium
The people heroically repelled
The onslaught of bloody disaster.
Our whole country was enveloped in
The frenzied flames of villainous invasion.
That time became historic, legendary.

A different epoch's now at hand for us.
Now giant factories stand, row upon row.
The creative charge of massive energies
Is ready for the feast of history.

Moscow has been transformed into
The capital of the world.

The ancient Kremlin, refuge of the tsars,
Within its chambers and wrought-iron doors
Preserves the spark of worldwide revolution,
The thunderous constitution of new worlds,
Along with valiant Reason and the strength of iron
hands,
Which knead the dough for masses of humanity.

(morning, 12 July 1937)

Birds of a New Kind
(Song of the Flight to the North Pole)

There, they've raised their wings
And spread their feathers out.
The cranes have started up
Their song, up in the sky.

A great clatter has also started
As new miraculous airships
Begin roaring, and with great tumult
Set about singing to the clouds.

Over the fields they fly.
And they fly over forests.
They fly over mountains,
Through fog and into the whirlwind,

And into the icy kingdom
Where lives the Great Blue Bird,
The talisman that will bring glory
To their beloved country.

They flew and flew some more,
And when they had finally flown
Into fierce snowstorms and cold
At last they came down to earth.

They grabbed hold of the Blue Bird
And put it in their gauntlets.
You know, this really happened.
It wasn't just a dream.

(night, early hours of 26 June 1937)

Round Dance of the Women Paratroops

Young women, girl friends all,
Darling swallow birds,
Communist Youth League buddies,
Valiant female eaglets.

Now hurl yourselves with daring
Down into seas of air.
Make the elements sing
In the void of sky-blue.

Fling yourselves now cheerfully
With the speed of thunderstorms,
Like the wild wind rushing
Headlong into blue vapours,

So that joyful chute strings
Are humming in your ears,

And your spirit senses
Stormy breakers crashing,

And your heart more brightly
Flowers with new vigour
And your heart burns hotly
With song on wings of fire.

(1 July 1937)

Women

> In any society the degree of women's emancipa-
> tion is the natural measure of the general
> emancipation.
>
> —Charles Fourier

Our world is creating new women too,
Beautiful, healthy and free.
We have no need for lovely Phrynes
Or other refined hetaerae of Athens
Offering Bacchic bliss, if you can buy it,
And a wet smack with a smile on drunken lips.

The times of Anachreon are gone.
There's no eccentrics any more
To dream, amid other fantasies,
Of Aspasia's charms, the lover of Pericles,
Or lazy, voluptuous odalisques
In harems of Oriental despots.

History now has swept all that away.
The sultan with his whims—his star has waned.
Mediaeval damsels also are no more
Languishing in their bracelets and their chains.
The dolls in powdered wigs have vanished too,
Mistresses of Watteau, of rich old men,
The playthings of illustrious princes,
Elegant whirligigs lacking mind and soul,
Pale tigresses of palaces and ballrooms
With artificial coral on insolent lips.

The beauties who flourished amidst the stupor
Of Moscow's former merchant quarter
Have melted away in the storm and thunder.
Their rosy-chubby corpulence
Could not withstand Fate's chariot wheels.
No more the folk-rite, inspection of the bride,
As in some paintings by Kustodiev.
These figurines for decorating beds,
Heads tilted sideways, birdbrains locked inside,
Have passed into the shadowed grave forever.

Entirely new breeds are flourishing
And joyfully they're striding ahead
With songs of good cheer on their lips
And golden sunlight in their eyes.

Brave women paratroops, whose daring skill
Can take entire cities when they will,
For all the people now they lead the way.

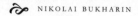

No strangers they to love, good times and joy
They're at home everywhere—work, battle, family.

(8 July 1937)

Sasha—Woman Tractor Driver

O, you cheerful Sasha, you,
With a head of hair so dashing,
With a song you're dancing
And with a song, plowing.
You drive your tractor with a song
Tearing over hill and valley.
With your proud and haughty soul
You tear off miles the way the wind
Tears leaves from golden aspens.

You work like one of the fellows,
Combative and thoroughly cheerful,
And sometimes you'll curse a guy out
For 'lounging around like some baron'.

With that little hand of yours
You do everything with skill,

And stubbornly you strive
To get results quicker than ever.

Wherever you set your hand to the wheel
Everything goes superbly,
Smoothly, well and quickly,
And you toss your head,
You chortle and laugh,
You dance and sing.

Your job title's '*traktoristka*',
You're known as dauntless Sasha,
But all that's not enough for you.
You're already holding your firm hand
On the wheel of a horse of the air
And luring your friends to do it too.

Already you're plunging downward
Your curly head leading the way
And with your sure and steady hand
You open your parachute.

Ay-da, Sasha-traktoristka,
Daring, dashing head of hair!
Proud blade of grass in the field,
Friend Sasha of the paratroops.

(night, early hours of 28 September 1937)

Mothers

The epoch of life, of life abundant,
All-powerful, all-conquering,
Crushing all dead things into dust—
It pulses in our burning hearts.

The time of joyful spring has come.
The axe's power will crash with a roar.
A kingdom of hopes and achievement's been born,
Of new eras for new, young generations.

The people rush into skirmishes with Nature,
Thrashing the villainous malice of all foes,
Working in harmony, loving ardently.

From Moscow itself to the port of Igarka,
The women here don't fear the men's embraces,
The new beginnings of a life of grandeur,

The fruit-bearing passions of love,
The heat and flame in the heart's blood.
Young mothers in our country are beloved.
They give the nation the gift of new youth,
Of shapely daughters and dauntless sons.
They'll cleanse the world of all Life's enemies.

Beloved wives, companions of the men,
Healthy and strong are the children they bear.
They sow emulation's seeds everywhere,
Completing the natural cycle of life

Amidst the splendid unity of Nature
There's a tremendous power—motherhood.
And that which Life produces, which Life gives,
Will live a long, long time, live endlessly long.

(9 August 1937)

κάλος κάί άγάδος
(*Kalos kai agados**)

E in si bel corpo più cara venia.
　　　　—Torquato Tasso, 'Jerusalem Delivered'**

We've dug out the stumps of poverty
With their strong, widely ramified roots,
With their diseases, wounds and deaths,
The miseries of the deaf and blind,
The heavy coughing of the doomed,
The misbegotten, crippled, deformed . . .

[Before me I see]
Health, strength and beauty,
Bodies supple and shapely,
In glowing nudity,
Their muscles elegant and sturdy.

A consonant harmony reigns throughout
In the smooth curves of these bodies.

With these clean lines life's rhythm assures us
That Beauty in the world's begun to sing.

This is creation of life that is beautiful,
With labour and inspired play,
Reunited with nature, our mother,
And with the flight of clear-skied thought!

Here there is courage, strength and skill,
Character of eye, intelligence, will,
And a goodly share of brave nobility,
Nor is thought napping behind these foreheads.

And these young wives and maidens fair
Are lovely as the flowers of spring.
With their bodies they bear love's crops
In nudity's radiance divine.

It's all here—set in wonderful proportions.
The music of bodies captivates the eye.
True human beings have grown up.
The beautiful is also the good!

(12 August 1937)

[*NOTE: Ancient Greek for 'The Beautiful Is Also the Good'.
[**NOTE: The quotation from the Italian poet Torquato
Tasso (1544–94) was also used as an epigraph by the Russ-
ian poet Konstantin Batyushkov (1787–1855), whose edi-
tors gave this meaning: 'In such a beautiful body there's an
even more lovely spirit.'—G. S.]

Flesh and Spirit

Unfortunately, madame, I observe that I am
composed of both body and spirit. And the
body is very strongly connected with the spirit.
Perhaps, with great wisdom, they could be sepa-
rated. But heaven did not decree that I should
learn to philosophize. And so, in my case, body
and spirit live closely together and share the
premises.

—Moliere

But related to culture in general is the tendency
of the mind toward the greatest multiplicity of
needs together with the means of satisfying
them.

—Hegel

Priests and monarchs of various faiths,
Crass unbelievers and fanatics too,
Have sundered us into flesh and spirit,
In order to mortify the flesh.

The vampires clothed in their black cassocks
Sharpened their flesh-cutting knives,
Fastened the stocks upon the body,
Wrapped hermit legs with iron chains
And put hair shirts and whips to use—
Those butchers of the living flesh!

Flesh was declared to be a vice
Originating in sinful Sodom,
Was threatened with dire punishments,
Blows of the sword, the fire in Hell,
Endless torture and execution
In the name of the Father and the Son.

The monks of various Christian sects
Along with the mullahs of Islam
And Buddhism's gaunt ascetics
Kept drilling in the same message,
Pounded away with the same behests
About the devilish sins of the flesh
That lurk on the pathway to pleasure.
The castrati and eunuchs in droves,
The jackals, clean-shaven and bearded,
The fakirs and stylites and saints
Repeated the message *ad nauseam*.

The world, they said, is blinded by deception
And by the pagan kingdom of Satan.
The sinful outer shell of spirit's
A vessel filled with grief and corruption.

And the wise sages of idealist thought
In the traditions of Platonism,
Of Gnostics and castrated mystics,
Drag the ends of the very same chain.

But Spirit is Flesh's luxuriant flower
Which fades in the shadows of midnight
Like a leaf without the tree roots,
For reality itself is Monist.
And so with word and deed we build
A great life for Body *and* Spirit,
For harmonious people's satisfaction,
The health of the strong, their own lives' captains,
So that they'll always flourish brightly,
That earthly joys and creation may grow,
With joyful labour, art and science,
With love and passion and friendly feeling,
Heroic valour in toil and labour,
And fellowship in both joy and sorrow.

(16 July 1937)

Fragments and the Whole

> Forever welded to a small, separate part of the
> whole, man himself is transformed into merely
> a part, not a whole . . . Instead of having his hu-
> manity stamped into his nature, he becomes
> something that merely bears the imprint of
> progress and science.
> —Friedrich Schiller, *Letters on Aesthetic Education*

In a succession of thousands of years,
In years of poverty and disaster,
What existed was not a person,
But countless disfigured cripples.

One spent his whole life as a cobbler
Formed no judgements higher than his boot tree.
Another turned two millstones all his days:
Behind their pointless turning he turned grey.
A third man plowed the soil from childhood on
And never visited the nearby town.

During the iron age of Capital
Men were further reduced, to smithereens,
To little cogs and screws in a machine.
A person became a number, a piece in a puzzle,
A bitten-off chunk of soul, a stump of body
In which the vital life was turned to stone,
In piles of prison-like apartment cells,
In the crazy hubbub of the cities,
Entirely torn away from living nature.
Deformed hysterics—that was all that grew there.

And in the villages, emptied of people,
Where brutish fear of the city prevailed,
A mildewed life, barbarically wretched,
Limped from one hut's doorway to another,
Like a blind old nag, ribs sticking out,
Walking in its sleep around
The same old pile of manure:
The wooden plow, the tavern, the priests.

* * *

The philosophers, the holy men of science,
Never knew the pains of physical toil.
They swam in the sphere of symbols alone
And worshipped the idol of empty abstraction.

But the new world of socialism
Brings back together, into organic wholeness,

The human fragments, the bits and pieces.
The existence of cripples in our land is disappearing,
Fragmentation and dividedness are dying out,
A new, creative person's being born,
A person who uses both brain and muscle.
This person doesn't snivel or grow sour,
But with vision embraces everything,
Is quick to emulate, participates everywhere,
In freedom and harmonious fellowship,
Within an integrated hero-people.

(11 July 1937)

Diversity

Thou dost belie him, Percy, thou dost belie him.
—Shakespeare, *Henry IV*

Ah, madame . . . let us go have supper now for
the good of these afflicted poor.
—Eugene Sue

How hard the hired liars cluck and cackle:
'Socialism is a barracks only, an anthill,
A mound of termites, no flowers, just burrs.'
(And other slander, in crummy canvas sackfuls.)
O, you aesthetes, you singers in praise
Of multicoloured diversity,
You are the eunuchs of impoverished thought,
Your bodies have no strength, produce no offspring.
Your world is one of false and base diversity,
A world of blood, banality and savagery,
Windowless, mouldy dwelling places, cellars,
Treasure houses of stench, decay, disease,

Districts ridden with bitter vice and next to them
The splendour of diamonds, gleam of silks,
Gold and bronze, Havana cigars,
Perfumed aromas, subtle and refined,
And bathtubs of tender pink marble.
Next to them, naked bones and gnawing hunger,
Cigarette butts in the gutter,
Stocks and chains for the defiant,
The mournful crutches of misfortune.

* * *

For some there's lobster, fine sauces and wines,
And tender fruits from beyond the sea,
Luxurious baskets filled with orchids.
For others, a rusty dipper and sorrow
Alongside the cancan and the champagne.
There we see thick necks and rolls of fat,
Wonders performed with plump, pink suckling pig,
Drunken luxuriance, a feast of Lucullus,
While poor children's faces are tinged with green.
There's war and peace, and blood and sweat,
The gaping holes of measureless poverty,
The vampire of insatiable greed,
The nauseating clamour of the hired minstrel's lyre.
Everything's full of contrast, quite diverse,
In the vain and idle world of property.
But that kind of striking diversity,
Where the scraping sound of stocks on ankles

Accompanies the clink of wineglasses,
We've shaken it off like Ahriman's* evil depths.
The great repair of humankind has begun.
We've a multiplicity of gifts and talents,
Passions, aspirations, inclinations,
All the joys of free, creative labour,
And don't forget heroic feats of valour.
Where troubles do not spring from the social order,
Where glorious sagas in real life multiply,
Legends of creative undertakings
And the most noble seeking: quests and searchings
Into fathomless infinities of worlds.
Diversity's our bottommost foundation.
Our enemy's the barracks of the fascists.
Where there rules a cretin, a hysteric,
Delirious ravings of a lowly gendarme,
The ideology of superman-beasts.
The sky there's greyer than a soldier's uniform.
Marching and drilling is the only god.
Outside the barracks entrance, by the slit of a
window,
A hired mercenary curses and belches.

(21 July 1937)

[*NOTE: Ahriman was the spirit of darkness and evil in the
dualistic religion of Iran, opposed to the god of goodness
and light, Ahura Mazda, or Ormuzd (Hormuz).—G. S.]

Vanity of Vanities

Vanitas vanitatum et omnia vanitas
('Vanity of vanities, all is vanity.')

—Ecclesiastes

If it is considered the ultimate in wisdom to
have a consciousness of the *nullity* of every-
thing, that might indeed indicate depth of life,
but it is only the depth of emptiness, as may be
seen from the ancient comedies of Aristo-
phanes.

—Hegel, *Lectures on the History of Philosophy**

All is the vanity of vanities.
Nothing in this world's of any worth,
Neither welcoming joy
Nor a sea of terrible troubles,
Neither what is true nor what is false.

That is how Solomon, ever so wise,
Formulated pessimism's lies.

But we could with equal justice
Put the formula in reverse,
Sing the praises of worldly grandeur
Amid infinity's pristine indifference.

Old man Seneca contended
That death was the ultimate ideal,
And Leibniz, the Pangloss of philosophy,
Sang songs to this 'best of all worlds'
Like a scholarly tailor praising the royal uniform,
Its gold embroidery expressing
The will of the Creator,
Architect of the world, and Father of all monads.

But the diarrhoea of philosophic pessimism
Comes from the parasites' fed-upness with life.
It's the katzenjammer of tired minds,
Scholarly doctrines of impotent men
In whom the flow of life has stopped.
The measure of the grandest heights of thought
For them's the measure of mere emptiness,
The stolid naivete of Pangloss.

The questionings of children, they say,
Are things that can't be answered.
Just give the sheep something to drink.

But joy and suffering both are held
In the storehouses of Being,
Not in the waves of oblivion,

But in the flames of seeking,
The flames of enquiring minds.

The highest joy of creation
Lies in the overcoming of suffering,
Activity that knows no end.

Life's fully justified in its own self.
It needs no sanction from some other source
Or any empty, naïve arguments.

(29 July 1937)

[*NOTE: Cf. Hegel, *Lectures on the History of Philosophy*, VOL. 1 (Lincoln and London: University of Nebraska Press, 1995), p. 401.—G. S.]

Flowering of Nations and Peoples

*In nova fert animus mutatas dicere formas.**

—Ovid

How many tribes and peoples our giant Union
embraces!
From snowy northern plains to dark-blue southern
seas!
The rapidly roaring rivers and silvery mountain
brooks
Send their multicoloured waters down to a single
sea.

So too its peoples, who flourish, now with the tur-
bulent springtime,
Have merged their forces into one, forever to be
blood brothers.
Uzbeks, Tajiks and Turkmen in the land of exhaust-
ing sun,

Visited once by Alexander, trampled by Tamerlane,
Where water has silvered the desert, and roads drill
the backbones of mountains.
Here lovely new flowers are given full rein to bloom.

On the pathways of ancient peoples, by the Cauca-
sus' rugged gorges,
Where the clangour of battles once rang, where the
vulture tormented Prometheus,
Under firm Kabardinian hands, a bright new life has
blossomed.
Those blossoms can be seen from distances far.

In ancient Colchis [Georgia] where, in search of the
Golden Fleece,
Jason once rushed with ill-omened Medea to battle
the dragon,
The Georgian has raised from decaying marsh,
From the stifling steam of swamps, the emerald of
new land.

On the ancient steppes of Ukraine miraculous
power plants rise,
And the people have troublesome Old Man Dnieper
on a leash.
In the taiga, on Siberian plains, on the banks of
swollen rivers,
In steppe lands, formerly wild—everywhere life's at
full flower.

Mongols, Yakuts and Buryats are reborn in flesh
and spirit.
They hurry along with others, within the great circle
of peoples.
In the wastelands of permanent cold, the Lapp and
the Nenets take heart,
And in their skies there's the echo of airplanes
buzzing like bees.

From under the tsar's savage knout, which held the
prison of nations firm,
In the forefront marches the Russian, leading the
circle's procession,
And grey-headed Moscow—the age-old scene of
torture and execution,
Of foul-smelling taverns and churches, of stupefied
boyars—
Has now become the capital of transformed nations
and peoples.
And by the walls of the Kremlin, Lenin's remains
are at peace.

(morning of 6 July 1937)

[*NOTE: Ovid's Latin phrase, the first lines of his *Metamor-
phoses*, Book I, might be translated as: 'The mind inclines to
speak of bodies changed to new forms.'—G. S.]

Pearl Necklace
(Song about Kabardá)*

The difficult years have sunk, down deep in the
River Lethe,
And never can there be, a turning back to the past.
Kabardá is happy now, flourishing with vigour,
From every morning's light to every dusk.

Against a vast abyss of dark-blue sky
There gleam the snow-white breasts of Mt Elbrus.
A caravan of clouds—they're half asleep—
Is sailing by, a flock of huge, slow swans.

And far off, covered by a tender smokiness
And cut transversely by the sun's bright rays,
The mountain ridges wear translucent haze
Of pearl whose sides are pierced by golden blades.

Serpent-dragons creep from mighty crags,
The pale blue and the emerald of glaciers.
The scales upon their icy sides are sparkling
Beneath the sun's great crown that's brightly shining.

And spread out down below, the green of valleys,
Where fields of crops give off a golden glow.
There, rivers wind like ribbons. After pouring from
the heights,
They've quieted the outbursts of their running.

II

The bloody years—their time has passed.
The struggle was a hard one.
Those landlord-nobles were tough nuts to crack,
And truly we had to drain the bitter cup.
In village or aul or Cossack camp,
In the mountains and at the passes,
In forest or canyon, or among cattail reeds,
The rifle and dagger ruled supreme.
Behind every rock or cliff lurked ambush
And everywhere we heard the click of metal.
Betal Kalmykov led them all,
Led all the poor folk into battle.
The land was abuzz with bullets
And blood flowed all around.

But after the heavy ordeal, as if from sleep,
New life has risen, new ground is broken.

The enemy Whites were routed in combat,
Their formations cut to shreds.
A rigorous broom swept through the region,
Though many died in those bitter fights.

When the losses were counted,
Betal, the leader of the poor,
Found that his father was missing.
He'd been shot down in the fields.

III

At last the concerns of battle passed.
Harmonious labour came gushing forth.
Betal
Mobilized
The people, big and small,
Persuaded them and pressed them
To put a quick end to old savagery,
To put in roads,
To put up bridges,
To bring in machinery,
Build hospitals, schools,
Make tiles for the roofs,
To practice seed selection,
Improve the livestock herds,
Sweep floors clean,
Introduce order.
They opened a bridge over the Baksan River.
It was the first iron bridge!

The ram would no longer drown in springtime floods,
Swept away by the water. Even herds of goats
Could go across, or a whole caravan.
It was a national holiday,
Triumphant mark of victory.
What rejoicing and singing there was
To see this wonder created first by the people!

IV

Already here in the capital, Nalchik,
For the young men and young women
A lovely Leninist town has been built,
Where everyone who can study
Must put in their time for learning.
And the aul, the mountain village,
Which had been cleansed
Of princes, nobles and mullahs,
Began sending its youth to the capital
To study and learn the sciences.
And wherever they were sent from
It had been decreed that some must be chosen.
More than a few tears were shed in parting
And probably some threats were made.
But soon there were wonders to behold
Great wonders, but not bad ones.
In the very next year
From all parts of the land
The people poured down in a wave

Like a flash flood from the hills.
All tears had been forgotten.
And the last bit of sanctimonious hypocrisy,
The yashmak, had disappeared.

V

Thus in good time Betal had forged
Cadres of solid metal.
The eaglets hastened to their native cliffs,
Having just learned to spread their wings.
On to the ordeal of long, hot work
Building honeycombs for an enormous hive.
A party law was applied here:
No party members can act like clerks—or whip
handles.
They must be foremost on the job,
Right in the thick of crucial tasks;
Otherwise things will go badly.
And so the work began to hum.
The young girls and young fellows
Were caught up in the fervour of the cause,
And so were the oldest old women.

* * *

Not only in the fields of corn
Or down where the watermelons grow,
Whether in forests or among flocks
Or in a mountain *saklya* hut,

Hanging over a precipice,
On one's own plot or in a kolkhoz
Or in a super-special sovkhoz,
Harmonious labour reigned everywhere
Along with comfort and good order.

VI

When the whole country marched against the foe
In one wide-ranging, connected front,
And the kulaks' struggle flared up
Beyond Kabardá's horizon,
The people of this land flowed like
A mighty river, into kolkhozes.
They didn't let the enemy open his claws,
Came down on him hard and wiped him out.
Right away a congress of elders was held,
With grey-headed Kabardá women present.
Each delegate was a hundred years old.
Their heads were covered with powder,
Their brows creased in wrinkled strips,
But their eyes glittered like the eagle's.
They were slender and graceful under their clothes.
And the elders' discussions went on.

* * *

They were loved and nurtured as honoured guests.
The women of all the government bodies
Followed after them, untiring as attendants,

Made their beds for them, looked after their horses.
This affectionate care touched their hearts.
The elders rode off to their mountain homes
On their spirited 'flying horses',
And the war cry was carried everywhere
Among the mountains proud and severe.

VII

Arisen from the shepherds of Kabardá,
Kalmykov strove for freedom,
Like an unbendable fighter,
Father of his native land,
Apprentice to the Leader of the Peoples,
A constant source of energy.
No slave was he to cursed wine
Nor did he smoke tobacco's poison.
Beneath starry skies he slept in a burka,
But always kept reading and studying,
And yet with a bullet on the fly
Could shoot an eagle from the sky

* * *

Out from behind the distant blue hills
In order to have a look at him
Before their own mortal hour,
Old men hurried to visit him.
Grey-headed granddads, blood brothers,
They came with wholehearted delight.

And from him they went off to die
And to tell, before their deaths,
With trembling hands
And tears in their eyes
That they had seen our great,
Our dear Kalmykov.

VIII

Betal cast his searching glances everywhere.
If, in passing, he noticed anything good,
He'd bring it to Kabardá. No second thoughts.
Like a busy magpie filling its nest,
He brought Swiss cows to Kabardá
And purebred English horses,
Merino sheep, many a precious head,
And powerful, fast-working combines,
From Holland the seeds of luscious flowers,
From Italy bees that give good honey,
Many tractors, big and strong,
And little portable motors.
He acquired quiet incubators,
Took many other initiatives,
Introduced model order everywhere,
Never intimidated by something new.

For party folk, including Young Communists—
The ardent younger generation—
He pronounced a rigorous law, energetically
Laying a difficult burden on them:

'Everyone must learn like an expert
The fundamentals of agro-technology
And know how to apply them like a fighter
In the construction of our new life.'

In the thick of the people Betal
Verified the use of this knowledge,
And whoever earned Betal's reproach
Felt truly ashamed and disgraced.

IX
To every party member was attached
A study circle of non-party people.
The whole population of Kabardá
Was educated as well as you could wish.
That's an illustration
Of the value of organization,
Of concrete leadership,
Destroying bureaucratic deformities.

* * *

New times began that were completely strange.
The land grew independent even of weather.
There came a year, a time of disastrous drought,
The threat of cruel harvest failure and famine.
The mass of the people, as one, went out in the
fields,
Dug networks of canals among the valleys

To bring the water down from the high mountains
And irrigate the whole land copiously.
The water now is tinkling like silver bells.
Kabardá revived and started singing.
It has produced a rich, luxuriant harvest.
'Look sharp, and see you bring all of it in!'
The young and the old—they're all dancing.
Such is the strong, guiding hand of the party,
Such is the might of the masses heroic,
With all their reserves of miraculous strength.
May Kabardá keep going forward forever,
This land of labour, happy, joyous, free.

X

People are now surrounded with caring
As with a soft, warm cloak.
The knot of poverty's been unravelled.
The cockroach type of life has ended.
The expectant mother or the sick man
No longer knows any sorrow:
All the neighbours, with no dispute,
Help them lovingly.
And the aged now are honoured,
As are warriors' dreadful wounds,
The tiredness after hard work,
Leftover scars of battle.
A loving eye keeps closest watch
Over the mother and the child,

And with good humour they respond
To children's endless pranks.

Often a strange thing happened:
In the morning, ever so early,
To a solitary old woman's house,
The province committee came for a meeting.
Where she lived—it was a real kennel.
Later on, they tore it down.
For this old woman, hard of hearing,
They built a brand-new home.

XI
The sun shines brightly over the pearl of the
mountains
Kabardá breathes with all its mighty heart.
The land has come out onto broad horizons.
It hears the running course of worldwide life.
In the village they're building model towns.
They call them something fancy, 'agro-city'.
They're digging ore out of the Earth's recesses,
And factory whistles utter their shrill cry.
Grain elevators rise into the sky
And *kombinaty*** have come into being.
They've put a collar on roaring river falls,
Tight-fitting collar: hydroelectric dams.
The hum of dynamos at the power stations
Keeps wildlife away from dangerous defiles.

* * *

In stanitsa and aul the immediate prospects
Glow with the fire of electricity.
In the houses, decorative carvings
Tell about the new life that has come.
Satisfaction has spread everywhere.
No trace is left of hoof prints of the past.
Science, engineering, the pen, the artist's brush,
Master craftsmen experienced at many things—
All come together in Nalchik, Kabardá's centre,
To lay out the course of the next Five-Year Plan.
Here culture grows not daily but every hour
Like a luxuriant forest of the tropics.
The honey's pouring right into your mouth,
Not off to the side and down your whiskers.
The people itself, a mighty and powerful blacksmith,
Is forging now a fate of its very own.

XII

Dear friends, let's dance, and do it ever so quiet,
The dance of the Caucasus, the Kabardinka.
Beautiful are the dark brows of our lasses,
And every day they're putting on new dresses!
Our lads are mountain eagles, proud and free,
Well-put-together, marvellous, handsome are they.
All of us, as one—we're always ready
For battle stern whenever the call goes out.

So let us dance, and do it ever so quiet,
The dance of the Caucasus, the Kabardinka.

* * *

Against the vast abyss of dark-blue sky
There gleam the snow-white breasts of Mt Elbrus.
A caravan of clouds—they're half asleep—
Is sailing by, a flock of huge, slow swans.

The difficult years have sunk, down deep in the
River Lethe,
And never can there be, a turning back to the past.
Kabardá is happy now, flourishing with vigour,
From every morning's light to every dusk.

(17–18 July 1937)

[*NOTE: See the explanatory note on Kabardá and Betel
Kalmykov, following the poem.
[**NOTE: Industrial complexes.—G. S.]

NOTE ON KABARDÁ AND BETAL KALMYKOV

In this poem about Kabardá, Bukharin pays special tribute to the 'leader of the poor' in that region, Betal Kalmykov.

Extensive information about Kalmykov does not seem easy to come by, but the limited amount available proves to be rather interesting. He was born in 1893, according to the brief article about him in the official Soviet encyclopaedia, and his date of death is given as 27 February 1940. (See *Bolshaya Sovetskaya Entsiklopediya*, VOL. 11, Moscow, 1973, p. 220.)

That article describes Kalmykov as 'one of the organizers and leaders of the struggle for Soviet power among the mountain peoples (*gortsy*) of the Northern Caucasus region'. The term 'mountain peoples' refers to the many small nationalities, often of Muslim religion, who historically found refuge in the mountains of the Caucasus.

The Kabardinians, or Kabardins, were and are the inhabitants of Kabardá, a region on the northern slopes of the Caucasus, east of Abkhazia and of the northern part of Georgia. They are a branch of a larger group of related peoples, the Circassians, or Cherkess. The Circassians gained fame in the Middle Ages as fierce cavalry fighters in the service of various Muslim potentates. Their horses, including the Kabardinian breed, also became famous.

According to the Soviet encyclopaedia, Betal Kalmykov was born to a Kabardinian poor peasant family. From the age of 14 he was a shepherd, and later became a worker. From 1912 on, he engaged in revolutionary activity among the mountain peoples. He helped to found and lead the organization Karakhaly ('The Poor'), a revolution-ary-democratic alliance of the poor among the minority nationalities of the mountains. The tsarist authorities took repressive measures against Kalmykov (although the ency-clopaedia article does not specify what they were).

After the Russian revolutions of February and Octo-ber 1917, during the year 1918, Kalmykov was a delegate to all five 'congresses of the peoples of the Terek region' and became a member of the Terek People's Council (Tersky Narodny Soviet). (The Terek is a major river that flows from the northern slopes of the Caucasus eastward to the Caspian Sea.) Kalmykov headed the work of the First Con-gress of the Nalchik District (*okrug*), which in March 1918 proclaimed Soviet power in Kabardá and neighbouring Balkaria. Nalchik is the main town in Kabardá, and its capital.

Kalmykov was a member of the Council of People's Commissars of the Terek region—first as extraordinary commissar for Kabardino-Balkaria and later as commissar for nationalities. Active in the civil war in the Northern Cau-casus, he was one of the organizers of guerrilla detach-ments. As a Red Army commander, he led a regiment and then a division.

After the defeat of the Whiteguards, in March 1920, he served as chairman of the Revolutionary Committee of Kabardino-Balkaria. From 1920 to 1930, he was chairman of the Executive Committee of the Kabardino-Balkar province (oblast). This autonomous oblast became an au-tonomous republic in 1936.

From 1930 to 1938 Kalmykov was first secretary of the Soviet Communist Party's Kabardino-Balkar province committee. The Soviet encyclopaedia article does not say why Kalmykov ceased to be first secretary in 1938 or what happened to him after that, but the Soviet historian Roy Medvedev reports in *Let History Judge: The Origins and Consequences of Stalinism* (a detailed study of the Stalin era) that Stalin's secret police organized a 'provocation' against Kalmykov.

Medvedev writes:

> Betal Kalmykov, the popular first secretary of the party's Kabardino-Balkar province committee, died in confinement. He was a personal enemy of Beria, but a great friend of Ordzhonikdize and many other party leaders. So an elaborate provocation preceded his destruction. Kalmykov's wife had formerly been married to a man who became a Whiteguard officer and [in the 1920s and 1930s, after the defeat of the Whites] that ex-husband was living in Paris. She had a son by him, who was living in Moscow. Under some pretext this stepson of Kalmykov was lured to Belorussia, arrested at a border station, and accused of trying to flee to his father in Paris. Kalmykov was then framed for participation in a 'conspiracy' against the Soviet regime.

Medvedev apparently had no information about where Kalmykov was held 'in confinement' or whether he was put on trial. Presumably the frame-up of Kalmykov occurred in or shortly after 1938, since that is the year when, according to the Soviet encyclopaedia, he ceased to be first secretary of the party in his home region. If the 1940 death date is true, one can only imagine what happened to Kalmykov between being framed-up and 'dying in confinement'.

Bukharin, writing in prison in 1937 about Kalmykov, of course had no idea that a sorry ending similar to his own awaited the man he described as the 'leader of the poor' and the hero of Soviet Kabardá.

Bukharin's portrait of Kalmykov reflects a kind of mini-cult that apparently surrounded the Kabardinian leader. A Soviet film, *Friends*, with music by Shostakovich, was based on Kalmykov's life and featured him as a typically beloved local party leader. Unintentionally, it was released in 1938, and after Kalmykov's arrest the film was of course viewed with disfavour, causing some difficulties for Shostakovich.

Medvedev's description of Kalmykov as a 'popular' leader is certainly confirmed by the portrait Bukharin gives in 'Pearl Necklace (Song About Kabardá)'.

Bukharin was apparently a frequent visitor to Kabardá. His poem 'On the Wild Boar's Track' describes a hunting trip there, and a 1934 photograph shows Bukharin with a group of 'alpinists' on Mt Elbrus (the highest peak in Europe), which was located on the western edge of Kabardá. Probably, Bukharin was personally acquainted with Kalmykov. They may even have been friends, and if so, that circumstance may well have contributed to Stalin's decision to destroy Kalmykov in 1938.

Medvedev mentions another possible factor in the downfall of Kabardá's leader: There were stories that Kalmykov, like many other local Soviet officials, began living 'like a grandee', having acquired 'the habit of commanding, of administration by fiat', and becoming 'cut off from the people'. This, says Medvedev, made it easier for Stalin to move against such local leaders, since Stalin 'could picture their fall as a result of the people's struggle against corrupt bureaucrats'. Medvedev writes that Mao Zedong used similar tactics against other leaders in the Chinese Communist Party, referring to them as 'those in authority who are taking the capitalist road'. [See *Let History Judge: The Origins and Consequences of Stalinism* (trans. Colleen Taylor) (New York: Alfred A. Knopf, 1972), pp. 414–15.]—G. S.

THE FUTURE

[Bukharin gave the above title to the five poems that he called 'series IX'.
[These poems express the author's vision of a future communist society.—G. S.]

The Universal Human Race

Oppression, wars, the cycle of boom and bust—
All disappeared like sores that long had flourished
On mankind's body, festering ominously
And growing worse with every century.

Moving their fighting columns in good, persistent
order
The sons of earth have rid the world of all these
bloody sores.

Gone are the huts of the poor, and prisons, and
laws,
Gone the barking of commands, armour and
swords.
Crowns are at rest in museums of antiquities,
With gods, the keys that never unlocked mysteries,
Hangmen of thought that once had great vitality,

Idols of Mammon monstrously transformed
Into the pale blue temples of Industry.

But now there are no gods, no princes either,
Only the orderly ranks of human comrades.
Now smoothly, noiselessly the Cosmos' mighty
elements,
Obedient, mute, for all their awesome power,
Are guided on their course by the turn of a wheel.

The people have splendid palaces, auditoriums
For games, for science, for art, for reading and
learning,
Marble-lined pools, all densely surrounded with
flowers,
Like ovals of mirrors set in colourful frames,
And observatories (pedestals for giant 'scopes).
Thought, Feeling, Creativity inspire all.

The worldwide circle dance moves decorously,
The dance of work and play, of brain and muscle.
Over our heads black cares no longer weigh.
Humanity keeps going forward, moving on,
And its creative works, like marvellous new fruit,
Hang from eternal motion's balance beam.

(11 August 1937)

Laurel Wreaths of Brotherhood

Man was to man a wolf,
But man has become to man a brother.
Fierce biting, slashing, the chewing-off of heads
By misbegotten, vicious, crippled souls
Has drifted off like poisoned charcoal fumes.

The dark and evil fires that used to glow
No longer flare along time's river's shores.

Descendants of the black, brown, yellow races,
Of so-called redskins of America,
Descendants of both Aryans and Papuans,
All are united by a single friendship.
They're working on a common mighty cause
With minds both skilled and capable—and daring,
One ocean of innumerable ideas
Surging with human ardour for creation.

Malice, hatred, perfidy are dead
And callous contempt, the vice of vainglory,
Soul-searing envy, and high-handedness,
And the accursed god of vindictiveness.

Instead, love's ancient god has settled in,
Dreamt of by the wise of ancient Greece.
The spirit of Eros and fellowship is reborn,
Linking all beginnings and all ends.
Here each rejoices at another's success
And rushes to assuage soul-searing pain.
Carried by life-affirming, creative urges,
They're flying forward on the wings of thought.
Base egoism here is laughable
Like a barbaric manginess of soul.

They march together, taking the high road
Of great and mighty deeds, not profiteering,
Creators of the mind's and body's riches
Crowned with the laurel wreaths of brotherhood.

(11–12 August 1937)

Life-Creativity

In the midst of Nature's everlasting forces
For the first time
All peoples of the world became conscious
Of their unified paths, rational and direct.

Their golden dreams
Were made a reality
Through struggle.

* * *

Through labour,
Through a creative sequence of strengths and
capabilities,
The reborn human race
Transformed

The old world in its entirety,
With its history of stale routine,
And cut the thread that was woven
By blind and bloody Fate.

Science's wizardry converted
The stern substance of matter
And the regal forces of the world—
Into material for human use.

With the fearless advance of knowledge
All that had seemed frightening
Revealed its true meaning
And was congealed in the shapely rhythm of
numbers.

The free human being, knowing no shackles,
Hears the music of many worlds in art.
And everlasting Nature
Looks with the eyes of the firmament
And smiles at Man, her son and king.

The battle with Nature,
With our great Primal Mother,
In affirmation of life,
Is led by the people of communism.

(12 August 1937)

Death and Life

> O death, from you there's no defense
> From king's heads too you take the crowns
> —Old Russian folk song

'Nothing in our life is frightening to him who has understood
That it is not at all terrible for a man not to exist in this world
Because as long as we exist there is no death
And as soon as death appears, there is no us.'
Thus taught the wise Epicurus.

About these words all-knowing Hegel instructed us
That Epicurus' thought is keen and will drive away the fear of death.

Our great teacher Engels in turn coined a phrase of his own:

'To live,' he admonished us, 'dear friends, means to die.'

Glory to those valiant men who met death without a tremor,
Glory to their fearless spirit, glory through all the ages!

But why renounce the possible advance of science?
Why set a dark limit on Reason, on thought's divine power?
For centuries man did not fly, now he flies like a bird.
In a hundred years perhaps he'll fly to the moon.
Who will prevent life's secret laws from discovery?
And the use of bio-leverage based on those laws?
Wise Bacon, the brilliant Lord of Verulam, said rightly:
'Our power of knowing is equal to Nature's might.'
Why then could not our wise descendants, destroying
The enemies of life on earth, 'trample death to death'?
For communism means an incredible growth of life,
Of health, creative powers, all the blossoms of pleasure.
Our distant descendants will undoubtedly struggle
For eternal youth, for life, against death's dark secrets,

And they will conquer this mighty fortress as well,
The one where, tradition tells us, Fatality wove its
nest.

(13 July 1937)

Infinity

πάντά ρέί
(*Panta rei*)
('Everything flows')

—Heraclitus

The world's everlastingness,
And its unendingness,
Mutual muffled reverberations
Of space and time.

Motion's wave
Is full of enigmas.
Today we solve
And overcome
One problem.
Another, tomorrow,
Running ahead like a wave,
Calls us into the deep.

Life is expanded
By these new callings.
They move apart and widen
The boundaries of thought.
Once more through the effort
Of thought and action
The chains of mystery
Are smashed to pieces.

That which was hidden
And covered in darkness
At a fearful distance
Has now begun to gleam
Like morning's beginning
Over haystacks on the ground.

What before was not needed
Is now a necessity
For people's lives,
And new challenges
Give rise to new tasks,
To a world of bold ideas,
All of life caught up in struggle,
A new boiling and seething.

And all the wellsprings
Of bodily pleasure
And creative thought
Spout from the depths.

That which appeared
Inaccessible
And insuperable
For ever and ever
Suddenly proves
To be easily solved.

As labour presses onward,
Fearless, undaunted,
Without any stopping
Or cowardly evasion,
Far into the distance we go.

The eternity of the Cosmos,
Its endlessness—infinity—
We drink to the full.

(13 August 1937)

APPENDICES

Bukharin's Letter to Anna Mikhailovna Larina, 15 January 1938*

[NOTE BY STEPHEN COHEN: What follows is the only letter ever found of the several Bukharin wrote to his wife, Anna Mikhailovna Larina, from prison. When finally retrieved 54 years later, it was for her a lacerating emotional experience and for all of us conclusive proof that he had written four manuscripts in Lubyanka. The letter is reprinted with permission from Anna Larina, *This I Cannot Forget: The Memoirs of Nikolai Bukharin's Widow* (New York: Norton, 1993).]

Dear Sweet Annushka, My Darling!

I write to you on the eve of the trial, and I write to you with a definite purpose, which I emphasize three times over: No matter what you read, no matter what you hear, no matter how horrible these things may be, no matter what might be said to me or what I might say—endure *everything* courageously and calmly. Prepare the family. Help all of them. I fear for you and the others, but most of all for you. Don't feel malice about anything. Remember that the great cause of the USSR lives on, and *this* is the most important thing. Personal fates are transitory and wretched by comparison. A great ordeal awaits you. I beg you, my dearest, muster all your strength, tighten all the strings of your heart, but don't allow them to *break*.

Do not talk carelessly with anybody about anything. You will understand my position. You are the person closest, dearest to me, only you. In the name of everything good that we have shared, I beg you to use all your strength and spirit to help yourself and the family *endure* this terrible phase. I think that father and Nadya should not *read the newspapers* during the days in question: let it be *as though they are asleep*. But you will know best what to do and what to say so that it will not be an unexpected horrible shock. If I ask this of you, believe me when I say that I have come to it through great suffering, and that everything that will happen is demanded by bigger and greater interests. You know what it costs me to write you such a letter, but I write it in the deep conviction that I must act only in this way. This is the main, basic and decisive factor. You yourself understand how much these short lines say. Do as I ask you, and keep a grip on yourself—be *like a stone*, a statue.

I am very worried about YOU, and if they allow YOU to write to me or to send me some reassuring words about what

I have said above, then THIS weight would fall somewhat from my soul. I ask you to do this, I beg you, my dearest friend.

My second request is an immeasurably lesser one, but for me personally very important. You will be given three manuscripts.

a) a big philosophical work of 310 pages (*Philosophical Arabesques*);
b) a small volume of poems;
c) the first seven chapters of a novel.

Three typed copies should be made of each of them. Father can help polish the poems and the novel. (A *plan* is attached to the poems. On the surface. They seem to be chaotic, but they can be understood—each poem should be retyped on a separate sheet of paper.)

The most important thing is that the philosophical work not be lost. I worked on it for a long time and put a great deal into it; it is a very *mature* work in comparison to my earlier writings, and, in contrast to them, *dialectical* from beginning to end.

There is also that other book (*The Crisis of Capitalist Culture and Socialism*), the first half of which I was writing when I was still at home. Try to rescue it. I don't have it here—it would be a shame if it were lost.

If you receive the manuscripts (many of the poems are related to *you*, and you will feel through them how close I feel to you), and if you are allowed to pass on a few lines or words to me, *don't forget to mention my manuscripts.*

It is not appropriate for me to say more about my feelings right now. But you can read between the lines how much and how deeply I love you. Help me by fulfilling my first request during what will be for me a very difficult time. Regardless of what happens and no matter what the outcome of the trial, I will see you afterward and be able to kiss your hands.

Good-bye my darling,

> *Your Kolka*
> January 15, 1938

P.S. I have the small photograph of you with the little one. Kiss Yurka for me. It's good that he cannot read. I am also very afraid for my daughter. Say a word or two about our son—the boy must have grown, and he doesn't know me. Hug and kiss him for me.

[*NOTE: Reproduced here from Nikolai Bukharin, *How It All Began: The Prison Novel* (reprint ed.) (Calcutta: Seagull Books, 2000), pp. 336–8.—G. S.]

Translator's Note on Bukharin's 'Chronological Listing' of the Prison Poems

Bukharin's 'Chronological Listing' includes the titles of the 'missing' first 14 poems, although we have no dates for them, for reasons explained below.

The dates of the poems that do have dates come from the typescript produced by the generous volunteer labour of Tonya, daughter-in-law of Anna Larina, Bukharin's widow. Tonya's typescript, incidentally, is usually but not always chronological, probably because the photocopies delivered to the Bukharin family were not in exact chronological order, and it was probably not always clear right away which poem followed chronologically after which. So in a few cases Tonya typed a poem (or poems) whose date put it (or them) slightly ahead of the next group of poems.

In his handwritten *Spisok khronologicheskii* ('Chrono-logical Listing') Bukharin did not put any dates. He probably felt he didn't need to, because in his handwrit-ten manuscript he had the date of each poem at the poem's end. That's the source of the dates that are in-cluded here. Thus, in the *Spisok khronologicheskii*, Bukharin was merely specifying the chronological order in which he wrote the poems. The dates themselves were in the poems. But since the first 14 poems are missing, we don't have exact dates for those.

As for the handwritten manuscript—if we go by descriptions given by Bukharin's daughter, Svetlana Gurvich-Bukharina (now deceased), who as a profes-sional historian had access to an official archive con-taining some of Bukharin's originals—he wrote at first on large, signature-size 'press sheets' (*pechatnye listy*), since that was the only writing paper the prison au-thorities allowed him initially. Presumably, he folded these large sheets, as is done in the printing process, until he had eight (or 16?) letter-size rectangles of blank paper, all folded together like a 'signature' used in book printing.

He sometimes wrote on the back as well as the front of these connected pieces of paper. In prepar-ing the English edition, we did not have access to Bukharin's handwritten originals, except for four pages—three of which are reproduced in the present edition of *The Prison Poems*. It seems that, as a result of efforts made by Stephen F. Cohen, letter-size photo-copies were made from Bukharin's originals and those photocopies were delivered by the archive officialdom to the Bukharin family in mid-1992. It was from those photocopies, showing Bukharin's minute handwriting, that Tonya made the typescript we have used to translate and edit the poems.

Список хронологический (о См)

1. Река времен.
2. Капуцин.
3. "Цивилизация".
4. Наместник Христ...
5. Две корки.
6. Слепое страдание.
7. Маркс.
8. Пир мудрецов.
9. Россия.
10. Бони.
11. Желтая контра.
12. Коля восстаний.
13. Диалог между раб. и Мефистоф-ем.
14. Ленин.
15. Праматерь - Природа.
16. Новые птицы.
17. "Идеал".
18. Хоровод парашютчиков.
19. Наследую.
20. Открытие клоун.
21. Архимедов рычаг.
22. Цвержение народа.
23. Мир электронный.
24. Женщина.
25. Биосфера.
26. Освоб. труда.
27. Впрод. пущец.
28. Осколка и цель.
29. Столица мира.
30. Ромб. челов-а.
31. Наука.
32. Смерть и Жизнь.
33. Без. пророк (Ницше).
34. Лира Царя. (Гейне).
35. Велик. Немец (Шейкам.).
36. Мастер (Леонард.).
37. Свет. рад. (Мариш).
38. Дв. Отц (Гете).
39. Хр. Слав Чел. (Бетх.).
40. Шторь и дух.
41. Хореева судьба.
42. (1-ки) Желч. Ониер. (Кабанер).
43. Поресенний предрасс.
44. Страфы.
45. Фарфук кузнец.
46. Спилое болото.
47. Многогреки.
48. Охрон. Испания.
49. Терн. пути (Сок Кит).
50. Промеч и Китай.
51. Vanitas vanitatum.
52. Метаморфоза.
53. Европа и Азия.
54. Горнип иер. борь.
55. Сумерки богов.
56. Масса.
57. Силиборум.
58. Golud. Форм.
59. Белые ночи.
60. Zoloro Осени.
61. Христ Царузи.
62. Черное Море.
63. Степные дали.
64. И Зайне.
65. Звезд над Вода...
66. Погон Афган.
67. Григор.
68. Краб.
69. На Зар. Заку.
70. Отарщика.
71. Береза.
72. На кабЛазу.
73. Гриоб.
74. Хадионел.
75. Зверуфа.
76. Седалоем.
77. Ролгой.
78. Надуф и.
79. Берл. Кид.
80. Сар. Лондон.
81. Нов. Море 15.
82. Продолов.
83. Дес. Мри.
84. Дура- Рад.
85. Мауру.
86. Висгелового.
87. Венир фрауб.
88. Каблож ки л.
89. Жидиверина.
90. Бесхопиму.
91. Фиве. хашул (Вджон).
92. Атост (Слипр).
93. Platans (Пушин).
94. Меда Едрецы (Ивар).
95. Маидач (Варам).
96. Колон (Пр. Жени).
97. Salvp. Страж (Мид).
98. Salvr Пог Сор (аулри).
99. Лам Гр (Mold).
100. Мани город.
101. Борьба миров.
102. Persia.
103. Воспоминан.
104. Белес снеж.
105. Газа.
106. Вногун.
107. Херже.
108. Разбун.
109. Каир.
110. Василиуль.
111. Заверт.
112. Заозеро.
113. Лунная ...
114. Дион Граж.
115. Леонидту.
116. Алб. Луни.
117. Красноярс.
118. Пен Морри.
119. Красногур.
120. В Урле.
121. Газа Солоуу.
122. Азгауз.
123. За Велик Ор.
124. Жиботину.
125. Мещерамин.
126. Золотол хроолин.
127. Горянсей Солб.
128. Эллада.
129. Выгаи Ипулиа.
130. Спартак.
131. Крещевин-на-Поит.
132. В кледи (Пурсал).
133. Предгои.
134. Гроза (Вел. Фр. рев.).
135. М огабрел (Ш. Фурь).
136. 1848.
137. Сериннилевский на пифе.
138. Коммуни.
139. Вшелог зов.
140. В смолвин.
141. Собдор.
142. Швот пахавп.
143. Мабрис. Верр.
144. Химшикко.
145. Винклу удалв.
146. Гелисеблон.
147. Вороп.
148. Ольясунин-ил.
149. Мариин Тильак.
150. Унилеграсс.
151. Надрасенен едала.
152. За хлебон.
153. Аделии под Мукдир.
154. Мераков.
155. Кулашун поошел.
156. Кулену.
157. Лавика.
158. Бура на море.
159. Севрнга солалв.
160. Сиерра.
161. Лавил.
162. Зайнь.
163. Чивтрл. Вейлеин.
164. Сириуш Ангитой.
165. Kolven.
166. Иочине.
167. Скрпа ти Литрьин.
168. Раиолу между угрел смертин.
169. Радулесуа.
170. Ворон.
171. Самы Градуу.
172. Ударник.
173. Цветь.
174. Подгравин Гораир.
175. Крисие Авсони.
176. Пограф Авсони.
177. Сон.
178. Борьба мор лет.
179. Сталинская Хурдия.
180. Зелмо.
181. Ментатилни.
182. Еврейсий девушае.
183. Неографион.
184. Берлину Тезгавае.
185. Древлий нейдар.
186. На мосуч.
187. Нозь.

BUKHARIN'S 'CHRONOLOGICAL LISTING'

[NOTE: This listing has here been set in database style. The left-hand data 'box' contains the number of the poem and the date. The numbers refer only to the poems in this book, from 1 to 173, excluding the missing first 14. (Bukharin's numbering actually went from 1 to 187, including the missing 14.) The centre box contains the title in English translation (or in a few cases, a non-English title). And the right-hand box contains the original title, usually Russian (transliterated), but in a few cases Latin or some other language. Occasional commentaries by me are interspersed, and it should be noted that in some instances the date that appeared at the end of the poem in Bukharin's manuscript differs slightly from the chronological order presented here, probably the result of errors in typing or the confusion resulting from the difficult prison conditions in which Bukharin was working.—G. S.]

DATE (IN 1937)* [*AS GIVEN IN THE TYPESCRIPT AT THE END OF EACH POEM]	TITLE (ENGLISH TRANSLATION)	(RUSSIAN ORIGINAL)
[no date available]	River of the Times	*Reka vremyon*
[no date available]	Capitalist Paradise	*Kapitalistichesky rai*
[no date available]	'Civilization'	*'Tsivilizatsiya'*

DATE (IN 1937)* [*AS GIVEN IN THE TYPESCRIPT AT THE END OF EACH POEM]	TITLE (ENGLISH TRANSLATION)	(RUSSIAN ORIGINAL)
[no date available]	Christ's Deputy	*Namestnik Khrista*
[no date available]	Two Rinds (or Crusts?)	*Dve korki*
[no date available]	Blind Suffering	*Slepoye stradanie*
[no date available]	Marx	*Marks*
[no date available]	Feast of the Cannibals	*Pir lyudoyedov*
[no date available]	Russia	*Rossiya*
[no date available]	Gods	*Bogi*
[no date available]	Iron Cohort	*Zheleznaya kogorta*
[no date available]	Cauldron of Revolts	*Kotel vosstaniy*
[no date available]	Dialogue Between a Worker and Mephistopheles	*Dialog mezhdu rabochim i Mefistofelem*

DATE (IN 1937)* [*AS GIVEN IN THE TYPESCRIPT AT THE END OF EACH POEM]	TITLE (ENGLISH TRANSLATION)	(RUSSIAN ORIGINAL)
[no date available]	Lenin	*Lenin*
End of first 14 [typescript numbering of poems follows (in boldface)]		
1. June 26	Nature—Mother of All	*Pramáter—Priróda*
2. June 26	Birds of a New Kind (Song of the Flight to the North Pole)	*Nóvye ptítsy (Pésnya o sévernom pólyuse)*
3. July 1	Ideal Types	*'Ideály'*
4. July 1	Round Dance of the Women Paratroops	*Khorovód parashutístok*
5. July 1	Heritage	*Naslédstvo*
6. July 2	Opening of the Treasure Troves	*Otkrýtie kladóv*
7. July 5	The Lever of Archimedes	*Arkhimédov rychág*

DATE (IN 1937)* [*AS GIVEN IN THE TYPESCRIPT AT THE END OF EACH POEM]	TITLE (ENGLISH TRANSLATION)	(RUSSIAN ORIGINAL)
8. July 6	Flowering of Nations and Peoples	*Tsveténie naródov*
9. July 8	Electron World	*Mir elektrónov*
10. July 8	Women	*Zhénshchiny*
11. July 9	Biosphere	*Biosféra*
12. July 10	Emancipation of Labour	*Osvobozhdénie trudá*
13. July 10	Journey by Air	*Vozdúshnoye puteshéstvie*
14. July 11	Fragments and the Whole	*Oskólki i tséloye*
15. July 12	Capital of the World	*Stolítsa míra*
16. July 12	Birth of Humanity	*Rozhdénie chelovéchestva*

Date (in 1937)* [*as given in the typescript at the end of each poem]	Title (English Translation)	(Russian Original)
17. July 13	Science	*Naúka*
18. July 13	Death and Life	*Smert i zhizn*
19. July 13	Mad Prophet (Friedrich Nietzsche)	*Bezúmny prorók (F. Nitzshe)*
20. July 14	The Lyre of Irony (Heinrich Heine)	*Líra irónii (G. Geine)*
21. July 14	The Great Unknown (William Shakespeare)	*Velíky neizvéstny (Vilyam Shekspir)*
22. July 15	The Master (Leonardo da Vinci)	*Máster (Leonardo da Vinci)*
23. July 15	The Brightness of Joy (Alexander Pushkin)	*Svétlaya rádost (A. Pushkin)*
24. July 16	The Eyes of Zeus (Goethe)	*Zevésovy óchi (Goethe)*

Date (in 1937)* [*as given in the typescript at the end of each poem]	Title (English Translation)	(Russian original)
25. July 16	Temple of Human Glory (Ludwig van Beethoven)	*Khram slávy chelovéchestva (L. Betkhoven)*
26. July 16	Flesh and Spirit	*Plot' i dukh*
27. July 17	Masters of Fate	*Khozyáeva sudbý*
28. July 17–18	Pearl Necklace (Song about Kabardá)	*Zhemchúzhnoye ozherélye (pésnya o Kabardé)*
29. July 18	An Old Prejudice Shaken	*Potryasénny predrassúdok*
30. July 19	Swifts	*Strizhí*
31. July 20	The Blacksmith's Apron (A Legend from Ancient Iran)	*Fartúk kuznétsa (legenda drevnego Irana)*
32. July 20	Swamps of Decay	*Gnílye bolóta*
33. July 21	Diversity	*Mnogoobrazie*

DATE (IN 1937)* [*AS GIVEN IN THE TYPESCRIPT AT THE END OF EACH POEM]	TITLE (ENGLISH TRANSLATION)	(RUSSIAN ORIGINAL)
34. July 22	Blood-soaked Spain	*Okrovávlennaya Ispániya*
35. July 22	Path of Thorns (Soviet China)	*Ternístye putí (Sovetsky Kitai)*
36. July 22	Prometheus and the Red Cap of Liberty	*Prometéi y krásnaya shápochka*
37. July 23	Vanity of Vanities	[Latin: *Vanitas vanitatum*] [Russian: *Suyetá suyét*]
38. July 23	Metamorphosis	*Metamorfóza*
39. July 24	Europe and Asia	*Yevrópa i Aziya*
40. July 24	The Bugler Plays Reveille	*Gorníst igráyet zóryu*
41. July 26	Twilight of the Gods	*Súmerki bogóv*
42. July 26–27	The Masses	*Mássy*

Date (in 1937)* [*as given in the typescript at the end of each poem]	**Title (English Translation)**	**(Russian original)**
43. July 27–28	Symphony of Cooperative Labour	*Simfóniya sotrúdnichestva*
44. July 29	Blue Ferganá	*Golubáya Ferganá*
45. July 29	White Nights	*Bélye nóchi*
46. July 29	Autumn Gold	*Zóloto óseni*
47. July 30	Crystal Kingdom (On the Summits of Tien Shan)	*Khrustálnoye tsárstvo (na vershí-nakh Tian-Shanya)*
48. July 30	Black Sea	*Chórnoye Móre*
49. July 31	Out on the Steppe	*Stepníye dáli*
50. July 31	In the Taiga	*V taigé*
51. July 31	Stars Above Ice	*Zvyózdy nad l'dámi*
52. August 2	Altai Rapids	*Porógi Altáia*

Date (in 1937)* [*as given in the typescript at the end of each poem]	Title (English Translation)	(Russian original)
53. August 2	Vultures	*Grífy*
54. August 2	Crab	*Krab*
55. August 3	At the Black Grouse Breeding Ground	*Na teterevínom tokú*
56. August 3	Hawk Moth Carousers and Revellers	*Brázhniki-gulyáki*
57. August 3	Birch Tree	*Beryóza*
58. August 3–4	On the Wild Boar's Track	*Na kabányem lazú*
59. August 4	Mushrooms	*Gribý*
60. August 5–7	Greed	*Zhádnost*
61. August 5–7	Brutality	*Zvérstvo*
62. August 5–7	Selfishness	*Sebyalyúbie*
63. August 5–7	Jealousy	*Révnost*

Date (in 1937)* [*as given in the typescript at the end of each poem]	Title (English Translation)	(Russian original)
64. August 5–6	Paris, Light of Wing	*Parízh legkokrýly*
65. August 5–6	Berlin Barracks	*Berlínskaya kazárma*
66. August 5–6	Octopus London	*Sprut-London*
67. August 5–6	New York, with Its Towers	*Nyu York v báshnyakh*
68. August 7	Adversaries	*Protívniki*
69. August 8	Elements of Spring	*Vesénniye stikhíyi*
70. August 8	Rainbow's Arch	*Dugá-ráduga*
71. August 9	Mothers	*Máteri*
72. August 11	The Universal Human Race	*Vsechelovéchestvo*
73. August 11–12	Laurel Wreaths of Brotherhood	*Ventsý brátstva*

DATE (IN 1937)* [*AS GIVEN IN THE TYPESCRIPT AT THE END OF EACH POEM]	TITLE (ENGLISH TRANSLATION)	(RUSSIAN ORIGINAL)
74. August 12	The Beautiful Is Also the Good	[ancient Greek: *Kalos kai agados*]
75. August 12	Life-Creativity	*Zhiznetvórchestvo*
76. August 13	Infinity	*Beskonéchnost*
77. August 13	Philosopher-Chancellor (Francis Bacon)	*Filósof-kántsler*
78. August 13	The Intellect's Love of God (Baruch Spinoza)	[Latin: *Amor Dei intellectualis*
79. August 13–14	Phalanx of Sword-Bearers (The Encyclopaedists)	*Falánga mechenóstsev*
80. August 14	Worlds in Formulas (Isaac Newton)	*Mirý v fórmulakh*
81. August 14	The Secret of the Human Race (Charles Darwin)	*Táina róda chelovécheskogo*

DATE (IN 1937)* [*AS GIVEN IN THE TYPESCRIPT AT THE END OF EACH POEM]	TITLE (ENGLISH TRANSLATION)	(RUSSIAN ORIGINAL)
82. August 14	'The Colossal Old Fellow' (Hegel)	*Kolossálny starík*
83. August 15	Land under a Spell (India)	*Zavorózhennaya straná*
84. August 15	Voice of the Buried Sun (Aztec, Inca, Maya)	*Gólos pogrebyónnogo sólntsa*
85. August 15	The Count in Peasant's Bast Slippers (Leo Tolstoy)	*Lápotny graf*
86. August 15	Dance of the Gorillas	*Tánets goríll*
87. August 17	War of the Worlds	*Borbá miróv*
[The 'Lyrical Intermezzo' starts here—poems of love & loss for & about Anna Larina]		
88. August 24	*Tristia*	[Latin: 'Sorrow']

Date (in 1937)* [**as given in the typescript at the end of each poem*]	**Title (English Translation)**	**(Russian original)**
89. August 24	Remembrance	*Vospominánie*
90. August 24	White Snows	*Bélye snegá*
91. August 24	Eyes	*Glazá*
92. August 24	Together	*Vméste*
93. August 24	To a Hittite Maiden	*Khéttke*
94. August 25	Parting	*Razlúka*
95. August 25	Nymph	*Nímfa*
96. August 29	Universal Love	*Vselyubóv*
97. August 30	Beginnings	*Závyazi*
98. August 30	Conception	*Zachátie*
99. August 30	Moonlight Sonata	*Lúnnaya sonata*
[End of 'Lyrical Intermezzo' (first part). Some 10–12 more poems of this 'cycle', appear later. They are mostly not grouped together, but we have noted them as 'Intermezzo' poems, for readers' information.]		

DATE (IN 1937)* [*AS GIVEN IN THE TYPESCRIPT AT THE END OF EACH POEM]	TITLE (ENGLISH TRANSLATION)	(RUSSIAN ORIGINAL)
100. August 30	John Brown (A Ballad)	*Dzhon Braun (balláda)*
101. September 1–2	Leningrad	*Leningrád*
102. September 2	Glory to Life	*Sláva zhízni*
103. September 3	Red Army Song	*Krasnoarméiskaya*
104. September 3	Red Air Force Song	*Pésnya lyótchikov*
105. September 4	Red Sailors (Red Navy Song)	*Krasnoflóttsy*
106. September 4	In the Grass	*V travé*
107. September 6	Anthem to the Sun	*Gimn sólntsu*
108. September 7	The Renaissance	*Vozrozhdénie*
109. September 7	Behind the Great Wall (China)	*Za velíkoi stenói*

DATE (IN 1937)* [*AS GIVEN IN THE TYPESCRIPT AT THE END OF EACH POEM]	TITLE (ENGLISH TRANSLATION)	(RUSSIAN ORIGINAL)
110. September 8	Schools of Painting	*Zhivopístsy*
111. September 9	Makers of Machines	*Tvortsý mashín*
112. September 9	Voices of the Past	*Golosá próshlogo*
113. September 10	Gothic Cathedral	*Gotíchesky sobór*
114. September 10	Hellas	*Elláda*
115. September 12	[From Ancient Egypt] A Priest's Lament (The Ipuwer Papyrus)	*Plach Ipuvera (yegípetsky papírus)*
116. September 12	Spartacus	*Sparták*
117. September 12	Peasant War	*Krestyánskaya voiná*
118. September 13	In the Cage (Pugachóv) [or: Pugachóv Encaged]	*V klétke (Pugachóv)*

Date (in 1937)* [*as given in the typescript at the end of each poem]	Title (English Translation)	(Russian original)
119. September 13	Predecessors	*Predtéchi*
120. September 13	Thunderstorm (The French Revolution)	*Grozá*
121. September 14	Dreamer (Charles Fourier)	*Mechtátel*
122. September 14	1848	*1848*
123. September 14	Chernyshevsky on the Scaffold [1864]	*Chernyshévsky na eshafóte*
124. September 14	The Paris Commune [1871]	*Kommúna*
125. September 15	1905	*Pyáty god*
[End of 'Predecessors' cycle; beginning of 'Civil War' cycle]		
126. September 15	At Smolny	*V Smólnom*
127. September 16	Sabotage	*Sabotázh*

DATE (IN 1937)* [*AS GIVEN IN THE TYPESCRIPT AT THE END OF EACH POEM]	TITLE (ENGLISH TRANSLATION)	(RUSSIAN ORIGINAL)
128. September 16	Ilyich at a Factory	*Ilyích na zavóde*
129. September 17	Tauride Palace	*Tavríchesky dvoréts*
130. September 17	Predators	*Khíshchniki*
131. September 17	In the Coils of the Constrictor	*V koltsé udáva*
132. September 18	White Church Bells [Ringing]	*Bély zvon*
133. September 18	Raven	*Vóron*
134. September 19	*Osmushka* (Eighth of a Pound of Bread)	*Osmúshka khléba*
135. September 19	Zhanna, Faithful and True	*Vérnaya Zhánna*
136. September 20	Earthquake	*Zemletryasénie*
137. September 21	The Latvian Rifles	*Latýshskiye strelkí*

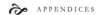

DATE (IN 1937)* [*AS GIVEN IN THE TYPESCRIPT AT THE END OF EACH POEM]	TITLE (ENGLISH TRANSLATION)	(RUSSIAN ORIGINAL)
138. September 21	[The Struggle] For Bread!	*Za khlébom*
139. September 21	Yudenich's March on Petrograd	*Yudénich pod Petrográdom*
140. September 21	Perekop [Battle of]	*Perekóp*
141. September 22	Kulak Perdition	*Kulátskaya pogíbel*
[end of 'Civil War' cycle]		
142. September 22	Idol [to Anna Larina—an 'Intermezzo' poem]	*Kumír*
143. September 22	Avalanche	*Lavína*
144. September 23	Storm at Sea	*Búrya na móre*
145. September 23	Northern Lights	*Sévernoye siyánie*
146. September 23–24	Dust-Devils/ Whirlwinds	*Smerchí*

DATE (IN 1937)* [*AS GIVEN IN THE TYPESCRIPT AT THE END OF EACH POEM]	**TITLE (ENGLISH TRANSLATION)**	**(RUSSIAN ORIGINAL)**
147. September 24	Downpour	*Líven*
148. September 24	The Land	*Zemlyá*
149. September 24	Young Woman [an 'Intermezzo' poem]	*Dévushka*
150. September 25	Sirin and Alkonost [an 'Intermezzo' poem]	*Sírin y Alkonóst*
151. September 25	The Colonies	*Kolóniyi*
152. September 25	Car Chase [an 'Intermezzo' poem]	*Pogónya*
153. September 26	Stone Tablets of the Five-Year Plans	*Skrizháli pyatilétok*
154. September 26	Conversation of Two Worlds	*Razgovór dvukh miróv*
155. September 27	Rádunitsa [an 'Intermezzo' poem]	*Rádunitsa*

DATE (IN 1937)* [*AS GIVEN IN THE TYPESCRIPT AT THE END OF EACH POEM]	**TITLE (ENGLISH TRANSLATION)**	**(RUSSIAN ORIGINAL)**
156. September 28	The Road [an 'Intermezzo' poem]	*Doróga*
157. September 28	Sasha—Woman Tractor Driver	*Sásha-traktorístka*
158. September 28	Shock Workers	*Udárniki*
159. September 28	Flowers	*Tsvetý*
160. September 28	'After Horace' [an 'Intermezzo' poem]	*Podrazhánie Gorátsiyu*
161. September 29	Economic Crisis	*Krízis*
162. September 29	After Ausonius (Spring) [an 'Intermezzo' poem]	*Podrazhánie Avsóniyu. Vesná.*
163. September 30	Dream [an 'Intermezzo' poem]	*Són*
164. September 30	Battle of Ideas (A Sonnet)	*Borbá mysléi (sonét)*

DATE (IN 1937)* [*AS GIVEN IN THE TYPESCRIPT AT THE END OF EACH POEM]	TITLE (ENGLISH TRANSLATION)	(RUSSIAN ORIGINAL)
165. October 1	The Stalin Charter	*Stálinskaya Khártiya*
166. October 1	Sunset	*Zakát*
167. October 1	*Meditationes*	[The title is in Latin]
168. October 2	To a Jewish Maiden	*Yevréiskoi dévushke*

[Bukharin designated the above entry as an 'Intermezzo' poem. The date on the typescript is unclear. What literally appears on the typescript is 'Sept.012,' but on Tonya's typed version of Bukharin's 'Spisok khronologicheskii' the words 'Oct. 2' are crossed out by hand, while beneath that, the words 'Sept. 4' are handwritten in Russian. She probably misread Bukharin's handwriting. Oddly enough, in a hasty handwritten Russian scrawl, 'Oct. 2' and 'Sept. 4' can look alike.]

| **169.** October 2 | Lament of Shame | *Postýdnoye* |

DATE (IN 1937)* [*AS GIVEN IN THE TYPESCRIPT AT THE END OF EACH POEM]	**TITLE (ENGLISH TRANSLATION)**	**(RUSSIAN ORIGINAL)**
170. October 3	Berlin Zoo [a group of 7 short poems]	[German: *Berliner Tiergarten*]
171. October 4	Ancient Land-scape [an 'Inter-mezzo' poem]	*Drévnii paysage*
172. October 5	On a Bridge [an 'Intermezzo' poem]	*Na mostú*
173. November 18	Night [an 'Inter-mezzo' poem]	*Noch*

Translator's Note on Bukharin's 'Systematic Listing'

Bukharin said, in his letter to Anna Larina of 15 January 1938, that on the surface the poems in his manuscript might seem chaotic, but 'a *plan* is attached to the poems.'

The 'chaos' can be seen if one reviews Bukharin's 'Chronological Listing' of the prison poems (see the preceding pages). From one day to the next the poet might jump from one theme to a totally different one.

For example, on 25 September 1937, he completed the poem 'Car Chase' (*Pogónya*), one of his charming love poems about Anna Larina, but on the next day he wrote about the Soviet Five-Year Plan.

Similarly, on 28 September 1937, he wrote a poem about 'Shock Workers' (i.e. the notorious

Stakhanovites, or exemplary workers, of the Soviet 1930s). The very same day he wrote one of his loveliest nature poems, 'Flowers'.

It is quite clear that the '*plan*' Bukharin referred to is embodied in what he called *Spisok sistematicheskii* ('Systematic Listing'), which indeed was 'attached' to the poetry manuscript—that is, it was one of the nearly 360 pages of handwritten manuscript constituting his book of poetry.

Following the present note, we reproduce a photocopy of one such page in the author's Russian handwriting: his final version of that 'Systematic Listing'. This page, incidentally, includes a small drawing by Bukharin, which may have been merely a typical old peasant drawn from his imagination, or it may have been his recollection of the appearance of Leo Tolstoy. (In a poem about Tolstoy he describes that grand figure of Russian letters as, indeed, looking like a typical old peasant: 'Grey-headed . . . with a spade-shaped beard./ Nose like a potato, big and broad.')

It should be noted that photocopies of only four handwritten pages from the poetry manuscript have been available to us in making this translation. Reproductions of three of these four pages in Bukharin's Russian handwriting are included in the present edition. The first is of Bukharin's proposed title page, reproduced in this edition facing the English-language title page. (It shows pigeons on what looks like a roof or ledge, perhaps the view from Bukharin's prison cell, as Stephen Cohen guesses.)

The second is the 'Chronological Listing' (*Spisok khronologicheskii*), referred to above.

Third is his final version of the 'Systematic Listing'.

(Another handwritten manuscript page in Russian is in our possession. It is an earlier version of Bukharin's 'Systematic Listing', but it is quite confused and unclear. His final version of the 'Systematic Listing', the third handwritten page in Russian, which we reproduce here, is what we have followed in deciding the order of the poems, as shown in our Table of Contents.)

In his 'Systematic Listing' Bukharin arranges the poems in *nine groups*, using a Roman numeral in the heading for each group. Occasionally in the typescript the author calls such groups of poems 'Series' or 'Cycles' (terms he seems to have used interchangeably). And he seems to have considered arranging the poems in more than a dozen groups before finally deciding on nine.

The nine groups are as follows, although Bukharin's 'series I' doesn't really count, because the 14 poems in that group are missing. Thus, in the present edition the poems are divided into eight, not nine, groups. (Bukharin used Roman numerals to designate the 'series' he had in mind.)

(I) Endings and Beginnings	(the 14 'missing' poems)
(II) Precursors	(13 poems)
(III) Civil War	(15 poems)

[NOTE: Most poems in groups (II) and (III) were written in September 1937. They were preceded chronologically in the writing process by about 100 poems, out of 173, dating from June to August of that year.

Nevertheless, these September poems appear as the *first two groups* in our edition. Bukharin specified that these two groups of poems should be the second and third parts of the book, but as we have said, the 14-poem group that Bukharin wanted as the first part of the book is missing.]

(IV)	Nature—Mother of All	(32 poems)
(V)	Heritage	(28 poems)
(VI)	War of Worlds	(28 poems)
(VII)	Lyrical Intermezzo	(29 poems)
(VIII)	Epoch of Great Works	(23 poems)
(IX)	The Future	(5 poems)

In most of the groups, we have followed the order Bukharin indicated in his 'Systematic Listing', with some slight exceptions.

In the groups entitled 'War of Worlds' and 'Epoch of Great Works' we have followed an order that differs more substantially from what Bukharin indicated. If one looks at the handwritten Russian of the *Spisok sistematicheskii*, one will see that in 'series VI' and 'series VIII' (that is, the 'War of Worlds' and 'Epoch of Great Works') Bukharin had a great many arrows moving poems from lower to higher positions. This suggests that he himself was having difficulty arriving at a logical ordering for these poems. If he had had the opportunity, free of oppressive prison conditions, to do a final editing of his poems, he may well have chosen some further rearrangement. We hope readers will agree that the ordering we have used in this edition, including for 'War of Worlds' and 'Epoch of Great Works', makes sense and is basically consistent with the order Bukharin outlined in his 'Systematic Listing'.

We must mention one particular exception. In the very last group of five poems, for which Bukharin chose the heading 'The Future' (*Gryadúshcheye*), he included a poem with a title in classical Greek, κάλος κάí ἀγάδος (transliterated into English, this would be spelled *Kalos kai agados*, ancient Greek for 'The Beautiful Is Also the Good'). It seemed to us that this poem belonged with four others about women and their emancipation, which we have grouped together near the end of 'Epoch of Great Works'. After moving 'The Beautiful Is Also the Good' to the 'Great Works' section, we replaced it by moving one of

Bukharin's 'Great Works' poems to the five-poem group about 'The Future'. This is the poem 'Death and Life', in which the poet speculates that in the future human beings will discover the means of indefinitely prolonging the life of the individual.

Пред.
Поэма о Ст.
Конца и начала

Река Времени
К-ва
«Цивилис.»
Пламенник Кр
Два хора
Обл. Огня
Марксъ
Мiр людской
Россiя
богъ
Тел. Кол.
Кор. Общ.
Диалог
Ленинъ.

— **Предъект** — своё еще 2 цикла на отдѣлъ

граждан. война

IV. Праматерь Природа

Прам. прир
Изобр. путеш.
Голуб. Сфера
— Бѣлые Кони
— Голуб Осени
— Круж. орбитъ
— Черное Море
— Страшное дѣло
— В Зимѣ
— Звезды над Щу.
— Пояса Альфа
Ураганъ
Гимн
— На Жел. Дор.
— Графически
— Береза
— На кабалу
— гримъ
1) Трава
Дес. Ури. и
Дра. Рад.
Мiр Недр.
Осудр.
О хромъ Кл...
Стрыдъ...
и Огня
о вы на мiре.
Сверк. стихiй
...

I. Наслѣдiе

1 — Наслѣдiе
2 — Солнце и Азы
3 — Заворож. страна (Инд)
4 — За Вел Ури. (Кит)
5 — Utro пора Солнца (англ.)
6 — Возрожденiе
7 — Живописецъ
8 — Творцу машинъ
9 — Наука
10 — Мастеръ (Милтон.)
11 — Фил.–камъ (Бэкон)
12 — Amor (Спинозъ)
13 — Фаланс (Этич.)
14 — Велик Кенз (Шекс)
15 — Мiр в дарѣ (Нют)
16 — Танецъ р. (Дарвин)
17 — Вел. Орг. (Уэльс)
18 — Без. Пруж. (Ницш)
19 — Мир. Шр. (Гейне)
20 — Сверх. рад (Пушк)
21 — Jel. Оги (Гете)
22 — Храм А. (Бетх.)
23 — Лам. Эрг (Мол.)
24 — Ужасное беды.
25 — Суверен богов
26 — Золотой проповѣ...
27 — Готический Собор (6) ♀
28 — Эллада (3) ♂

≠ VI. Борьба Мира

1. Призывник.
2. Фордъ-ги Куккловичъ — Разговоръ
3. Джон браунъ — Fortland(?)
4 — Ленинградъ
5 — Идеалъ
6 — Жадность
7 — Звѣри
8 — Себялюбie
9 — Революцiя
10 — Пафос. лич.
11 — Берлинск. Каз.
12 — Студ. Лонд.
13 — Кон. Мiра с б.
14 — Охр. Исп.
15 — Тери. кург. (Каз)
16 — Прол. и Кр. Маи
17 — Горье. шр. горъ
18 — Масса
19 — Потряс. недръ.

20 — Ромб. чело. б.
21 — Танец горой
22 — Борьба мира
23 — Красноармъ
24 — Нѣш. мер.
25 — Красноармеецъ
26 — Крыша набѣгъ
27 — Нь. Кавказ

VII. Мiрiч. Интермеццо

1 Trittia
2 Вiолон.
3 Бѣлоснѣж.
4 Глаза
5 — Вилисъ
6 — Хердже
7 — Разлука
8 Налуда
9 Вселенной
10 Забавы
11 Качели
12 Луна Сон.
13 Cicalа Муз
14. Гиен Солн.
15 Кулихар

16. Октавина
17 Сирiн и Алко...
ни...
18. Поляне
19. Радужнику
20. Дорога
21. Преображенiе Горизонтъ
22. Подграфами Автомн.
23. Сон
24 Борьба лесовъ
25. Meditationes
26. Эфиосонъ Гиг...
27. Эрлин даiроу
28. Ниса...
29. Ночь

VIII. Эпоха Велик Раб.

1 — Орбл. Труд.
2 — Арх. Вавил...
3 — Мейлинъ...
4 — Смер. Сотр...
5 — Хор. Сутбй...
6 — Стол. Мiр.
7 — Пол. нУшер.
8 — Хорвiй Марш.
9 — Плуг в Ду
10 — Оск. и цвѣт.
11 — Могопр.
12 — Женщ.
13 — Цвѣт. карол.
14 — Маяки
15 — Cлѣдуй в буду...
16 — Vanitas
17 — Эпиан. Огр.
18 — Кутающихся houseller
19 — Jeens
20 — Схрифуть Некилъ...
21 — Сама. Транскрипцiя
22 — Удаленiе
23 — Восстанавливаю Хорамъ

IX. Грядущее

1 — Всесловущъ
2 — Белорграфъ
3 — Καλός και ἀγαθός
4 — Животворницъ
5 — Ректоментъ
6
7